残傷の音

STILL
HEAR
THE
WOUND

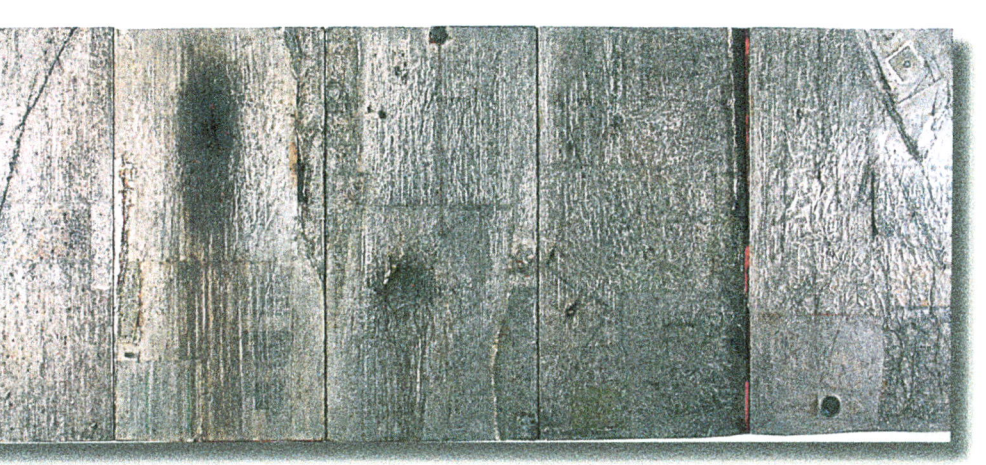

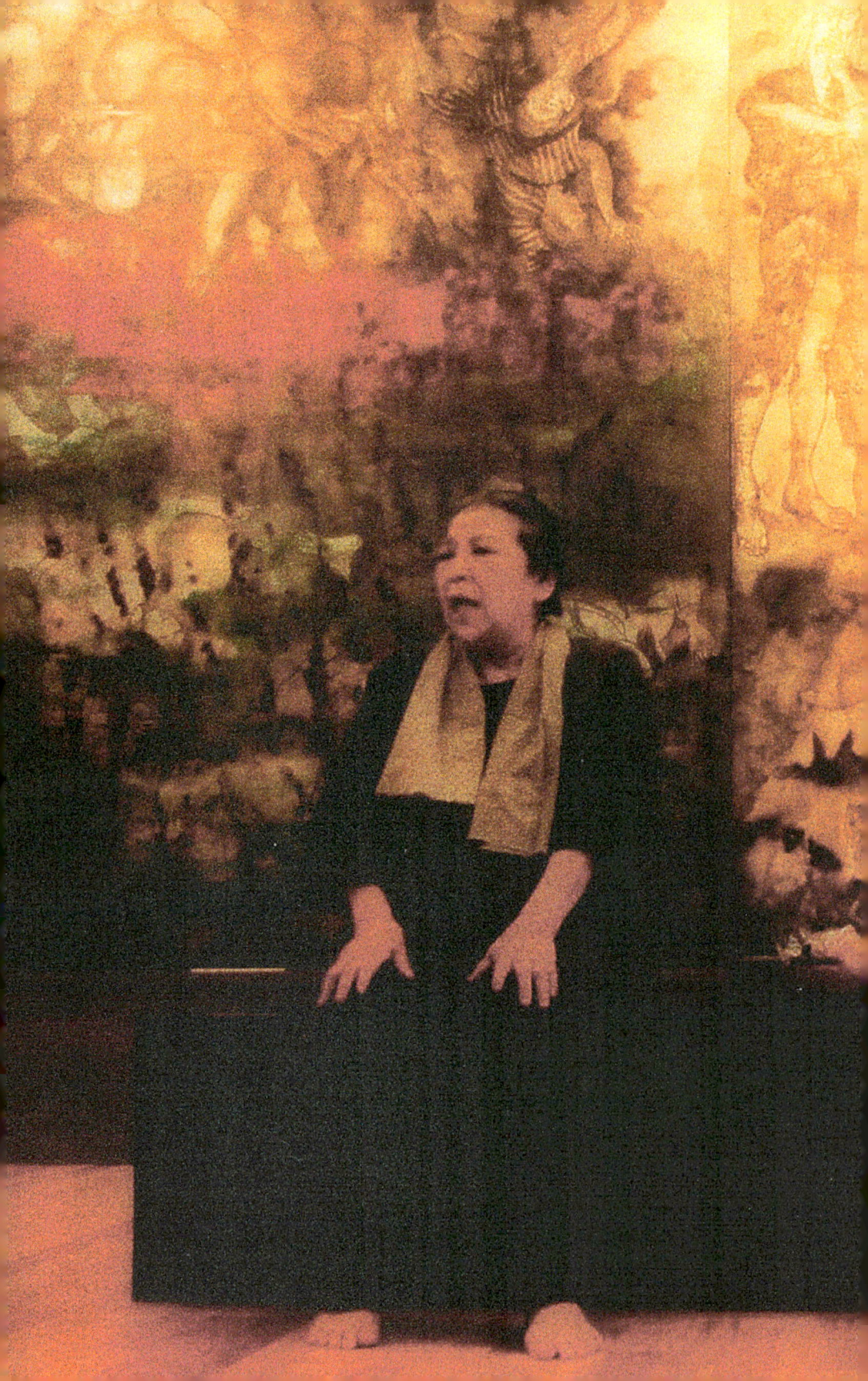

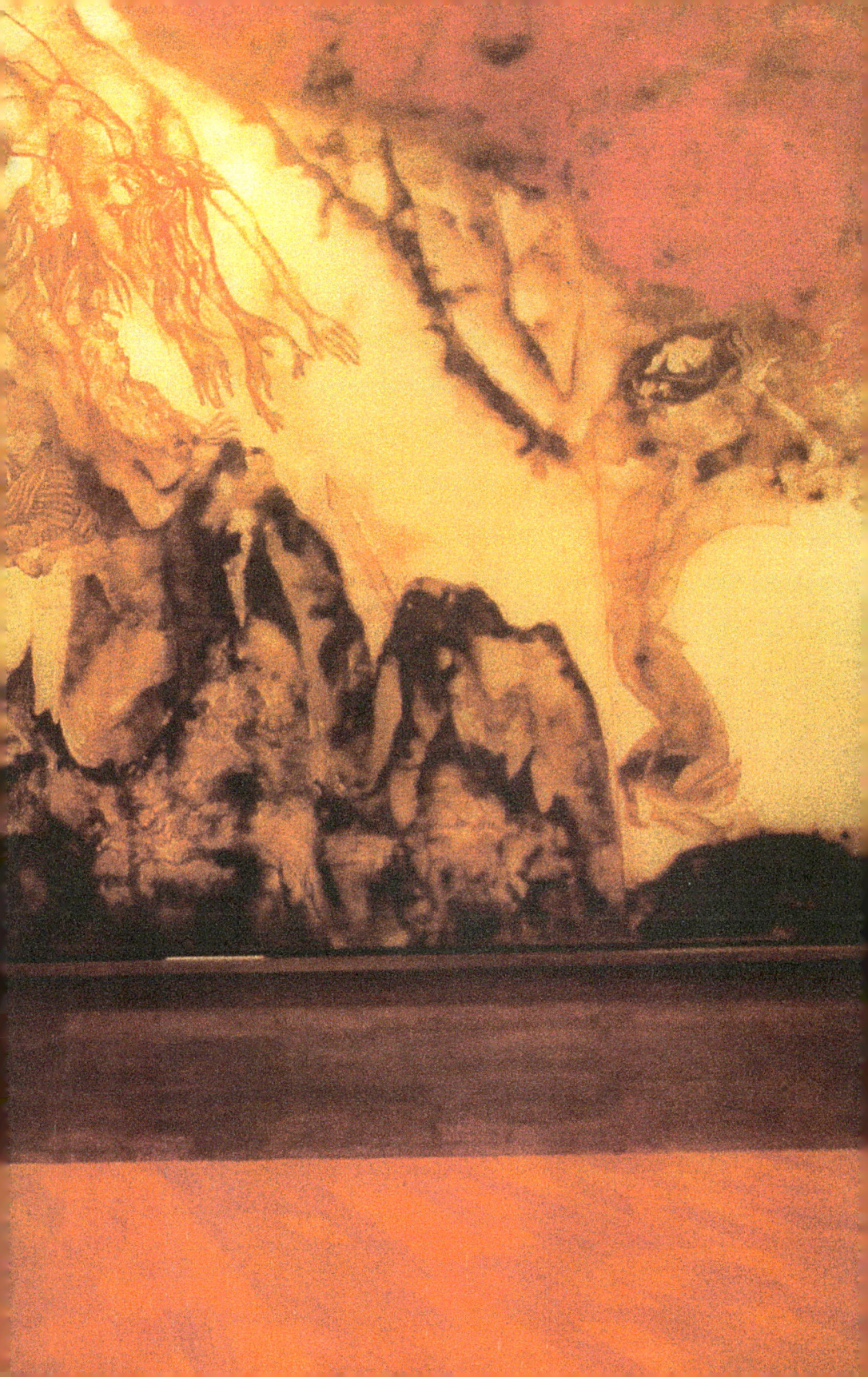

The Cornell East Asia Series is published by the Cornell University East Asia Program (distinct from Cornell University Press). We publish books on a variety of scholarly topics relating to East Asia as a service to the academic community and the general public. Address submission inquiries to CEAS Editorial Board, East Asia Program, Cornell University, 140 Uris Hall, Ithaca, New York 14853-7601.

We gratefully acknowledge support from the Kyoto Seika University Publishing Subsidy Program, 2015. We also acknowledge Iwanami Shoten in Tokyo for their generous assistance.

Number 181 in the Cornell East Asia Series
Copyright © 2015 Cornell University East Asia Program. All rights reserved.
ISSN 1050-2955
ISBN: 978-1-939161-61-1 hc
ISBN: 978-1-939161-81-9 pb
ISBN: 978-1-942242-81-9 ebook
Library of Congress Control Number: 2015945077
Printed in the United States of America

Spread: Kitajima Sumiko, *Nipponjin?* (Japanese?), still image from a performance with the *Battle of Okinawa*, by Maruki Iri and Toshi, Sakima Museum, May 5, 2005. Photograph: Kuniyoshi Kazuo.

∞ The paper in this book meets the requirements for permanence of ISO 9706:1994.

STILL
HEAR
THE
WOUND

TOWARD AN ASIA,
POLITICS, AND ART TO COME

selected essays edited by
LEE CHONGHWA

translation edited by
REBECCA JENNISON & BRETT de BARY

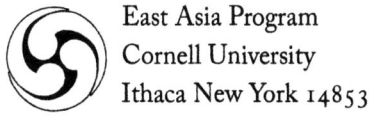

East Asia Program
Cornell University
Ithaca New York 14853

CONTENTS

PART II

LIST OF IMAGES

PREFACES

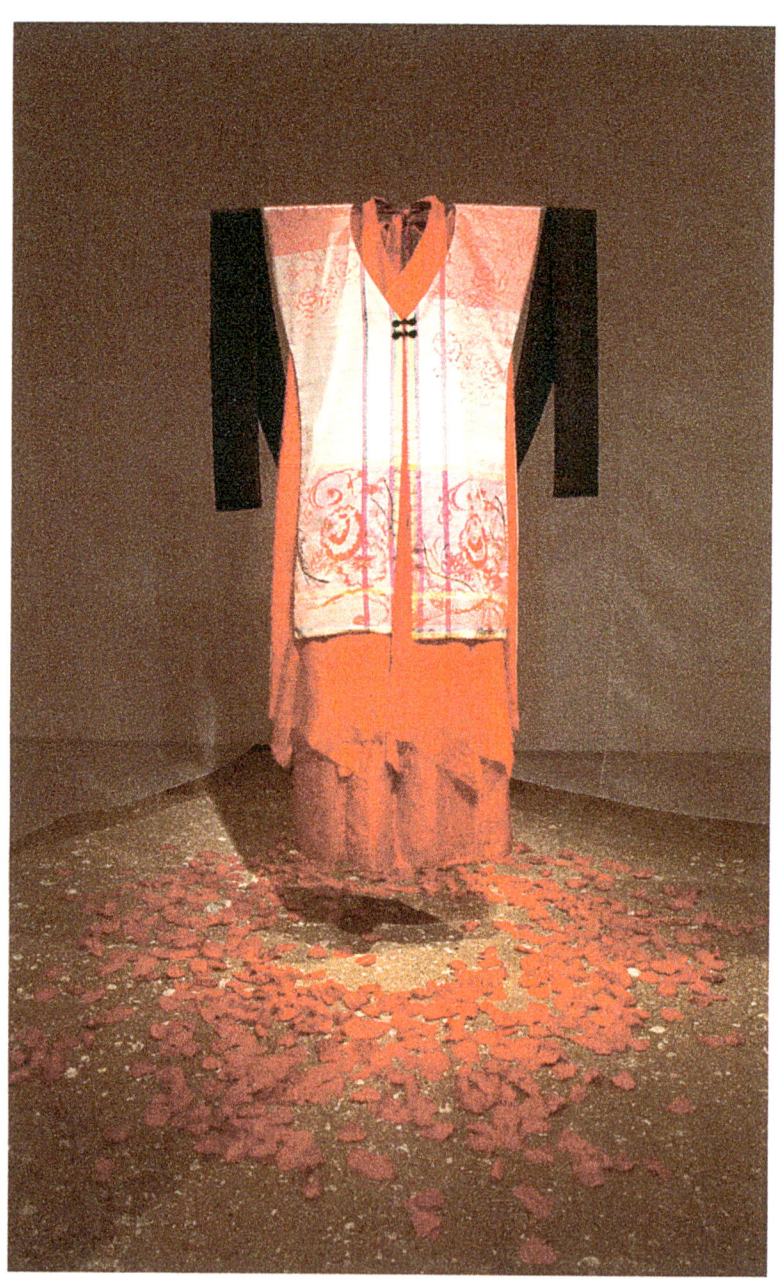

Oh Haji, *Sange* (Scattered Flowers), 2005.

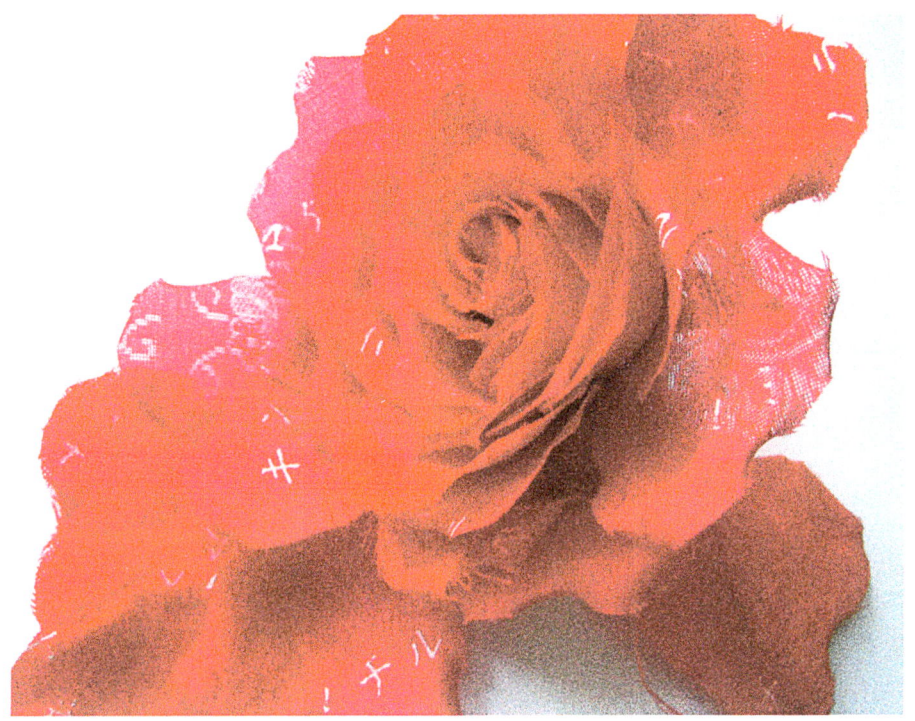

Oh Haji, *Sange* (detail), 2005.

Still Hear the Wound

Expanding Dialogues on Asia, Politics, and Art

Rebecca Jennison

O n a warm day in March 2007, a group of scholars, artists, curators, and a musician/composer gathered in front of the Sakima Art Museum in Ginowan City, Okinawa. Many of us had come by plane, either from Tokyo or Osaka, to Naha, and then by bus or taxi from central Naha, winding our way along roads lined with chain-link fences that surround Marine Corps Air Station Futenma to the entrance of the museum. At the far end of the museum's courtyard, still scattered with stones that we would learn were part of Kinjō Mitsuru's project *Voices of the Stones*, was a large *kameko-baka* or "turtle-backed" tomb indigenous to the Ryukyu Islands. Now and then, the sound or shadow of a plane overhead reminded us of our proximity to the Futenma landing strip.

In 2004, I had traveled to Okinawa and to Henoko, the coastal fishing village where the construction of a new airstrip on an offshore coral reef inhabited by the endangered dugong—part of a proposed plan for the relocation of Futenma Air Station—is still being protested.[1] On that trip, I had seen the fence that begins on land and vanishes into the sea, marking the border between the fishing village and Camp Schwab, and the beach where Marines trained in tanks on the sand before being deployed to Fallujah, Iraq. Two and a half years later, standing in the lobby of the Sakima Art Museum, I was intensely aware that through the Asia, Politics, Art project I would

---

1. At this writing, local citizens and their supporters continue their nineteen-year peaceful protest to stop the construction of the offshore airstrip.

learn much more about Okinawa's past and present, a place where colonial, postcolonial, and postwar histories in East Asia continue to intersect in complex ways.

Takahashi Yūji launched the event with a piano performance in the lobby, where Teraya Yūken's creation, *You-I, You-I,* a kimono dyed in the traditional Okinawan *bingata* style—with colorful images of V-22 Osprey aircraft and parachutes intermingled with the more familiar floral and animal motifs—is still displayed. Shinjō Ikuo describes Takahashi Yūji's performance of an original composition inspired by Nakaya Kōkichi's poem, "The Last Note," in detail in the essay he has contributed to this volume, "The Contours of Sound." Similarly, other essays that follow discuss works by Ito Tari, Yamashiro Chikako, Oh Haji, Soni Kum, and Takamine Gō that were presented in workshops held at the Sakima Art Museum that afternoon and at the second workshop in September 2007. Readers are encouraged to both read the essays and view the works on the DVD that accompanies this volume.

In "The Contours of Sound," Shinjō writes of the life of Nakaya Kōkichi (1936–1966), the poet whose work inspired Takahashi to create the musical composition he performed, and makes reference to people whose lives and deaths have been "erased from the front stage of Asian politics," a theme that runs through this volume. According to Shinjō, "These are also people who wait with bated breath in a disappearing 'past' for a time that will recall their lived experiences in word, sound, and form. What else is asked of us other than to listen to the silent call of the mourned?"

As Shinjō and others here suggest, one aim of the Asia, Politics, Art project has been to shed light on those whose lives and deaths unfolded on the backstages of East Asian politics and history, and who call out to be remembered and mourned. One thing that makes this collection of essays and artworks unique is that scholars working in a range of disciplines were asked to engage in conversations with practicing artists: academics working with the written word and artists working in a range of materials and media including textiles, film, and performance art were challenged by one another to express themselves in new ways. In his essay, Shinjō also beautifully elucidates the view that in a region still haunted by divisive politics, art has the potential to become a bridging point that can enable us to rethink or reimagine interconnected histories in East Asia, and "resist the very regime of 'national history.'"

While the essays and artworks included in this volume speak for themselves of the significant "research outcomes" of this unique, collaborative project, it might also be said that they also document a timely critical cultural history that not only explores the work of a group of artists and activist-scholars based in Japan, but that also probes connections linking past histories to ongoing geopolitical tensions to lives being lived in present-day East Asia. As a reflection of this focus on intersections between humanities-based research and the works of contemporary artists, this volume includes a number of images and a DVD of interviews with the artists, thus making it both an editorial and curatorial project.

In one sense, the writers and artists whose works are presented here might be perceived as being of the periphery, as many of them are located at a distance from both the center of the nation-state (and state-sponsored cultural projects that advocate a more "monoethnic Japan") and the contemporary art world in New York or Tokyo, and more than half of the participants are either from Korea or Okinawa, or are *zainichi* Korean.[2] But from another perspective, this project, and the works that still continue to emerge from it, must be understood in very different terms that radically disrupt any simplistic binary mapping of center and periphery, as part of a different stream, or streams, of critical cultural and contemporary art production which perhaps has no center, and which is helping to remap and revision our twenty-first-century world.[3]

Each participant in the Asia, Politics, Art project no doubt has her or his own narrative of encounters that led to participation in the project. I myself came to know poet and scholar Lee Chonghwa in the late 1990s through my research and collaborations with scholars and artists engaging with questions of cultural diversity, feminism, postcolonial histories, and critical theory. In the early 1990s, I participated in the Asia Women and Art Collective, an informal study group and collective established by artist Tomiyama Taeko to explore intersections between feminism, postcolonial histories, and contemporary art.[4] Monthly meetings were held in a small café near Yotsuya in

---

2. The term "*zainichi* Korean" literally means Korean residents of Japan. See Sonya Ryang and John Lie, eds., *Diaspora without Homeland* (Berkeley: University of California Press, 2009); and Tessa Morris-Suzuki, *Exodus to North Korea* (Lanham, MD: Rowman and Littlefield, 2007), for excellent accounts of the historical background and formation of diverse Korean diasporic communities in Japan. Also see chapters 4–6, this volume. In *Questions of Travel* (Durham, NC: Duke University Press, 1996), Caren Kaplan warns of such simple binaries.

3. Artists, critics, and curators whose works help unravel and make visible complex layers of diasporic experience, contested histories, and current geopolitical conflicts are too numerous to touch on in detail here. To mention a few: Yong Soon Min, Margo Machida, and Dinh Q. Lê.

4. Tomiyama Taeko (b. 1921) established Hidane Kōbo in 1975 and has collaborated with Takahashi Yūji on a number of multimedia works since then.

Tokyo; my own research for that project led to works and curatorial projects by Asian American artists Yong Soon Min, Theresa Hak Kyung Cha, and Margo Machida, who were exploring questions of history and memory, gender and ethnic identity in their works.[5]

Later in the 1990s, at a conference coordinated by Nishikawa Nagao at the Institute of International Language and Culture Studies, Ritsumeikan University, Ikeuchi Yasuko and Lee Chonghwa began discussing the possibility of collaborating on further projects that might explore questions of gender, ethnicity, and representation in contemporary art in the East Asian context. The research project "Theoretical Approaches to the Study of Gender and Performance Art: On Asian Women Artists" (パフォーマンス・アートとジェンダーに関する理論的研究　－アジア女性アーティストを中心に¯) was initiated by Ikeuchi in 2002; this project enabled us to conduct dialogue and collaborate with artists, performance groups, and scholars in Kyoto, Tokyo, Seoul, and Seattle.[6] In 2004, Diaspora and Art: The Korean Diaspora project, headed by Suh Kyongsik of Tokyo University of Economics, and *Borderline Cases: Co-responses on the Borderlines*, coordinated by artist Shimada Yoshiko, brought together artists, scholars, and curators from Korea and Japan in a groundbreaking symposium and exhibition in Tokyo. In that same year, Oh Haji co-curated an exhibition of works by young artists of the Korean diaspora from Japan, Europe, and North America at the Kyoto Arts Center, *Orientity*.[7] Clearly, a certain momentum was building as ongoing conversations among innovative artists, activists, and researchers engaged with feminism, postcolonial theory, and art were being generated.

In 2006, when Lee Chonghwa invited more than a dozen scholars and artists to participate in the Asia, Politics, Art project, the response was enthusiastic. The first workshop was held at the Sakima Art Museum and followed

---

5. Through Hagiwara Hiroko, I met Yong Soon Min and learned of the Godzilla, Godzilla West, and SEORO collectives and many curatorial projects, including *Memories of Overdevelopment—Philippine Diaspora in Contemporary Art* (Plug In Editions, Canada; University of California Irvine Art Gallery, Wayne Baerwaldt; 1995) and Margo Machida, Vishakha Desai, and John Tchen, *Asia/America: Identities in Contemporary Asian American Art* (New York: New Press, 1994).

6. See reports on the Performance Art in East Asia Research Project, edited by Ikeuchi Yasuko, Ritsumeikan University. For summaries of the reports, see https://kaken.nii.ac.jp/d/p/14594025.en.html

7. See *Deiasupora, aato no genzai—korian deiasupora o chuushin ni* (Diaspora and art today—on the Korean diaspora), Tokyo University Economics Research Center, June 2005; *Borderline Cases: Women on the Borderlines*, A.R.T./ F.A.A.B., Tokyo, 2004; *Orientity*, Kyoto Arts Center, 2004 (https://orientity.wordpress.com/).

two teach-in events in Tokyo and Okinawa; it was the first of seven workshops and marked the beginning of a series of dialogues and collaborations
that led to the publication of *Zanshō no oto: Ajia, seiji, art no mirai e* by
Iwanami Shoten in Tokyo. Now, thanks to generous support from Kyoto
Seika University and the Cornell East Asia Series, selected essays and artworks from that volume appear for the first time in English here.[8]

Lee's call for participants to consider new meanings of "Asia," "politics,"
and "art," and to explore interconnections between these three terms in response to works by participating artists, is what led to the twelve essays in the
original volume, and a DVD of interviews or works by seven of the artists.
The styles and aims of the responses are diverse; together they help us to reimagine the three terms and to see new connections between them at a moment when the Abe government's revisionist views of history and resurgent
nationalisms are once again sparking heightened tensions in the region. Before turning to brief notes on the essays and DVD in this volume, some
comments about the vision and early works of Lee Chonghwa may provide
readers with a clearer sense of the context from which *Still Hear the Wound*
emerged.

During the course of the Asia, Politics, Art project, the number of interested participants grew from two dozen to nearly a hundred. One reason for
this is Lee Chonghwa's vision and practice as a poet and political philosopher.
Following the publication of her earlier work, *Tsubuyaki no seiji shisō — Motomerareru manazashi/kanashimi e no, soshite himerareta mono e no* (Murmurs
as political thought: In search of ways of seeing the sorrow, and things hidden, 1997), Lee had become known for her stance and practice as a *shisakuka*
(思索家 or thinker), *shijin* (詩人 or poet), and *seijishisōka* (政治思想家 or
political philosopher).[9] As we will see, Lee's "Words for a Preface" is also an
expression of her stance and serves to introduce the essays and artworks that
readers will discover in this volume.

---

8. Generous support from the Asia-Pacific Research Center at Seikei University, Tokyo,
made it possible to conduct the research seminars held in Okinawa and Tokyo, as well as to
publish the original volume of essays with DVD: *Zanshō no oto: Ajia, seiji, art no mirai e* (Tokyo:
Iwanami, 2009).

9. Lee Chonghwa, *Tsubuyaki no seiji shisō —Motomerareru manazashi / kanashimi e no, soshite himerareta mono e no* (Murmurs as political thought: In search of ways of seeing the sorrow,
and things hidden; hereafter, *Tsubuyaki*), reprinted in a volume with other essays (Tokyo: Seidosha, 1998). *Tsubuyaki* is structured around four poems—three by well-known Korean poets that
treat critically important periods of Korea's modern history, and one by Lee herself, thus linking
defining moments in private and public memory.

The title of this volume itself provides further insight into Lee's unique poetic strategies. *Still Hear the Wound* is a translation of a compound invented by Lee for the original title of this volume, *Zanshō no oto* (残傷の音). The character for *zan* (残), used to suggest "things that remain, are leftover or are lingering," is combined with the character *shō* (傷), also read as *kizu* (wound), to create a new compound, *zanshō*, literally "wounds that still remain." Alongside the character for *oto* (音), or sound, the phrase conveys a visceral sense of the sound/vibrations of wounds that still remain and resonate—an unexpected juxtaposition of the senses of touch and sound that, as Brett de Bary explains so eloquently in her essay, "Afterthoughts, 'After-Life,' on the Occasion of Translation," alerts readers to ways that Walter Benjamin's notion of synesthesia might prove useful in reading the essays.

When *Tsubuyaki* was published in the journal *Shisō* in 1997, it immediately caught the attention of many intellectuals, writers, and artists. This unique, poetic essay was published at a time when debates about war remembrance and reconciliation of the "military comfort women" issue were growing more heated.[10] Lee recalls feeling that in a context increasingly fraught with polarized debate, there was too little space for dialogue, too little attention being given to the question of what new ways of looking at (*manazashi*) or listening to victims of wartime trauma might make it possible to better understand and embrace their sorrow. In *Tsubuyaki*, Lee was making a call for new language and new ways to engage in dialogue about these issues; over the years, *Tsubuyaki* itself would become a bridging point for such dialogue.

Like many readers, French literature scholar Ukai Satoshi was struck by the unconventional form of *Tsubuyaki*, and noted the sense of "surprise and vitality" he felt upon first encountering the text. Ukai describes the context in which the text was written as follows:

> "The winter of 1997." As with every date, this is a sign. What period, and just what it concretely represents, memorialises, remembers, is, in the end, unclear. Surely a secret will always remain, for structural reasons. However, this date, for me, is inextricably linked to its function as a symbol of the days of this era, where the atmosphere has

---

10. There are numerous accounts of these developments, but for a short summary in English about the "revisionist history" movement of the late 1990s and a discussion of the reemergence of these problems, see Nakano Kōichi and Yamaguchi Jiro, "Japan-Style McCarthyism and Threats to Academic Freedom," YouTube, October 6, 2014, https://www.youtube.com /watch?v=TNjWHwCQbcE.

become suddenly thin, and an unbearable sense of suffocation has begun to creep over our society.[11]

In the midst of an "unbearable sense of suffocation" that was sparked by the emergence of the historical revisionists' (*jiyūshugishikan*) movement, Ukai and many other readers felt that Lee's call or demand for a different kind of gaze, or way of seeing—and, I would add, listening—could open up a different way of approaching these questions. Lee's poetic sensibilities and rigorous philosophical inquiry made *Tsubuyaki* "a text which at first glance seems nothing but permeated by sensation and even sensuous, and yet, in fact, has a remarkable intelligence coursing through every fiber of its being."[12]

Lee herself describes the form and style of *Tsubuyaki* as a collage of "murmurs." The hybridity of the text, its poetic breath and voice—or what Gayatri Spivak might call its "protocol"—is unique and evoked numerous reviews and responses at the time. While an intensely personal, poetic text, *Tsubuyaki* was simultaneously Lee's call to create new forms of collectivity that, "unlike more conventional notions of collectivity, are not perfectly completed, always of the moment, but continuous. Not a society, not the state, not a static collective, but a space, or a sphere, or a world, where it is possible to have—and to share—such a gaze."[13]

Like *Tsubuyaki*, "Words for a Preface," the first work from the original volume that readers will encounter here, is written in Lee Chonghwa's poetic style. In one sense, it is a highly unconventional preface to a volume of essays; in another, it constitutes the perfect bridging point between Lee's earlier works and the essays and artworks. Like *Tsubuyaki*, it is a carefully composed collage interweaving Lee's own poetry with excerpts from three other works by Kim Sowol, Shin Tongyop, and Kim Shi-jong. Lee's "Words" links images of wild *jindalle*/azaleas, the flower that is found all over the Korean peninsula and is often invoked in modern Korean poetry. Through juxtaposing and linking these poetic texts and images, Lee creates a work with its own unique rhythm and breath and invites readers to "hear the wounds" that still resonate at multiple levels over a spectrum of historical periods and geopolitical locations.

---

11. Ukai Satoshi, *Aru "manazashi" no keiken* (The experience of a certain gaze), *Gendai shisō*, August 1997, reprinted in Lee, *Tsubuyaki no seiji shisō*. I am grateful to Paul McQuade for his excellent translation of Ukai's essay and insightful comments on *Tsubuyaki*.

12. Ibid.

13. Ibid.

Along with "*jindalle*/azaleas," the word *kentai* (献体) appears throughout "Words for a Preface." While the word *kentai* is commonly used in Japan to refer to the donation of a body for medical research, Lee's emphasis here on the body or bodies as "offerings" seems to give the term a new and unique meaning; thus, we have translated it throughout the text as "body offering." Lee's "Words for a Preface" and the notes that follow also remind us that the period during which we engaged in this collaborative project coincided with the period of time of waiting for the moment when the remains of Murayama Toshikatsu, Lee's close friend and colleague who helped initiate the project and who died suddenly in 2006, were finally returned to his mother.

In his commentary on *Still Hear the Wound*, political philosopher and scholar Kamejima Kōichi notes the connections between Lee's 1997 text, *Tsubuyaki*, and both "Words for a Preface" and Lee's conversation with musician and composer Takahashi Yūji, "On Not Letting Death Die," that also appears in the Preface of this book. Kamejima explains that Kim Sowol went to Japan in 1923 and barely escaped "the demagogy and brutal murder of Koreans (after the Kanto earthquake) and returned to Korea." He raises questions about the translation of these texts from Korean into Japanese, and points to the significance of including the third *jindalle*/azalea poem written in Japanese by Kim Shi-jong in 1953. Lee's inclusion of the "third azalea" reminds us of the complexity and significance of Lee's own choice to write in Japanese.[14]

Like Kamejima, I have come to see the threads that connect these texts. I might add that just as Lee uses her unique poetic language and style to create collages of words that link past and present, private and public memories, the artists whose works are presented here also use visual and material vocabularies to give expression to intersecting personal and unofficial public histories. Like the transport and transposition of images in "Words for a Preface," the visual images in these works also begin to circulate and converse with one another. Similarly, the essays that engage with these works, while shedding light on the "backstages" of Asian politics and history, engage with the artworks in a spirit of dialogue.

Lee turns to reflections on the vast numbers of people who died far from home "on the road," victims of war and colonialism, and explains her own experience of sensing "a sound that seems to enfold them ... a sound that covers those who have died." Here Takahashi Yūji refers to the multi-

---

14. Kamejima Kōichi, "*Zanshō no oto* o yomu" (On reading *Still Hear the Wound*), unpublished comments, Political Science Study Group, Department of Law, Seikei University, July 23, 2009.

directionality of sound and its movements, noting that it is "impossible to say whether a sound is 'here' or 'there.' ... Sound is essentially a process of fading away. By the time we've said we hear it, it is just a memory."

In "The Contours of Sound," Shinjō Ikuo draws on his experiences of performances by Takahashi Yūji and Ito Tari at the first Sakima workshop in a powerful essay that elucidates the dialogues or unexpected encounters sparked by these two live performances. For Shinjō, Takahashi Yūji's musical composition created and performed in response to Nakaya Kōkichi's poem "paved the way towards the beginning of a call-response relationship" that characterizes the Asia, Politics, Art project and its attempt to "link the political, social, sexual, economic, ethnic, and racial—in effect, the innumerably defined—divisions that we live in Asia today, within a space-time of collaborative artwork."

In her live art performance, *I will not forget you*, feminist performance artist Ito Tari pays homage to Kim Soon-duk, a former military comfort woman who passed away in 2004. Shinjō vividly describes Ito's performance in front of Maruki Iri's and Toshi's mural painting, the *Battle of Okinawa*; he notes that for several fleeting moments the encounters sensed and experienced in that space opened up "the possibility of politics ... as a physically intimate exercise."

Ito's performance also inspired Satō Izumi's essay, "Deaths That Are Not Remembered." In her response, Satō interweaves an account of another Korean woman who was forced to work as a military comfort woman in Okinawa, Beh Boungi. As if illustrating Shinjō's point that Okinawa has continued to be "the locus of military massacres and a front-line military base ... in postwar Asia," Satō explains that it was Takazato Suzuyo, founder of Okinawan Women Act against Military Violence, who met and helped Beh Boungi and who still supports victims of military sexual violence around present-day U.S. military bases in Okinawa. Ito Tari, inspired by what she learned about Beh Boungi at the Sakima workshop, began incorporating her story and reports of recent incidents of sexual violence in Okinawa around U.S. bases into a new performance artwork, *One Response*, as early as April 2007.[15]

---

15. The video documenting *I will not forget you* included in the DVD here begins with a *telop* ("television opaque projection device," or text superimposed on a screen, such as captions, subtitles, or scrolling tickers. This term is frequently used in Japan.), and three dates: 1937 (the date when Kim Sun-dŏk was forced to become a military comfort woman), 1945 (the end of the war), and 2006 (the year that the performance was created). The performance at Sakima Art Museum could not be filmed with sufficient lighting, so Ito chose to include a video recording of an earlier version of the performance held at PA/F Space in Tokyo in 2006, filmed by Desirée Lim.

Yano Kumiko attended the second Asia, Politics, Art workshop at the Sakima Art Museum, held in September 2007, and saw works by Okinawa-born video and performance artist Yamashiro Chikako. Yano's poetic essay is a response to Yamashiro's "Okinawa Complex Volume 1—Ibano Beach, Urasoe City" and helps us glimpse the lives of Okinawans affected by ongoing military and commercial development in and around the U.S. bases through the eyes of a creative artist. Yano also examines her own positionality as she views these works. This essay can be read alongside the interview of Yamashiro in *Still Hear the Wound II*, in which the artist speaks about filming *Shore Connivance (Mokuninhama)* and *Seaweed Woman (Aasa Onna)*, the character Yamashiro invented and filmed at several locations along the coastline of the main island of Naha, including Henoko.[16]

In "Specters of East Asia," playwright Choi Jinseok explores links among the histories of Okinawa, Taiwan, and Korea, focusing on the unnamed and unremembered Korean conscripted laborers who died in faraway places "on the road." Choi also reflects on his own personal history as a third-generation *zainichi* Korean and raises questions about ways that the pressure to assimilate into Japanese society might be linked to the movement for Okinawan independence. Choi has gone on to create and perform in original theater works, to publish translations, and, more recently, to publish a book in response to a growing number of incidents of hate speech directed at *zainichi* Koreans.

Music and film critic Higashi Takuma discusses representations of Okinawa in films by Takamine Gō and photographs by Higa Toyomitsu. Higashi critiques divergent representations of Okinawans as seen in Gō's films that sometimes feature rock musicians from the band Condition Green, who often played for U.S. servicemen in Kōza, and the *Minatogawa Man* displayed in the Okinawan Prefectural Museum. In his provocative reading of these works, Higashi invokes Benjamin's "Angel of History" and cites Caren Kaplan's discussion of discourses on location, thus enabling him to situate local discussions of the politics of representing Okinawa in a larger framework.

Ikeuchi Yasuko's in-depth response to works shown by Soni Kum at the

---

16. Shinjō Ikuo, "The Ethics of Ecstasy: The Art of Yamashiro Chikako," and Kondō Kenichi, "Seeking Okinawa's Real Face: The World of Yamashiro Chikako," both in *MAM Project 018* (Mori Art Museum, 2012). Ayelet Zohar, "Camouflage, Photography and [In]visibility, Yamashiro Chikako's 'Chorus of the Melodies' Series (2010)," *Trans Asia Photography Review* 3, no. 1 (Fall 2012). Also my "Unspeakable Bodies of Memory: Performance and Precarity in Recent Works by Yamashiro Chikako," *Journal of Kyoto Seika University* 44 (2013).

first Asia, Politics, Art workshop provides readers with many insights into the background of Kum's montage of images and fragments from different film sources and image fragments that in turn underscore Kum's struggle to negotiate "the conflicting versions" of history that she encountered growing up as a third-generation *zainichi* Korean. Building on extensive interviews with Kum, Ikeuchi goes on to develop new readings of both Kum's *Foreign Sky* and Oshima Nagisa's *Death by Hanging*. The dialogue between Kum and Ikeuchi has continued in recent years as Kum has gone on to complete her PhD and to produce new works.

In my own tentative comments in "'Postmemory' in the Work of Oh Haji and Soni Kum," I try to show how these third-generation *zainichi* artists negotiate and express cross-generational memory, drawing on Marianne Hirsch's writings on "postmemory" of Holocaust survivors. I explore ways in which these third-generation *zainichi* artists have created unique materials and metaphors that help them explore questions of diasporic identities, as well as private and public memories and their works in the context of other contemporary art of the diaspora. Both artists have continued to produce breathtaking works that are being exhibited in and outside of Japan.

Unfortunately, in our effort to see that information about the Asia, Art, Politics project reached English-speaking readers in a timely fashion, we were unable to complete translations of all the essays in the original volume. We would have liked to include Jung Yeong-hae's insightful reading of Kinjō Mitsuru's *Voices of the Stones*, Kinjō's collaborative project commemorating those who died in the Battle of Okinawa. In her essay, Jung asks, "Is it a memorial? Is it a place of repose for the souls of the dead? Is it a prayer?" While pointing to the intersection among performance, ritual, prayer, and contemporary art practices seen in many of the works shown here, Jung's piece is also formed around her own poetic response to Kinjō's work and links it to the history of her own family, who come from Jeju Island. We have included Kum Soni's interview of Kinjō Mitsuru in the DVD attached here. For Kinjō, *Voices of the Stones* was a collaborative act of expression through which participants came to experience "sounds and reverberations ... not just skimming along the surface, but swimming in deep water." In his view, to "preserve the work in a fixed form, as art" would have undermined its real purpose and value. Kinjō states:

> If it had become permanent, the life force that, well, dwelled there, would eventually lose its sense of purpose. ... We felt that it would be

unbearable to see it permanently stuck there as a mere gesture/object of artistic expression. ... Something there allowed us to come to a momentary sense of understanding—something that shouldn't remain a permanent fixture (art object).

It was that fleeting moment, when it seemed that the stones were speaking, that was important, and stays on in the memories of those who experienced it. The ephemeral, performative aspects of *Voices of the Stones* perhaps signal a series of interconnected "states of precarity," something that is conveyed in various ways in all of the works introduced here. There is the initial precarity of the memories and lives of those lost, the fleeting and sometimes "risky" performative acts by the artists, and the impermanence of the works themselves that can only be partially documented, but not fully preserved, as art objects.

Essays by Uema Canae, Abe Kosuzu, and Kim Hyeshin were also included in the original volume, but could not be translated in time for inclusion here. Canae, curator at the Sakima Museum, whose support throughout this project was invaluable, writes of Okinawan artists whose works resist commodification and discusses ways in which the Sakima Art Museum has functioned as a space of remembrance and exchange. Her essay is a response to drama, music, and dance performances by Kitajima Sumiko, Iha Kumiko, Iha Sadako, and Nejimei Hiromi at the second workshop held at the Sakima Art Museum. A scholar of American and Caribbean studies and peace activist, Abe Kosuzu, explores recurring images and metaphors of "skin" and "nation" in the works of participating artists. Art historian Kim Hyeshin discusses and compares works by Oh Haji and Korean artist Yun Suknam, uncovering nuanced resonances in their works. We hope that these essays will be translated someday.

Finally, a few notes on the production of the DVD, *Still Hear the Wound*: The interviews, filming, and film editing were all done by Soni Kum in Okinawa and Tokyo. In their responses to Kum, Oh Haji, Yamashiro Chikako, and Kinjō Mitsuru all speak very openly about their motivations for creating the works and about their unique creative processes. The transcriptions and English translations of the interviews were done by Hirano Oribe, Andrew Harding, and Jooyeon Hahm. Soni Kum also undertook the painstaking task of designing and inserting English subtitles. In addition, as Kum's segment in the original DVD was much shorter than the others, she has created a new version here. Readers will find additional information about recent works by the artists in the contributors list.

In addition to segments on five of the artists, we include Soni Kum's film interpretation of *Still Hear the Wound II*, with images of the Maruki's *Battle of Okinawa*, a soundtrack by Kum, music composed by Takahashi Yuji, and a translation of "The Last Note" by Nakaya Kōkichi.

ACKNOWLEDGMENTS

Needless to say, a project like this cannot be realized without the help of many people. We are extremely grateful to Lee Chonghwa and Iwanami Shoten for granting permission to translate and publish selections from the original *Zanshō no oto* volume, and to Lee Chonghwa for her generous support of the translation project. As we begin and end with the works of the artists, we are all greatly indebted to Oh Haji, Yamashiro Chikako, Ito Tari, Soni Kum, Kinjō Mitsuru, Kitajima Sumiko, Miyagi Akira, and Takahashi Yūji for permission to use their works. We also thank Yumiko Chiba Associates, Maruki Hisako, and the Sakima Art Museum for their generous permission to use reproductions of the artists' works. In addition, Shinjō Ikuo, Choi Jinseok, Ikeuchi Yasuko, Higashi Takuma, Satō Izumi, and Yano Kumiko have generously granted permission to translate and publish their essays.

Generous support from the Center for Asian and Pacific Studies at Seikei University made the initial workshops possible, and now, thanks to support from Kyoto Seika University and the Cornell University East Asia Program, we are able to publish these works in English. Kiriyama Yoshio's advice and support at every stage of the volume's production is deeply appreciated. Thanks are due to Hirokazu Miyazaki, director of the East Asia Program at Cornell, for his vision in launching a Translation Studies initiative within the program, of which this collaboration has been an inaugural activity. We thank Joshua Young of the East Asia Program for his keen interest in this initiative, and for his administrative and technical help. Mai Shaikhanuar-Cota of the Cornell East Asia Series offered expert help with every aspect of production, including our cover design. The Central New York Humanities Corridor, with a grant from the Andrew W. Mellon Foundation, funded a workshop at which Lee Chonghwa discussed the Art, Asia, Politics project with invited speakers: we thank Richard Calichman, Ellie Choi, Pedro Erber, Andrew Harding, Arnika Fuhrman, Victor Koschmann, Meera Lee, Mizutamari Mayumi, Paul McQuade, Joshua Pilzer, and Naoki Sakai for their participation. Because the essays and artworks made reference not only to Japanese, but also to Korean and Okinawan contexts, we often cast our nets far and wide in attempting to resolve translation problems. Postgraduate student Hirano Oribe of Kyoto Seika University offered steadfast help and illuminating insights. Asakawa Shiho's untiring support facilitated communications with authors and artists in Japan. Youngmin Kim, Meejeong Song, Watanabe Naoki, and Christopher Ahn also offered indispensable help. Kasai Hirotaka, Kasai Shima, and Park Jin-Han kindly discussed interpretive questions with Cornell translators at a graduate seminar in Fall 2013. Dianne Ferris provided reliable and congenial assistance with formatting.

Thanks to Brett de Bary, who coordinated seminars at Cornell in 2010 and 2013, the idea of publishing selected essays from the original volume was born. Without her ongoing encouragement and impressively painstaking attention to every word and thought, we would not have been able to complete work on this text. Finally, we thank Moira Roth, whose early and enthusiastic response to the DVD, and whose own groundbreaking work on the power of art to untangle "obdurate histories," have been a great source of inspiration and support throughout.

Of course, none of this would be possible without the help of translators willing to take on the often daunting and difficult challenge of rendering these works in English. It is thanks to the hard work of extremely talented graduate students that these translations have found their way into print. We thank Ryan Buyco, Andrew Harding, Miyako Hayakawa, Junliang Huang, Keiji Kunigami, Jillian Marshall, Paul McQuade, and Andrea Mendoza of Cornell University, and Jooyeon Hahm of the University of Pennsylvania, for their contributions. Postgraduate student Hirano Oribe of Kyoto Seika University offered patient and careful responses to our questions. Yutaka Yoshida's profound grasp of Lee's poetic voice and uncanny ability to find near-equivalent phrasings of the most difficult passages in English enabled us to include Lee Chonghwa's "Words for a Preface." Gayatri Spivak has described the task of translation—not only but perhaps especially from non-Western languages—as both "impossible and necessary." I have recalled Spivak's words countless times, and like Spivak, hope that some readers will be inspired to go back to the original Japanese (and Korean) for their own taste of the sounds and sensations of these languages.

EDITORS' NOTE

Asian names are given in the normal order of family name followed by surname, except in the case of artists or authors who prefer to use the English
order. Macrons are included on long Japanese vowels, except in the cases of
place or personal names familiarly used in English (e.g., Tokyo, Ito Tari). In
romanizing Korean names and words in this volume we have generally followed the Revised Romanization system, in accordance with the trans`litera-
tion conventions used in the original Japanese volume. We depart from this
where an alternative romanization is preferred by artists or authors featured
in the volume, or where citing precedents in English-language publications.

Afterthoughts, "Afterlife," on the Occasion of Translation

Brett de Bary

In retrospect, I note, and realize, that the brief essay that follows has been a preliminary attempt to prise out the "logic of resonances" (that is, a political and ethical philosophy) that seems to me to inform the structure and activities of the project known as Asia, Politics, Art. My effort itself is, of course, simply another translation project, in which I have admittedly relied on a strand of post-structuralist translation theory familiar in the North American academy. Nevertheless, I have performed the translation in the belief that it is important to try to articulate—as Rebecca Jennison also urges in her prefatory essay—what is distinctive and "new" about the Asia, Politics, Art project. It embodies a spirit of political activism that also insists on a certain indirectness, and a space somehow apart. We need to further explore this difference from the activism of earlier historical moments, recognizing in it a creative response to social and historical conditions—as well as to the availability of new and different cultural resources—specific to the early twenty-first century.

At the beginning of an interview with the performance artist Ito Tari in 2013, Lee Chonghwa, this volume's editor, proposed exploring the topos of "lingering," "remaining behind"—a topos of the "residue" and perhaps the "remainder." "Your action leaves something behind," she said of Ito's performances. "There's something in the so-called 'expression' or 'image' there that we can't get inside, and can't appropriate for ourselves—as if there was another body there, and a time that envelops it."[1] Lee likens such a perfor-

---

1. Lee Chonghwa in the interview "'Kasetsu' no hifu: Pafuōmansu ātisuto Itō Tāri, 40-nen

mance to the "site of life" itself, for "to live," in her view, is always a matter of "remaining" or "living on" in the face of accumulated memory.

Lee's insistence here on defining human life as a kind of "afterlife" sets forth the question of continuity in discontinuity, that is, in a profound sense, "sounded" throughout the volume of essays *Still Hear the Wound: Toward an Asia, Politics, and Art to Come*, presented in translation in this volume. This guiding evocation of a sound (音) of lingering or "remaining" wounds is produced by a compound invented by Lee for the occasion (the compound 残傷 that connects the characters for "wound" and "to remain" is not part of the formal Japanese lexicon). It offers the volume to readers in a gesture of poiesis and synesthesia. Within the context of this English-language volume as an instance of translation, then, we might recall the moment of synesthesia in Walter Benjamin's well-known discussion of translation—a process Benjamin, in a manner not unlike Lee, would take to be a form of afterlife. In translation, Benjamin wrote, drawing on an image evoking both touch and sound, "meaning is touched by language only the way an Aeolian harp is touched by wind."[2] Letting this glancing, vibrating contact between Benjamin's harp and wind further invoke in us an association with resonance, we come back again to the theme of *Still Hear the Wound*. For in the volume, as in the series of events Asia, Politics, Art upon which the book's essays are based, the actions of hearing, listening, responding, and, more broadly, resonating are proposed as indispensable for any Asia to come.

While it might seem obvious that *Still Hear the Wound*, whose essays deal with artworks about relations among Korea, Okinawa, and Japan, intervenes in Japan's fraught contestation over its twentieth-century national history from a transnational perspective, it does so with a difference that must be emphasized. Rather than fashioning itself as a contribution to the now-voluminous body of scholarly, historical writing addressing questions of Japan's responsibility for colonial violence and war crimes, that is, the Asia, Politics, Art project seeks precisely to enact and activate a response that resonates on multiple registers and in multiple expressive modalities, going beyond the conventional writing and rewriting known as history.

To be sure, the project shares with conscientious historians a sense of the

---

no kiseki" [Trying on other skins: Tracing performance artist Itō Tāri's 40-year career] in *Tosho Shinbun* (Tokyo, July 6, 2013), 1.

2. Walter Benjamin, "The Task of the Translator," in *Walter Benjamin: Selected Writings, Volume 1, 1913–1926*, ed. Marcus Bullock and Michael W. Jennings (Cambridge, MA: Harvard University Press, 1996), 262.

urgent need to counter the movement toward historical revisionism that has only intensified in Japan in recent years. Yet in this instance, the linking of what is broadly called art to politics and Asia is a call to go beyond the discursive. This is not only because the collection's title, in its synesthesia, alludes from the start to the different sensory modalities necessary for "hearing the wound." It is also because here any facile, if commonsensical, equation among memory, writing, and history is rejected.

Perhaps what is different about Asia, Politics, Art, then, is this insistence that, on a more fundamental level, history can only be a bodily experience. This would explain the pivotal role in the project of performance and installation art (often too ephemeral to have been reproduced in this volume, and created for the most part by minority artists lacking the considerable material resources required for mainstream art production). It also explains the project's steadfast attention to the inescapable paradox Benjamin has defined, in his work on translation, as afterlife. As Samuel Weber has written, Benjamin's work on translation sought to challenge the Romantic notion of art, or the "symbol," as a realm of perfection, immutability, and eternity, albeit within a secular framework. Rather, Benjamin (in a spirit Weber aligns with the Baroque) called attention to singularity and finitude in relation to signification and language. From a temporal perspective, signification involves incessant movement through material media that are never identical, and therefore, it inexorably involves loss. This loss becomes even more apparent in the movement across different languages that takes place in translation. For Benjamin, "the original can be said to outlive itself" in translation, but only "while being condemned to live on and away in the foreign language," Weber writes. Thus, "as a singular event, the translation is destined to 'go under' and be absorbed in the history of the foreign language." Far from being a natural, organic continuity, history, like translation, is for Benjamin "marked by an irreducible finitude." For in the German Baroque conception, history (like the individual and his or her signifying activities) was always subjugated to death. For the Baroque, in Benjamin's words, "death draws the jagged line of demarcation between physis (*Natur*) and significance (*Bedeutung*)."[3]

In this vein, we might say that something about the bodily experience of history stressed by Asia, Politics, Art is illuminated when we consider it in

---

3. Samuel Weber, *Benjamin's -abilities* (Cambridge, MA: Harvard University Press, 2008), 69.

relation to Benjamin and the German Baroque. By seeking an encounter with the past in sensuously engaging works of art, the project, as we have observed, turns aside from a quest for transparency in history. Moreover, by continuously representing the past in terms of the body/bodies of the dead (whether of a colleague, or of the "deaths far away" that are also elegized here), the project justifies its detour from transparency by specifying the relation between living and dead to be one of aporia. This is why, in the artworks and the discussions of them here, we find everywhere exhibited simultaneously a tenacious attachment to the individual body of the departed, with its experience of irreversible decline and death, accompanied by a determination to remember and commemorate—to forge a relationship in the here and now between that body and what survives, "remains," and might generally be named "life." In Benjamin's spirit, we might conclude that—whatever the relationship fashioned in the face of such undeniable discontinuity—it can never be simply a "natural" or "organic" one, but can only be a relation of poiesis.

On the basis of these considerations, and turning to one of the specific tropes that calls to us powerfully from this collection, we might ask what else about history is conveyed by the words "body offering" that occur in its prefatory poem, "Words for a Preface: *Jindalle*/Azaleas or Flowers for *Body Offerings*." In the most immediate sense, as Jennison explains, "body offering" (献体 or *kentai*, a compound used to designate a body donated to medical research in contemporary Japanese) is a reference to the young scholar and translator, Murayama Toshikatsu, who was a founding member of Asia, Politics, Art. Murayama died suddenly in 2006, as the project was being launched, at the age of thirty-eight.[4] In what might be seen as one of the many resonances associated with the project, Murayama's body was returned to his mother from the hospital where it had been used for research, around the time that this volume was first published. Figuratively, the term "body offering" is thus doubly allusive, referring at once to Murayama himself, and to the book that is dedicated to him.

Insofar as the book takes up questions of history, however, we might further deduce that, since a body offering must be donated or given up, what is implied here is also that history involves giving something up, or having

---

4. Murayama's published work consisted primarily of translations, especially of critical theory and gender theory (an area in which he worked collaboratively with Takemura Kazuko, among others). As Lee notes, Murayama's first single-authored work, *Toward (Invisible) Desires: In Dialogue with Queer Theory*, was published shortly before his death.

something at stake—thus risk, exposure, or even a certain loss or wound. Not only is the idea of giving up evocative of (even a possible translation for) the term *Aufgabe* or "offering" in the original title of Benjamin's "Task of the Translator" (*Die Aufgabe des Übersetzers*), but it also reminds us of Benjamin's interest in the Baroque notion of death or loss in history that Weber has pointed out. What we must understand is that there is a "lack of reciprocity, symmetry, equivalence" in the individual's relation to history in this view.[5]

Such reflections only serve to amplify the association between the "body offering" and the "wound" in this volume's title. In that respect, the Asia—or transnational—evoked by *Still Hear the Wound* has much in common with concepts of community "opened by a wound" that are being explored in other critical and artistic circles at this time. For example, some feminist scholars have tried to conjoin the notion of bodily vulnerability (as a condition for political solidarity) elaborated by Judith Butler with Robert Esposito's or Hélène Cixous's notion of the "wound" as symbolizing a community's commitment to expose itself to "the contagion of otherness," as opposed to fixating on its immunity and safety.[6] Thus we might surmise that the face-to-face encounters between scholars and practicing artists out of which this book grew required of them, in however modest or symbolic a way, a certain bodily experience of history, at the very least in the form of exposure to mutually unfamiliar media of expression.

In that vein, we should also note that "Words for a Preface" is a poem by Lee whose passages are here interwoven with fragments of other poems by the modern Korean poets Kim Sowŏl and Shin Tongyop and by the contemporary *zainichi* poet Kim Shi-jong. Its positioning at the beginning signals the importance for the project as a whole of poetic language and the figural, or to a poetic mode of relationality whose primary characteristics will be resonance, association, and rhythm. The small white boat, the ear-shaped cup, are vessels set afloat upon the sea in a gesture of commemoration that entrusts messages to its rhythms. This is the sea that separates the scattered bodies of those who died "far away" in the era of colonialism and war, and that also separates Korea, Okinawa, and Japan. And yet it is also the sea that

---

5. Weber, *Benjamin's -abilities*, 68.

6. Joana Sabadell-Nieto and Marta Segarra, "Impossible Communities: On Gender, Vulnerability and Community," in *Differences in Common: Gender, Vulnerability, and Community*, ed. Joana Sabadell-Nieto and Marta Segarra (Amsterdam: Rodopi, 2014), 9. Sabadell-Nieto and Segarra refer to writings on the "wound" and community by Robert Esposito, Hélène Cixous, and others.

connects in separating, and is an unstable boundary. Just as the small boat leaves only an ephemeral wake, or trace, on the water, so the sea is "the same everywhere" (as one of Tawada Yōko's narrators has asked, "How can one say where the place of foreign water begins when the border itself is water?").[7] The poem offers inaugural images for the volume that are rhythmically repeated, yet transformed as they are dislocated into changing contexts, as is the case with the cited fragments of Korean and *zainichi* poetry. The repetitions constitute an arrangement, not of exact or symmetrical parallels, but of resonances, generative echoes.

Rebecca Jennison has already explicated here the effect of Lee's rhythmical repetitions, twisting lines, and dislocations on a second leading trope, that of the azalea—positioned as interchangeable with, and of equal significance to, the trope of the body offering. In an extremely perceptive essay, "Politics and Aesthetics of the Wound: Performative Narratives of the People by *Zainichi* Korean Artists," Eun Yung Jin and Bo Seon Shim have unraveled the politically complex semiotics surrounding the symbol of wild azalea, or *jindalle*, in modern Korea. As they explain, the wild azalea should not be confused with the rose of Sharon, the official national flower of South Korea that is mentioned in the national anthem. Nevertheless, the wild azalea, sometimes coded as a "repository of emotion" and "feminine" complement to the rose of Sharon, is often associated in modern Korean poetry with intensely nationalistic emotion. Similarly, in North Korea, the wild azalea is not an official national flower, but is commonly used to evoke national emotion, as in the revolutionary dance work *The Azalea of Our Nation* (or in the clip of wild azaleas from North Korean director Jo Kyong Sun's 1982 film *Wolmido*, incorporated into Soni Kum's video work, *Beast of Me*). In Lee's twisting and intertwining lines, hallowed azaleas are made interchangeable with the secret "metamorphoses" of women, and the play of "goddesses" who appear in a citation, in Murayama's *Toward (Invisible) Desire*, from Jean Genet's "Alberto Giacommetti's Studio": "In this studio a man is dying, consuming himself, and before our eyes turning himself into goddesses." The transport and transposition of these images through different associations, along with the invocation of metamorphosis, allow the male dead, the playing women, goddesses, and azalea petals to freely circulate and appear and stand

---

7. Tawada Yōko, "Where Europe Begins," in *Where Europe Begins*, trans. Susan Bernofsky and Yumi Selden (New York: New Directions, 2002), 123.

in for each other. By so doing, Lee, as Jin and Shim state, overturns the traditional association of the azalea with the idea of a "simple dichotomy between male and female."[8] Azaleas are divested of the connotations of heterosexual romance that customarily naturalize heteronormativity at the crux of nationalist affect.

Lee's use in her poem of "red, red *jindalle* flowers" from Kim Shi-jong's "Azaleas," published in 1952 in Osaka, deserves attention because it performs another type of shifting. In the first two lines, "red, red *jindalle* flowers" are associated by the poet with "our homeland" (in Kim Shi-jong's case, the island of Jeju from which he fled with his family at the time of the 1948 massacre). Yet the following two lines shift the referent for the beloved symbol to Japan, using the pointer or deictic "this": "my azaleas / I have seen / these flowers blooming / on *this* Japanese soil, too" (emphasis mine). I completely agree with the wording of Jin and Shim's assertion that, with this rhetorical gesture, Kim Shi-jong allows azaleas to bloom "anywhere."[9] Rather than completely disavowing the poetic image's affective power, he disassociates it and dislocates it from any specific land, such as the nation-state. Jin and Shim's choice of the word "anywhere" here, is strikingly similar to those in the proposal made by Gayatri Spivak, in her discussion of the "strenuous imagination" required to think beyond nationalism. Observing the indigenous people with whom she has worked in India, Spivak does not seek to deny the existence of affect, of a feeling of "rock bottom comfort in one's language and one's home," or even "one's little corner," "anywhere" it exists. Nationalist ideology "hijacks" and "conjures" with this emotion, says Spivak, when it is simply a sense of "thereness" that could be transported elsewhere.[10] (Describing the oral formulas by which indigenous women, singing as she walked with them to a fair in Kolkata, referred to the city by one name after another, in a series of rhythmical substitutions, she writes, "Here, then, is a thinking without nation, space-names as shifters, in a mythic geography because of the power of the formulaic.")[11] Kim Shi-jong's poetic vision thus

---

8. Eun Yung Jin and Bo Seon Shim, "The Politics and Aesthetics of the Wound: Performative Narratives of the People by *Zainichi* Korean Artists," in *Korea Journal*, Volume 55, No. 1 (Summer, 2015), Seoul: Korean National Commission for UNESCO, 95.

9. Ibid., 97.

10. Gayatri Spivak, "Nationalism and the Imagination," in *Differences in Common: Gender, Vulnerability, and Community*, ed. Joana Sabadell-Nieto and Marta Segarra (Amsterdam: Rodopi, 2014), 35.

11. Ibid., 38.

shifts the location and setting of the beloved "red, red *jindalle* flowers" to "this" Japanese soil, in a similar gesture.

It goes without saying that—with the nevertheless significant exception of Murayama—the deaths commemorated in these essays are the result of colonial, and by extension wartime, violence. In them we repeatedly encounter images of "comfort women" abandoned in the battle zone by the retreating Japanese army, of Korean porters executed by that same army for staving off hunger by eating stolen rice grains in Okinawa, of anticolonial guerilla fighters who died too far from relatives to be buried by them, of suicides in the Battle of Okinawa, and, most challengingly, of victims on both sides of the 1948 Jeju Massacre whose stories were suppressed for so long. Reencountering these dead in art, albeit as spectral presences, is what is entailed in the process of "still" hearing the wound.

As their title suggests, for Jin and Shim the trope of the wound allows an unresolved tension to be maintained throughout the volume as it confronts these memories of violence. The wound still heard in this collection is also still unhealed. Its manifestations in the present belie the linear temporality of the nation state, since it symbolizes a violence (within and between nation states) which repeats and returns. As they note, the Asia, Politics, Art project has insistently sought to connect the past and the present, "but not in a linear manner."[12] Moreover, they describe the volume as animated by the continuous pressure its "performative narratives of the people" exert against "pedagogical" narratives deployed by the Japanese nation-state, whose assimilative ideology produces and reproduces the unity of the nation by erasing difference. In this sense, they insightfully comment on *zainichi* playwright Choi Jinseok's essay, "Specters of East Asia." By foregrounding the existence of hitherto unacknowledged dead still in unmarked graves in Okinawa ("comfort women" and Korean laborers forced to work as army porters), they maintain, Choi complicates the story of the "victims" of the Battle of Okinawa. For Koreans were also killed by Okinawans serving the Japanese army. Okinawans, while themselves discriminated against under Japanese colonialism, also discriminated against other ethnicities like Koreans under the sway of assimilationist ideology. For Choi, acknowledging the existence of mutual discrimination between minorities (which he refers to as "embracing the otherness within") productively "splits" and contests the pedagogical narrative of

---

12. Jin and Shim, "The Politics and Aesthetics of the Wound."

national unity, and is the necessary foundation for new relations among *zainichi*, Koreans, and Okinawans.[13]

Yet, as some critics have asked, does synesthesia not ultimately resolve differences in a synthesis? Does the volume's commitment to resonances, in this sense, seek a harmony that turns aside from conflict, from the struggle for restitution and justice?[14] I believe the participants in Asia, Politics, Art would wish neither to deflect, nor reject, the pertinence of this question. As a project that has consciously avoided situating itself as a direct intervention into the controversy over the official state narrative (that is, has deliberately turned away from its institutionalized language, modalities, and spaces for debate), it has avowedly sought a different space for itself. In this way, it is experimental, its success or failure still an open question.

Yet a few concluding thoughts might helpfully be brought to bear on these deliberations. One returns us to our opening considerations of Benjamin, synesthesia, and translation, and to the image of the wind and Aeolian harp. For the touching of the harp by the wind certainly produces a resonance. For Benjamin, however, this "touch of translation" must always be (in his words) "glancing," "tangential," and fleeting. This is because, as we have mentioned earlier, it is the fundamental work of language and signification to constantly depart and move on. Even more vividly in the case of translation between languages, the "tangential encounter" can give rise to multiple afterlives, because so many possible meanings are at stake. This is the view of Weber, who observes that Benjamin's "tangential encounter" refers to the way the "interplay of the different *possible* meanings of the original text and of the translation" produces not a single meaning but a *"difference of meanings* which, like a difference of opinion, signifies precisely through its disunity." Benjamin's German word *Berührung*, Weber further notes, can be translated as "contact," "touch," or "glancing," but "can also signify, paradoxically, the

---

13. Here I have recapitulated the argument by Jin and Shim, who draw on Homi Bhabha's distinction between the pedagogical and performative narratives of the nation. Ibid., 87–91.

14. In a discusson of Tanizaki's use of synesthesia, Thomas Lamarre points out both the romantic and reactionary potential of synesthesia, which can be taken to symbolize the organic unity of the modern nation. "There is an ideological critique of the synaesthetic strategy. Basically, it calls attention to the synthesis that accompanies synaesthesia. Which is to say, it is the terms for the unification of the senses that become problematic—the 'syn' of synaesthesia." See Thomas Lamarre, "The Deformation of the Modern Spectator: Synaesthesia, Cinema, and the Spectre of Race in Tanizaki," *Japan Forum* 11, no. 1 (1999): 28.

'state of being moved,' as by an *emotion*."[15] In these envisionings, resonance is a mode of affective touching that can be both light and glancing and take place within a play of differences.

Jean François Lyotard's definition of the "figural," in contrast to the "discursive," can also shed light on how the commitment to resonances of the Asia, Politics, Art project, with its insistence on bodily participation, might be understood as something other than "harmony." For Lyotard, the crucial difference between "discourse" and "figure" lies in contrasting uses of, or approaches to, the signifying medium. For Lyotard, the "discursive" is that which, in its aim to convey a clear message, signifies according to invariant rules of a language or genre, and in the process erases the "opacity and density" of the signifying materiality. By contrast, the realm of the "figural" involves "a libidinal involvement with an object in its density and spatiality," one that gives rise to an "excess" of meaning.[16]

Lyotard's comments on deixis and the figural are particularly interesting in relation to our discussion of deictics above. For he points to the disjunction between the status of deixis within the systematized rules of language (discourse) and deixis as the gesture of the living body in space. As Vlad Ionescu understands it, "the closed system of language inevitably inhibits the referential dimension, that is, the 'here' and 'now' of the desiring body in its position of denotation." The living body, that is, always occupies a space that cannot be completely absorbed into textual and linguistic space. The figural, precisely because it engages the "desiring body in its relation to signs that are plastic, visual, and dense," possesses a certain capacity to break through conventionally codified space.[17]

Since each work of art, in its materiality, occupies a singular time and space, while creating symbolic and imaginary spaces through its significations, the work of art is often seen as modeling alternative social spaces. Certainly the Asia invoked by Lee Chonghwa at the close of her dialogue with Takahashi Yūji, also included in this volume, seems to be this kind of space. As she says in her concluding statement there, "We create art that is a response, and in that sense, a ritual ... perhaps, that is what I would call 'Asia.'"

Insofar as a response implies a relation, it can designate a sociality, here

---

15. Weber, *Benjamin's -abilities*, 95.

16. I rely here on Vlad Ionescu, "Figural Aesthetics: Lyotard, Valéry, Deleuze," *Cultural Politics* 9, no. 2 (2013): 146.

17. Ibid.

provisionally termed "Asia." Moreover, in light of the volume's concern for processes of commemoration and mourning, Lee's use of the term "ritual" brings in the concept of affect and, indeed, the concept of a plurality of human bodies that any possibility of "resonance"—as a process by which human bodies *affect* each other—implies. This "Asia" is not so much a specific place as mode of relating to others and to the Other within.

If one can see *Still Hear the Wound* as a kind of ritual, we will need to recognize the sociality it hopes to create and re-create by situating that ritual where, in Benjamin's words, "death draws the jagged line of demarcation between physis (*natur*) and significance (*bedeutung*)." This volume's unwavering gaze at the bodies of the dead, according to this logic, cannot be described as melancholy, politically passive, nor defeatist, but generative and anticipatory—a way, in Lee's carefully chosen words, of "not letting death die."

Note: I would like here to express my personal thanks to Rebecca Jennison for the exceptional generosity she displayed at every stage of our work cotranslating and coediting this volume. Without her unsurpassed knowledge of art by women activists in Japan, her penetrating insights, and the extensive network of contacts she mobilized to assist with our project, it could not have been completed.

Words for a Preface

Jindalle/*Azaleas or Flowers for* Body Offerings

Lee Chonghwa

with "Azaleas"

Kim Sowol (1902–1934)

Sinking

Still submerged, with a clear membrane spreading on and in the sea

Softly I place a small jar on the way

The sea left me like a lump of pus, undissolved, dancing and crawling

The membrane that covers me looks like a small ear-shaped cup

A small white boat

to shore, to land, onto the soil

The earth is not yet warm

I pour *sake* into the white ear-shaped cup

Dig into the earth   trace the footsteps of memory

the rest transferred and left

Burial in transition

"I will become a ghost and wander the earth,

and if that too is not possible,

I will pay a visit in someone's memories."

(from the last words of Jo Mun Sang, Korean prison guard for
the Japanese Imperial Army, executed for war crimes)

We dance and crawl together with him, tracking his traces in their dreams

Living is a place that moves   looking for and transferring graves

When you go away

Sick of seeing me

I shall let you go gently, no words

From Mount Yak in Yonghyŏn

An armful of azaleas

I shall gather and scatter on your path

Road of *Jindalle*/Azaleas

Jindalle/azaleas   delivered from distant memories
Memories of   giving birth   treading   burying
of death / far away
and the "play" of the goddesses

This is a dream as well; we offer
that "intersection between the pleasure of reading and erotic pleasure"
of which Murayama Toshikatsu (1967–2006) wrote in
Toward (Invisible) Desire,
and the secret metamorphoses of the women—themselves like petals—
who play among us as we live treading on the azalea petals
that are also the crowded, exposed bodies of the dead;
offerings for this mourning ritual to stay alive with the dead,
for our irreplaceable friend Murayama-san

The time of waiting for the *body offering*

The time for those sleeping testimonies to stop breathing again,

to be alive, tolerating

to become corporeal

The time to dissolve and release the lumps of those distant memories

for the time of the *body offering*

The gaze from the dead

This life addressed by the dead

treading on azaleas

Waiting for the contingency of death

The woman-ness of death

For the appearance of this woman-ness of death

Intoxicated by the lukewarm breeze that blows then

we tread   on the petals of the azaleas

Step by step away

On the flowers lying before you

Tread softly, deeply and go

"... here everything is precarious and about to collapse,

everything is tending to

dissolve, everything drifts: now, all this is somehow apprehended in an

absolute reality. When I have left the studio, when I am out in the street,

it is

then that nothing of what is around me is real anymore.

Shall I say it? In this

studio a man is slowly dying, consuming himself, and

before our eyes turning

himself into goddesses."[1]

The transformation or "metamorphoses" of the goddesses

The curtain that gazes at them on a strange shore

Time for the hem of the curtain that was born from

the Korean wear, *chima*, of grandmothers

to become the woven crest of white-braided hair

The ends of the long strands of hair

appearing from anywhere   somewhere we don't know

memories of the hair   show no trace   leave no trace

memories of needles/hair   the touch of their shadows

Each petal that flickers and is then scattered

Toward distant memories pregnant with needles

The "play" of the goddesses
crawling   flowing   floating   slumbering   dancing

From the body that has become a needle
come bodies that transform   intermingle   transmogrify

the bodies that "metamorphose"

The dead who are playing   the playing goddesses

Azaleas blooming in crowded clusters that dance and crawl
The moment when those *jindalle* flowers turn into the *chima jogori*
of the Korean women

Chima jogori

I wear you

I cut you

I wear and sever what you memorize

After this long time of waiting for the *body offering*

on a summer morning when leaves on the tree planted and grown

in your place,

in place of friends who love you,

flicker in the blinding light

it was you who gently visited, flowering yourself with petals

into your mother's hands   Murayama-san

Even if I never again   see his dear face

May those   bright flowers

Bloom in the hills and mountains.

Even if I never again   hear his sweet songs

May his   pure breathing

Live on in the forests and fields.

You who walk the fields in desolation.

When the snow melts on the road   fill yourself with wind
When the wind dies down   fill your heart with love

Even if I never again   meet his dear shadow,
May his soul   shed tears and go away
and bloom in the hills and fields

Shin Tongyop, "On the Hills and Mountains," from the collection of poems
Asanyeo (1963)

The azalea flowers smiling, red, from the hands of your mother as she held you
"—'but you ... ' he said. 'What were you doing?'
—I was watching her. To help her, to show respect for this woman who had
brought death with her into the depth of the night.
To care for this woman in the midst of falling, all the way into death"[2]

Without one single regret
Without anything left behind
You have to   just as you were   live the time of the *body offering* once again
Nothing to regret, nothing left behind   no longer anything to hide
Flowers for the *body offering*

I make an offering of azalea flowers

The *body offering*
A new birth given in a strange body   the space of the *body offering*
And what lies beyond that time

Life that transforms itself

From the dead who came later   once again to the dead
The quiet negotiations that begin in the place beyond

And, as I dream that life and death might be secretly inverted

When you go away
Sick of seeing me
I shall not shed a tear

Come closer   as if crawling onto the earth   as if spilling forth blood
Jindalle   jindalle   jindalle

(Spring 2009, Lee Chonghwa)

Translated by Rebecca Jennison and Yoshida Yutaka.

APPENDIX
NOTES ON "PLEASURE OF READING"
FROM *TOWARD (INVISIBLE) DESIRES* by Murayama Toshikatsu

Three Azaleas or *Jindalle*

Jindalle   jindalle   jindalle

Concerning the three *jindalle*: There are countless poems about *jindalle*, the springtime flower that blooms everywhere on the Korean Peninsula and fondly in Japan as well. Among them are "Mountains and Rivers of *Jindalle*," a poem by Shin Tongyop (1930–1969), published in 1959 (though not mentioned directly in my text) that, as if to trace the scars of the Korean War, dedicates the azaleas blooming amidst the fragments of bones of the half-buried who died far from home to those guerilla soldiers who fought in the mountains in solitude.

And there is the inaugural poem in the first issue of *Jindalle*, a journal published by a group of *zainichi* Korean poets in Osaka in the 1950s.

> ...
>
> *Red, red jindalle flowers*
> *On the dark, dark skin of the earth, our homeland*
>
> ...
>
> *May you burst into bright red flame*
>
> *Even if trampled upon   even if crushed*
> *Don't forget the seasons   my azaleas*
> *I have seen   these flowers blooming   on this Japanese soil too*
>
> ...

Interweaving these poems with Kim Sowol's "Azaleas" (1920s), a love poem for a parting lover written with irony and in the rhythm unique to the Korean language, I have dared to read it as a body addressed by the dead.

THREE BOOKS

Three books that are left in my hands. *Children of the Earth—Literature, Politics and Nationhood* (Mark Shell, translated by Murayama Toshikatsu and others, Misuzu Shobo, 2002), a book that I just happened to start reading one day, and *Thinking Past Terror: Islamism and Critical Theory on the Left* (Susan Buck-Morss, translated by Murayama Toshikatsu, Misuzu Shobo, 2005) that he tenderly handed to me with his thoughts about the translation.

On that rainy evening before the dawn when he collapsed, while speaking of his dream to produce a DVD for this volume, he bashfully wrote his name in his one original work *Toward (Invisible) Desires: In Dialogue with Queer Criticism* (Jinbun Shoin, 2005). Now, as I read bits of these three books in turn and at once, with my heart beating quietly, I am waiting to hear words that might be a response to the (style of) the work of Murayama-san who was able to breathe in some form of life with both subtlety and strength through the act of reading and translating.

THREE DATES

Dates that still cannot be recorded
Allow me to record them here
He collapsed at dawn on October 7, 2006
    (August 16 by the Lunar Calendar)
and on October 11 he was taken off life support
And then
on August 6, 2008
on a hot summer day
after waiting so long for the *body offering*
he comes back into his mother's hands.

Kang Sun's translation of Shin Tongyop's poem in "*Dakkoku wa tachi sare*," taken from Kim Eung-Gyo's *Kankoku gendai shi no miwaku* (Shinkan sha, 2007) was used in the original text. Our English version was translated from the Japanese.

Please see the summary of the contents of "*Jindalle*" in *Jindalle/Karion* (reprint, Fuji Shuppan). Kim Sowol's "*Jindalle*" was translated from Korean to Japanese by Aoyagi Yuko (unpublished). The English translation, slightly modified to fit the format of Lee Chonghwa's poem, is by David McCann, from the *Columbia Anthology of Modern Korean Poetry* (New York: Columbia University Press, 2004).

The "play" of the goddesses refers to the works by the artists that are introduced in this book (please see images and DVD).

The words "play" and "metamorphosis" used above are quotations from Murayama Toshikatsu, *Toward (Invisible) Desires*.

NOTES

1. Jean Genet, "Alberto Giacommeti's Studio," in *Aruberuto Jiakometti no atorie* [Alberto Giacommeti's studio], trans. and ed. Ukai Satoshi (Gendai kikakushitsu, 1999). The English text is from *Selected Writings of Jean Genet*, ed. Edmund White (New York: Harper Collins Publishers, 1993).

2. Jean Genet, "High Wire Artist" [*Tsunawawatari geinin*], in *Aruberuto Jiakometti no atorie*. Translated from Japanese to English. Originally published in French in 1957. The original text reads as follows:

"—Et toi, me det-il, qu'est-ce que tu faisais?

—Je regardais. Pour l'aider, pour la saluer parce qu'elle avait conduit la mort aut bordas de la nuit, pour l'accompagner dans sa chute et dans sa mort. (Jean Genet, "Le Funamble," in Œuvres complètes 5, Gallimard, 1979, p.18).

On Not Letting Death Die

A Prefatory Dialogue between Lee Chonghwa and Musician/Composer Takahashi Yūji

LEE: I'VE BEEN thinking that when we get together today, we could talk about sound.

Takahashi [hereafter TY]: Sound?

Lee: Yes, sound. In Japanese the word is *oto* (音).[1] You kindly set some of my poetry to music a few years ago. One of the compositions is called "For You—Island." I actually have it with me here. The word I am thinking of in Korean is *sori*. It's something relating to these matters that I've been wanting to talk about ... just a feeling I've had, for some reason.

How to talk about sound? You were telling me that when you compose, you "want to create a certain moment, in order to get started." It's the same with writing. Hasn't it been said that writing means "creating a situation"?

I guess, if I were to put it differently, I might say that today I want to think about the question of "creating" something. Creating something is a process at which one is simultaneously present and absent. ... It's the site of a certain kind of death. Death in the sense that death is something that makes us no longer here, and yet it is something from which we can by no means be absent. In that sense, one might say that both death and artistic creation

---

1. Translator's note: In the following, Chinese characters have been inserted in parentheses beside a number of different words related to sound that are used by Lee and Takahashi. These ideographs are shared (although their usage, nuances, and meanings can differ) across both the Japanese and Korean languages that form a point of reference for Lee and Takahashi as they discuss the philosophical, cultural, and political implications of "sound." Needless to say, since such careful attention is directed to the ways in which different words can be associated with each other, as well as their differing nuances, the translation of such passages has necessarily involved a greater than usual degree of interpretation.

involve, as well, a kind of life, being alive, breathing. I go around in circles thinking about this ... but when I do, there is always sound that comes to me.

TY: Sound comes ...

Lee: The sound doesn't come *from* me. It seems to come *toward* me from some place. I can't tell the direction, but I hear it "coming" from somewhere else. Isn't there an expression just like this in Japanese? You add the verb *kuru* ("to come") to the verb *kikoeru* ("to hear"). Literally, this means something like "coming to be heard" (*kikoete kuru*) and resembles the expression "coming to visit" (*otozurete kuru*). So in this expression, sound really does "come." Of course, I'm only talking about this in the Japanese language today.

TY: Yes. "Coming to be heard" (*kikoete kuru*) and "I hear it" (*kiku*) have different meanings in Japanese. *Kikoete kuru* conveys the idea of "accepting" or receiving something, while *kiku* means something has hit its target.

When you *see* something, you focus on it and the things around it blur. But in the case of sound, if you try to listen to one sound out of a totality of sounds, it's actually harder to hear it.

Lee: I guess so. But at the moment I want to stick with sound, without having to reduce it to something else. I mean, what you just said seems to have to do with the physical basis for the perception of sound. I'm not sure how well versed I am in that kind of thing. ...

But it struck me just now that when I used the Japanese expression *kikoete kuru*, you said it meant "to accept," in the sense of receiving something somewhere. In my own Japanese language world, the words *kikoete kuru* carry with them a sense of "from somewhere or other," or "at some point," or "I just realized that. ..." In other words, they convey unmistakably that something "is," don't they? In that moment when something is transformed from being over there, or far away, to "right here," that's the moment of, "Ah, it is coming to be heard." In that very instant the past and the present collide with each other. They ... how does one put it?

TY: They become interchangeable.

Lee: Exactly! They become interchangeable, yes. Thanks! Interchangeable. That's the situation of *kikoete kuru*. Just a minute ago I said I wanted to avoid making this a discussion of the physiological. Of course, I'm not discounting something like your "physical" presence here, or mine. But the instant we use an expression like "the eyes," it seems to me the body actually stops being the body and becomes something else.

Because I'm talking about that moment when what was here is now over there, or what was there is now here ... that very moment when the two become interchangeable and suddenly the sounds are uttered, "*Kikoete kuru*." This might seem like a kind of passivity, but I don't think so. You just talked about the moment when one begins to "receive" sound. This suggests there is already something harbored within, something contained there, something like that ... but *kikoete kuru*. I'm not talking about hearing words, but something like rhythm. What "comes to be heard" is first a kind of rhythm. A rhythm.

TY: I see ...

Lee: We can call it "rhythm," beat, tempo, or whatever. In Korea, rhythm refers to something that can be "long" or "short." It's a matter of relative length. ...

TY: "Long and short." ... That is *chandan* in Korean. ...

Lee: Yes. *Chandan*. Before words, there is *chandan*.

When I spoke about death before, it's because for a long time I've been thinking about the term *kakushi* (客死) or "faraway death."[2] The countless dead who perish on the roadside, in vast numbers, and whose bodies are still there, as if they had simply fallen asleep, or vanished. I think of their remains strewn here and there, and their ... souls, I suppose I should say. What I'm concerned about is not how these dead should be honored, or mourned. Not at all. I'm saying that the question of *kakushi* and the question of sound overlap in some way. There's no form one can find for *kakushi*, anywhere.

TY: Yes, in the same way that it is impossible to say a sound is "here" or "there." Because by the time we say we have heard a sound, it's already over. Sound is essentially a process of fading away. By the time we've said we hear it, we are talking about a memory. Think about a cat. ... When a cat pricks

---

2. Lee refers to her August 3, 2006, discussion of the term *kakushi* (客死), at the eleventh event in the series of lectures titled A Gaze from Sixty Years after the War's End, held at the Ginza Nikon Salon that year. At that time Lee Chonghwa presented the lecture, "Otozureru kioku, okuritodokeru kioku" (Memories that arrive, memories that are sent to arrive). We here reproduce the ideographs for *kakushi* since, according to Lee, she is deliberately introducing a word now rarely used in contemporary Japanese (although it would be familiar to speakers of Korean). The word *kakushi* (客死), carrying its traditional meaning of "to die while a guest," "to die while traveling," "to die on the road," "to die while absent from one's own home," continues to be used by Lee throughout this *taidan*, for both its rhetorical force and conceptual implications. It has particular significance for her argument since its meanings can even encompass the notion of "to be absent at/from one's own death." It thus raises the ethical issue of how to deal with the unknown or unrecognized death, with the anonymous death of the individual within a mass death, with deaths in natural catastrophes, and so forth. (Translator's note based on interview with Lee Chonghwa, Ithaca, New York, March 2015.)

up its ears, it's not because it sees something. It's listening to something behind it. ... That tells you something about sound.

Lee: Of course. I say it is something like a "shade" (気配) that appears.
Yes, I think that's the word I want ... something one feels intently in the presence of.

TY: A shade, yes. This is why at times something "comes to be heard."
And if you think of it that way, can't we say that, indeed, there is something
contained within *chandan* or rhythm, something that opens up? By the time
we are able to hear it, there is already something being carried along with it.
It's not as if it came entirely from elsewhere. There is probably a certain link
with memory, in this sense.

But just as we can read words in different ways, we can hear sounds differently. Can you remind me of the Korean word for *hibiki* or "echo"?[3] Didn't
I hear that the Korean word for "echo" also carries the sense of a needle
(Chinese character 鍼) being thrust through an opening? And there is a tin-
gle that is set off. At the same time, the hole a needle goes into is referred to
by the word for "jar" (Chinese character 壷) in Korean. This is why the same
word came to mean a "vital point" (*kandokoro* in Japanese, written with the
Chinese character 勘所) in acupuncture or a "crux." And the term for "vital
point" originally meant "point of feeling" (written with the Chinese character 感所, also read *kandokoro* in Japanese). The same word can refer to any
place that is slightly indented. One locates a "point" and passes right through.
It is where an echo arises. We find the same words are used in talking about
needles, or acupuncture, and sound.

Lee: I'm not sure I want to pursue the association with *hibiki*, as a word
for "echo," in Japanese. The sound I have in mind is closer to what we call *ul
lim* (to cry or groan) in Korean.[4]

TY: There's a numbing sensation that occurs. It occurs at the moment the
needle suddenly penetrates ... or, no, by the time you notice it, the needle has
already gone in.

Lee: As a child I loved to sew with needles. But my mother always said,
"You should give that up. Girls who sew too much end up badly. Do something more active. Go play outside." She wasn't happy about my sewing. She

---

3. Translator's note: Takahashi uses the Japanese word *hibiki* written with the Chinese character 響.

4. In discussing the *taidan* text in Ithaca, New York, in February 2015, Lee noted that at this
point in the discussion she wanted to avoid pursuing the associations between *oto* (音) and
hibiki (響). This was because *hibiki* has customarily been used with nationalistic overtones in
modern Japanese songs and other cultural texts.

was a strange mother in that sense. Elsewhere I was praised for sewing ... a feminine virtue. But she told me I would meet a sad fate. ... It's linked to unhappiness. ... Don't do that kind of thing. She probably didn't think of it this way, but I wonder if, growing up in a very patriarchal society, she'd heard some warning like this. ... I've wondered about that.

People would also often say, "The needle is a living thing." If you make a mistake and put it in the wrong place, the needle pricks you. And if you aren't paying attention, the needle will go right into your body. ... That was the scariest thing people said.

TY: Yes ... and they say the needle will go all around inside you.

Lee: They said that ... and I really thought it was true! I think I still believe that. I have nightmares about it. I dream I have a needle going around inside me. I'm still kind of chary with needles. I set them down really carefully. After just a bit of time passes, I'll count all my needles. Just in case something's missing. If I can't find one where I've been keeping two or three, I'll look all over frantically.

Surprisingly enough, needles are circulating in bodies in some of the artworks of friends I've made during our Asia, Art, Politics project. Oh Haji's work puts the ordinary needle to marvelous uses. Needles become flowers, and flowers bloom. ... The needles are hidden behind them. Or needles (or is it the flowers?) can become a *chima*. Inside, the *chima* is full of needles. ... They are leaping and dancing about. Then the *chima* lightly enfolds them. This is the *chima* of Oh Haji's grandmother, who passed away.

In Soni Kum's work, we also find a body full of needles. In one work, Kum appears carrying cloth on her back. She seems to move like a needle, with a twisted expression on her face. One has the sense the needles are trying to burst out. And, yes, in her piece called "Slumber" (which she performed in Tokyo and the Philippines), Kum herself is wrapped in white cloth and she has filled with balloons made out of condoms with a red, blood-like liquid. In this case Kum's body acts like the needle. Holding a needle in her mouth, she bursts the balloons open with a pop, and the blood-like liquid drips all over her body covered with the white cloth. Needle and body have become one, and the needles that twirl and swirl around inside the body—all of this is expressed through the woman's body.

Couldn't we see Ito Tari's work this way, too? It's just the same. Ito estranges her own body. Isn't it like stabbing it with a needle? Her body enfolds something that at some point pierces its way out, and estranges that body.

We could speak in the language of critical discourse and call this violence or pain, but in the end I'd just say that we see a woman bearing needles within. There must be some reason why we see this same kind of body in all three artists' work. It wasn't something they agreed upon ahead of time. And yet they are all preoccupied with it. I want to see it as a kind of grief for the dead. For all those who have disappeared into the heavens. Some kind of body that harbors the needles or has even swallowed them, bursts up through woman in all these works. They may be the needles of a distant, far-off memory, or this may be a dream about needles moving through the body. ... There is a fear, a shiver, that is provoked by it. The words "rhythm" (旋律 or *senritsu*) and "shiver" (戦慄 or *senritsu*) sound alike in Japanese ... or we could speak about the Korean *ul lim*, to cry or groan. That's why I always count my needles. To be sure I'm not missing one.

So look how our strands have come together ... all because you brought up needles! I hadn't mentioned them at all. But this always happens when I talk with you, Yūji. ... You provide these openings. The needle pricking a point brought it all together. That needle produces a ring or reverberation ... and this is how sound arises.

If we were to move from here to the matter of the words you mentioned ... when people think of words, they always think of meanings. But when I used "rhythm," I was thinking of it in a certain way—not the rhythm of classical or modern poetry, but something else. Rhythm, as a realm that precedes intelligibility ... how do we relate that realm of rhythm to words? If we were to speak of this in the context of art, we might say that in the instant something takes shape as a "work of art," it becomes a kind of language. It becomes words. Aren't there moments when we are looking at a work of art and we have that sense of something "coming to be heard" (*kikoete kuru*)? By contrast, in the case of sound, we just have something like random piles of words. ... How about thinking about it that way?

TY: Piled-up words?

Lee: I once jotted down a note to myself. A person (*hito*) is alive, a living being who is a "human." In Japanese the word is *hito* and in Korean it is *saram*. *Saram* means a "person who is alive." So we are talking about "person," "shade," and "sound." The way I think of it, when a sound arrives or a sound appears, there is a moment when no one is there. Sound might just be what stays around, like a remainder, when anything "humanistic," anything tied up with the human and human thought, has disappeared. Sound circulates between the human and what we might call the ghostly. That is why sound encompasses something like the idea of the "shade." Because of this, I never relate sound, in and of itself, to memory.

TY: They are not the same, that's true. ...

Lee: Somehow I have that sense. However, let's go on and consider how sound could be thought of in relation to mourning. When there is mourning, people often talk about "voice." A person's voice. In these instances, the voice is seen as a kind of medium we borrow. But for me, as soon as the word "voice" is introduced, things get a little too human-centered. ... I mean, the smell of the human is very strong here. In turning to sound, I'm looking for something less defined than "voice." ...

A person who dies an anonymous death joins masses of other departed spirits. Is there a way we can mourn these countless dead? Can we grieve for them, memorialize them, call out to them, be open to them ... respond to them somehow? We need some way of mourning that allows us, the living, to bring them along with us in our everyday lives. But unless we can actually put ourselves in contact with something like the *sound* that surrounds those dead, what we do will be no different from the conventional prayer, in which words of mourning, once they have been uttered, are simply repeated. I want to stay close to the deaths, to be cut off from them as little as possible. So I'm trying to think of mourning in a different sense.

I remember that when the playwright Kisaragi Koharu passed away, you said, "I'm saying goodbye, for now." ... I'm looking for something like that "for now." When someone dies, people say, "O-yasumi nasai" ("good night" or "rest well"). But I am thinking of something before that ... something like "for now."

TY: Something should stay behind as a remainder, something that hasn't been so completely formalized it can be forgotten. How to keep that from happening is the problem. But once you attach a meaning to something, you fix it in a certain way and the process stops there.

Lee: When you were composing the music for "To You—Island," you said you wanted to hear my voice.[5] And also when you composed "To a Friend on a Distant Island."[6] What were you thinking about "voice" then?

---

5. *Anata e—shima: Dansei gasshō to koishi no tame ni* (To You—Island: Composition for Male Chorus and Pebbles), poetry by Lee Chonghwa and musical score by Takahashi Yūji. Conducted by Tanaka Nobuaki. The piece has four parts: "The Sea," "Stones (*birure*)," "Wind," and "The Wind's Dwelling." It was performed on November 26, 2005, in the Great Hall of the National Olympic Youth Center.

6. *Tōi shima no tomo e— Yun Dongju Tayasuku kakareta shi* (To a Friend on a Distant Island—Yun Dongju's *A Poem That Came Easily*), poetry by Lee Chonghwa and musical score by Takahashi Yūji. Conducted by Tanaka Nobuaki. Tokyo Philharmonic Chorus 50th Anniversary Concert, Series 4, 2005.

TY: I wanted to understand how the poems could be read. Poems have a rhythm and resonance. There has to be something there beyond one line of words after another. I usually try to figure that out. And there is a ritual in Jeju Island, isn't there? About receiving something from the ocean and sending it off again.

Lee: Ah ... the ritual called Chilmeoridang Yeongdeunggut. ...[7]

TY: Yes, I needed to know about that, and there were other things. ... I was just waiting for something to emerge from all of it.

Lee: Yes, waiting for you don't know what. I wait like that, too. And then there is the moment of *kikoete kuru*. Without the "sound," all my thinking and pondering comes to nothing. But maybe the best part is when I *don't* hear anything. The needle stops for a split second.

When you are composing, is there actually a moment when something turns into sound? That's what I want to ask you. You create sound, so, I am wondering ... do you remember how I once told you I didn't think of you as a "pianist"? Of course there are pianists who play the piano, but that's not the sense I have when you perform. No, instead it seems as if the piano is doing something to your body and I can't even tell where the sound started.

TY: [Laughter.]

Lee: Does the sound come from the piano, or from the small figure sitting there? Something living comes out of that inexplicable mixture.

The sound is always a little unexpected, a bit strange. It always seems to diverge just a little from the score, as if the sound itself is a bit uneasy. It's coming from somewhere, but we're not sure where. The moment when we feel *that* is the best ... yes, that space of not knowing where it's coming from.

In Korean, we have the word *maaru. Maaru* refers to sounds that come out of the mouth, so it means something a little different from written words. It's a kind of mark of being alive. There was a time when people would say, "Why don't you 'do a *sori*'"? They didn't ask a person to "say something" or "tell us something"; they would say, "Do a little *sori*." It referred to something

---

7. Translator's note: The Chilmeoridang Yeongdeunggut ritual is held on Jeju Island each spring, and consists of two ceremonies, held two weeks apart, in which local deities are asked to ensure a good catch from the sea for the coming season. The first, the Chilmeoridang rite, "welcomes" the goddess of the wind and other gods, who are entertained for two weeks and then "sent off" in a second ceremony, the Yeongdeunggut ritual, in which straw boats are launched into the sea.

like sound surging out. When this was attached to a form, it became "*pansori*."[8]

About *sori*. Words are simply improvised, to the rhythm, but here improvisation is almost like having no words, since they just disappear as the singer utters one after another. The most important thing is the sound that one "comes to hear." The uttering comes in undulations. That's what people mean by *sori* when they say, "Do a little *sori*." This *sori* creates a sort of rhythm and something in it really resonates.

One way to mourn those countless people who perished along the wayside is to walk (歩く). Just walk. We could think about walking as the kind of sturdy treading suggested by the word *fumu* (踏む). To tread on the ground is to live—because we have to walk to survive. Whether we're conscious of it or not, every day we walk. When we ride on trains, meet friends, go to work or to school, we engage in this act of walking. This in and of itself becomes a way of mourning the dead.

But in the context I am talking about, to tread or *fumu* can also mean "trample over" (*fuminijiru*, 踏みにじる).[9] Yes, to actually *trample over*. The activity of walking has both these aspects. And when something is trampled upon, just at the point where it is about to disappear, it starts to heave itself up again. When people talk about memory they are referring to something like this.

Walking in everyday life, even though we do it all the time, is something people almost always forget about. This kind of walking belongs to the realm of unawareness, oblivion. People do not remember every step they take when

---

8. Translator's note: *Pansori* refers to a mode of musical storytelling that rose to prominence in seventeenth- and eighteenth-century Korea. The storytelling is accompanied by a drummer.

9. Translator's note: Lee suggests here that the characters for *fumu* (踏む) and *fuminijiru* (踏みにじる), insofar as they represent different ways of "stepping," offer insights into how we might see the activity of walking (歩く) from a more existential perspective. While she contrasts the two, both words also carry positive connotations for her in terms of mourning. *Fumu* (踏む) suggests to step with sturdiness or resiliency. This sturdiness implies that a certain forgetfulness about past traumas may simply be a necessary way of continuing to live. On the other hand, the character for *fuminijiru* (踏みにじる)—a character often associated in modern Korean poetry with the subjugation of Korea under Japanese colonialism, as Lee points out in other writings—suggests a violent trampling. In a deeper sense, to see life as trampling is to understand that all human life is sustained over and above previous human lives and is indebted to them. To be mindful that our very activity of walking/living is a form of indebtedness to the dead, and to the sacrifices of those who were victims of violence, is what is involved in seeing our own walking as a form of "trampling over." Of course, the specific reference here is to *kakushi* in Asia. Many thanks to Hirano Oribe for explicating the poetic and philosophical resonances of these terms.

they walk. But what if we talk about walking from the perspective of what is trampled over? This, on the contrary, becomes a way of remembering.

Asia as a totality—and it's still like this now—is full of places where people met a "faraway death." Very few people died in the place they were from; most died in a place they didn't know. But, in Asia, aren't people who don't die in their own place treated as "others," and told not to come home? They are feared. They are something unclean. They are that kind of being. It's for these beings that we must continue to grieve. Can't we see our walking, which involves trampling something underfoot, as a form of mourning?

I want to see the realm of sound, even though it overlaps in many ways with the words used to talk about mourning, as still different from them. That's why I say that, whenever humans are involved, we are not talking about sound. Then no sound "comes to be heard." We could put it this way: sound exists only "when the human doesn't exist," when "humanism" and the world of meaning vanishes. ... This is when sound somehow appears, when something "comes to be heard." This is why I have been distinguishing what I call "sound" from the realm of memory. It is in the absence of the human that sound somehow emerges, "comes to be heard." I am thinking about how to create that kind of sound.

TY: Creating sound. But what you are talking about is not the same as making sound out of nothing, right?

Lee: What about the word *koku* (哭, to grieve)? Does that refer to a sound? The cry made when someone dies. The word itself is like sounds: *Ko! Ku!*

TY: That is probably the way some rituals evolved. Rituals connected to a certain etiquette of mourning. And there were also written words eulogizing the person who died. Such traditions are for the most part linked to official ceremonies. Because writing or making inscriptions are forms of expression linked to authority. There are other ways to mourn or remember the dead, but those are again different from paying tribute to someone or from speaking out about certain injustices.

We were watching the news about Gwangju in May 1980 (people refer to this as the "Gwangju uprising," "rebellion," or "revolt," depending on their political perspective), as it was happening on Japanese TV. What I remember most clearly was watching a large group of people in a truck, all tied up together. The truck was going off somewhere. We wondered where it was going. And the moment the truck turned and went outside the frame of the camera, it disappeared beyond that space. Somewhere else. But that place beyond became connected to a lot of other things. That "no place in particular" can be reborn anyplace, everyplace.

Lee: It's like the place of "death" and of "faraway," the place of "sound."

TY: And to connect these to many other things, so that what happened in a particular time and place doesn't just end there, isn't just enclosed inside that culture or tradition, but rather expands it. So that something that is here and something in another place are...

Lee: You mean not making a death fixed. Not letting that death die...not allowing it to die. "Faraway deaths" are deaths that scatter and spread. That's what "on the roadside" means. Roads are everywhere, and they are there because people lived so many deaths on them.

So I wonder if there is a way to mourn all of those deaths that does not let them die, rather than mourning the death of each single "I." Before, "faraway death" was something that was excluded or erased, eliminated. And so even the word *kakushi* (客死) has almost disappeared from Japanese language. Now death is a matter of belonging—it's "my," "someone's," "your," "our" deaths. But, as you just said, Yūji, couldn't we transform this into "not letting death die," into a different kind of space where cultures intermingle and resonate? The sites of *kakushi*, in and of themselves, connected to all these deaths.

By mourning in this way, by thinking of these deaths not as something in the past but as coming along with us into the present, we can also think of the here and now in terms of what once was, somewhere else. It's the moment of transference, when one becomes something like a medium. I'm avoiding a word like "make the past present" (現在化) for a reason. Because there, a subject of this "making present" would become necessary. That's not what I'm thinking of. For example, Oh Haji, Soni Kum, and Ito Tari use their bodies to perform, bodies that are different from this body of mine. So it's rather mysterious. While something from the past is brought into the present, what is here in the present seems to go away somewhere. At that moment, one is estranged from one's own body.

Women sometimes say, "My body is not really my body."

Or "my body is not mine." These are words that suddenly burst out along with a sigh, in a moment of suffering, or great worry, or deep hurt. It is there before your very eyes. The passage of time itself has been chiseled into the body. It is the moment when, despite the body's unmistakable materiality, the words, "My body is not mine" burst forth. In the same way, I am thinking of how we can make "faraway death" something that endures, by "not

letting death die." This is different from the idea of memorializing, of pre-
serving the memory of something. It's a way of mourning that is "to continue." Not letting death die, by *continuing*.

Proceeding in this way, we can reach a way of mourning death that is
different from those that are institutionalized, privileged, or linked to power.
And what may emerge from this, apparently by coincidence, are "Asia" and
"art." I am thinking of something like the artworks by the women I mention
above, or Yūji's compositions. I am thinking of these as emerging in offerings
to those who died far away. Voices that we receive, that have "come to be
heard." Voices found unexpectedly, like sounds picked up by chance. I have
been sensing these things that cannot be explained for some time. They've
stayed with me. And I've been thinking that the best I can do is to simply
make an effort to express them in words.

TY: Yes, words are so difficult. When we say something with words, it
always becomes something different. So we want to stop at a point just *before*
everything has been expressed in words. Yet this is different from ambiguity.

Lee: Nothing is "fixed" or promised, but there is continuing.

TY: Continuing. Not cutting something off. Asking how to suggest
something that cannot be fully expressed, while using words that have the
function of making things clear. With poetry, that might be possible. But if
you try to explain or analyze that with other words, however far you get, you
just end up going in circles.

Many different reverberations come rising to the surface. Here, in this
book, the contributors have done many different things. It is not always
clearly stated ... but something new is born out of that. Maybe this is what I
am referring to as "sounds," or "echoes."

Lee: But even so, I actually do want to give this a form. As a kind of
ritual. But something different from what the word *gishiki* conveys in Japanese.

TY: Yes, yes. Something like "form" just cannot be avoided, but it should
be form as that which provides an occasion, or opportunity, for others. It is a
place where something else opens up, something different.

Lee: When I think about how to sustain this in a way that does not let
death die, I think of something that can involve a minimal number of people. How to find a minimum that becomes a kind of maximum? As we
continue to live, or have to go on living—and if we are to speak of this in
terms of some kind of ethics—then we must acknowledge our need at this

very moment in history to find a way that allows us, with the least effort and greatest potential, to make connections. We create art that is a *response*, and in that sense we might call it a ritual. That's what I'm feeling. And perhaps, that is what I would call "Asia."

TRANSLATED BY BRETT DE BARY AND REBECCA JENNISON.

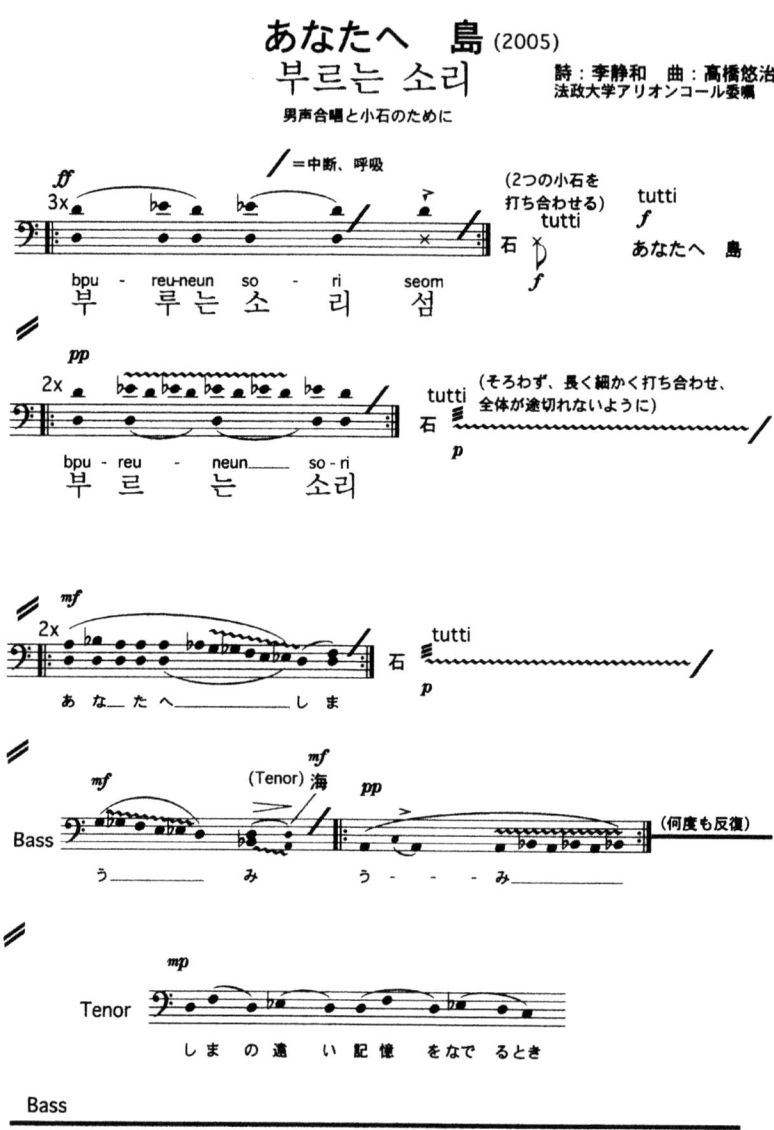

Takahashi Yūji, *Anata e shima* (For you island), detail of musical score, 2005.

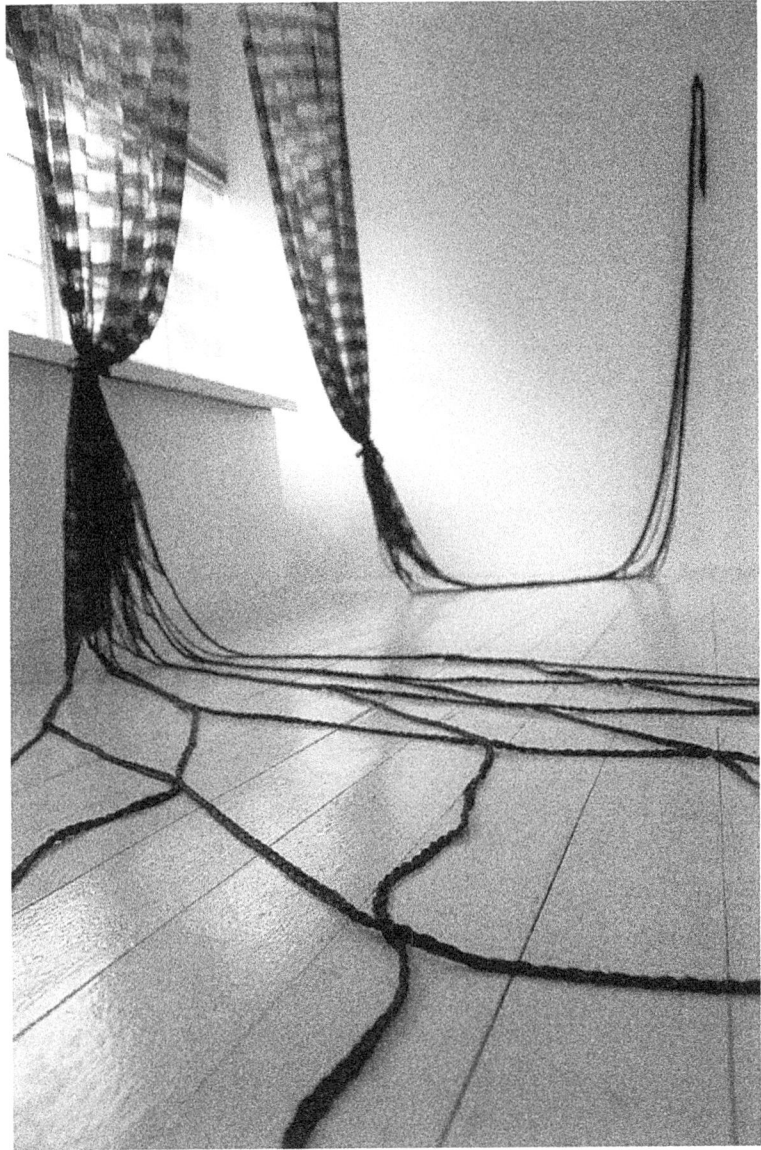

Oh Haji, *Kanojo no mitsumeru fūkei* (The landscape at which she gazes), *Orime o suri nukerumono—chinmoku no toki—phillippine no tabi kara* (Things that slip through the weave—silence—from travels to the Philippines), mixed media installation with silk, brass hooks, i-kat printing, i-kat discharge dyeing, macrame, Voice Gallery, Kyoto, 2008.

PART 1

CHAPTER 1

The Contours of Sound

A Place Connecting the Music of Takahashi Yūji and the Performances of Ito Tari

SHINJŌ IKUO

1. IT'S RAINING

It's raining, even far, far away
Even on tiny, tiny creatures
It rains and rains

IT WAS 1966 when, in the year of his death, a young man named Nakaya Kōkichi wrote this in Okinawa.

What were the kinds of scenes that flashed before his eyes at the moment his life came to an end? What kind of sounds reverberated in his ears? We find no trace of this, even in *Namaeyo tattearuke: Nakaya Kōkichi ikōshū* (*Name! Stand and Walk! The Posthumous Writings of Nakaya Kōkichi*, published by San'ichi Shobō in 1972). But within this memoir, published by his bereaved friend in the aftermath of Okinawa's "reversion to Japan," there are clear indications of the masochistic and remorselessly condemnatory speculations of a young man who understood all too well that his ideals of political revolution were being destroyed from the inside out, as liberation from the oppression of U.S. military occupation was being entrusted to the "reversion" movement.

3

To live the "postwar" in Okinawa can be nothing other than a contradiction in which one despises the fictitiousness of such a temporal category, but at the same time finds it necessary. This much is made clear by Nakaya's words, which question the "postwar" that we ourselves currently live. This fundamental question undoubtedly plagued Nakaya himself, but the question he raises is very far from an accusation; it is closer to a whisper.

There is one musician who has listened closely to Nakaya's whispers, almost as though he has sensed the rain that falls far away in closer proximity. During the opening of the first workshop in Okinawa that formed part of the Asia, Politics, Art project, Takahashi Yūji spoke in his subdued voice about a song he wrote which was triggered by Nakaya's "Saigō no nōto" (Last note) in *Name! Stand and Walk! The Collected Memoirs of Nakaya Kōkichi*, a book which he happened to pick up at a second-hand bookstore in Tokyo in the 1980s. This almost unimaginable encounter between Nakaya Kōkichi's writing and Takahashi Yūji's music anticipated the Asia, Politics, Art project and led to it finding its contours in sound. The fact that it has been sound, more than anything, that has provided a definitive outline for the contemplation of, and aspiration after, the kind of resonant empathy that this project desires proved to be incredibly fortuitous.

It was initially thought that the song Takahashi Yūji presented to us, titled "Last Note," would be casual background music to announce the opening of the Asia, Politics, Art project, but as we started to follow Nakaya Kōkichi's words—which accompanied the piercing notes of a piano played in the gamelan scale, with a hint of string and percussion instruments, and female vocals (with shamisen accompaniment by the late Takada Kazuko)—each and every one of us was so moved by this unsuspecting voice trembling over the meticulously polished floor of the Sakima Art Museum that we became caught up in reliving past memories not our own, and were captivated by the repetition of a pain and lamentation we were soon to encounter.

There is no doubt, of course, that it was the frustration of his ongoing dream to see a revolution in occupied Okinawa that led Nakaya Kōkichi to commit suicide. Okinawa then "reverted" back to Japan as though his death had never happened. This is what happened, there is no doubt.

In a time which continues to try to jettison and erase, as if they were just noise, those memories which come to terms with and struggle with its past, Okinawa's present remains a fraught one. And yet, when the words that Nakaya wrote in the moments before he died that tragic death are once again revisited through Takahashi Yūji's music, that which has been left behind in the past is recalled in the present. The suspension of those events that remain unfinished business are anticipated through this kind of second life and second death, and the unfinished lives of those of us who continue to live in an Asia of divisive politics will be rediscovered through the bridging point of art. It is then that words and songs will resist the very regime of a "national history" implicated in death and the act of forgetting, overcome the wall that divides space and time, foreground the possibility for cooperation and coexistence realized in empathy, and continue to lead those of us living in Asia today to the farthest reaches of memory.

2. GETTING HELPLESSLY, UNAVOIDABLY WET

The beginning of a new poiesis via the collaboration of poetry and song. Takahashi Yūji's music stands as clear proof of this beginning, calling Nakaya Kōkichi's words back from the shadows of history. It also strikes me that in the continual war zone that is Okinawa, the countless dead that have been killed in the history of "postwar" Asian wars are called into the midst of our project, beckoned by the sounds composed by Takahashi.

Death is not finished, and the dead are yet to return. An unexpected evening begins to envelop us, as if announcing this very fact.

> It's raining, it's raining
> It's raining, even far, far away
> Even on tiny, tiny creatures
> It rains and rains
> Even the rocks are wet
> Even the sky
> Even my fingers are wet
> Helplessly, unavoidably
> Wet
>   Nakaya Kōkichi, "Last Note"

"It's raining." ... What is opened with these words, and at the same time lovingly enclosed by them, is none other than the unfinished temporality experienced by those who live, have died, and have been killed in Asia's politics of division. That the name of Okinawa is remembered as a frontline base for the Korean and Vietnamese Wars—in other words, as an alternative name for the departure point of violent massacres—cannot be recalled without feelings akin to shame or embarrassment. In "postwar" Asia, Okinawa has continued to be the locus of military massacres and a frontline military base. In this respect, it cannot be denied that Okinawa has existed, and continues to be made to exist, as a front line/link to the violence encroaching on the lives of those living in Asia. That being said, it must not be forgotten that this front line of violence, this Okinawa that continues to be an alternative name for war, has claimed those living in Okinawa itself in its fires of war. Unveiling the tragic double meaning of this endless infighting, Nakaya's "Last Note" questions us who are in the present.

In the time lived by Nakaya Kōkichi, returned to us by Takahashi Yūji's music, "it rains and rains." Just before his death it seems that it never stopped raining in the depths of Nakaya Kōkichi's body, but rather than a metaphor for some heroic call for revolution, it seems that this is first and foremost a rain that fell in Nakaya's heart as a prayer, however fruitless it may have proved to be, to alleviate the vicious heat suffered by the bereaved who were burned alive.

Nakaya had lost his niece in the U.S. fighter plane collision at Miyamori Elementary School in 1959. This incident, also known as the Ishikawa Jet Crash, refers to a tragedy in which a U.S. F-100 jet plane lost control and plummeted into Miyamori Elementary School in Ishikawa prefecture, central Okinawa, killing seventeen and injuring well over two hundred. In this incident, which has been largely ignored—even forgotten—in "postwar" Japan, Nakaya was brought face to face with the burned corpse of his beloved niece.

Deeply affected by what he saw at the morgue that day, Nakaya later found himself imprisoned in the recollection of those images. This experience was to be described by Nakaya, who now had to live the remainder of his short life repeatedly dealing with spiritual crises, as engendering a turning point in his thinking. And yet the event lacks a number of particularities for it to be referred to as such. Or perhaps, it is precisely because it lacks so many particularities that the incident transformed into a force that repeatedly threatened him within the dark depths of his self, forcing him to relive the scene time and time again. For Nakaya, it was undoubtedly in this very sense of lack that the burned corpse of his niece came to be a constant encroachment on the present, a central location as the manifestation of continuing war in "postwar" Okinawa. And yet, the corpse lacks many things itself. The burned corpses described in "The Death of My Niece," a text included in his posthumous writings, have a similar lack of definition.

There are no legs. None. Its legs are gone. As for its hands, its hands are gone too. There is nothing above the wrist. Is it a man? No, a woman. Oh, it doesn't have genitals. There's nothing. Ah, its eyes, its eyes are full of burnt sand. Its charred, disfigured nose is full of sand as well. How about its guts? I wonder if its guts are okay? Ah, no, it has none. Its insides are empty.[1]

Among these "empty" corpses is his niece. Nakaya writes, "Her dirty teeth, the only thing left intact, protrude from where the lips used to be on her incinerated face. A tooth in the middle is hidden by the gum, and can't be seen."[2]

In this visceral response to the voiceless murmuring of the "incinerated face," it is possible to find Nakaya's "postwar" as well as a political resistance to Okinawa's "reversion" to Japan. It was this Nakaya who, in his dedication to the "reversion movement," was torn between the extremities of hope and despair, and afflicted with an exasperated sense of confusion. Is it any wonder that in what would be his final work he poignantly hopes for rain? There can be no doubt that this rain was intended to envelop his own soon-to-be-deceased body, as well as the scorched remains of his niece. "It's raining, it's raining, even far, far away / Even on tiny, tiny creatures / It rains and rains." Is this rain anything other than an incessant, insistent prayer? The rain that falls "even on tiny, tiny creatures" must also be one that soothingly covers all those caught in the blaze.

And yet, surely it is not just Nakaya and his niece that should be wrapped in this salve of rain. This rain must fall universally on all the speechless dead killed on the battlefields of a fictitious "postwar" era.

There is no reason, for example, why this "far away" that Nakaya envisaged could not be Jeju Island in 1948. There is also no reason why it couldn't be Gwangju in 1980. In fact, it seems likely that what Nakaya envisaged was an expanse of rain that generously covers all the lands afflicted by the fires of war, and all who survived—or died—in them. In Hiroshima, Pyongyang, Mindanao, Chongqing, Dresden, Nanking, Nagasaki, Gaza, Tokyo, Fallujah; in every war zone. This rain must fall on the innumerable "empty" corpses. This rain that falls "far away" must, then, also "rain and rain" on those of us who find ourselves in Okinawa today.

---

1. Nakaya Kōkichi, *Namaeyo tatte aruke: Nakaya Kōkichi ikōshū* [Name! Stand and walk! The posthumous writings of Nakaya Kōkichi] (San'ichi Shobō, 1972), 30–34.
2. Ibid.

In each land disproportionately drenched by this rain are those who have burned to death like tinder, disfigured beyond recognition, whose corpses remain undiscovered, erased from the front stage of Asian politics. Yet at the same time, these are also people who wait with bated breath in a disappearing "past" for a time that will recall their lived experiences in word, sound, and form. What else is asked of us other than to listen to the silent call of the mourned?

Takahashi Yūji's music paved the way toward a beginning of precisely this call-response relationship. We might say that through Takahashi's music, the Asia, Politics, Art project was able to clearly ascertain its own ideal as an attempt to link the political, social, sexual, economic, ethnic, and racial—in effect, the innumerably defined—divisions that we live in Asia today, within a space-time of collaborative artwork. What is important is that we now recall those that we have not met before, and the times that they lived, and together face the difficulty of reliving those times. What is required is none other than a "politics of supplication" ("*motome no seijigaku*," in Lee Chonghwa's words) in which we submit ourselves, unreservedly, to the resonance of empathy within our bodies, and explore our coexistence with people whom we may well be harming and distancing ourselves from in the process of categorizing who this "we" actually is.[3] Of course this request is not an easy one to fulfill, but it is precisely in this request that sound and word can be crystallized into things that are truly alive, and at the same time proffer all the transformations needed on the body itself.

With regard to this possibility, I would like to recollect something articulated some thirty years ago by Takahashi Yūji himself: "When we reflect from the present on the formative history of the songs, poetry and plays produced during the Vietnam War, or of literature written in Korea since the period of resistance to Japanese rule, it is necessary to scrutinize the method and practice of cultural formation with a wide lens," he writes in a particularly evocative text titled *Ikiru tame no uta* (Songs to live by). He continues,

Poetry and song are the primary stages of cultural formation. Not printed poetry, but the poetry of words and rhythm, of thought crystallized in clear, easily quotable images, poetry as songs that define the gestures of word and rhythm as a vehicle of melody. Poetry and

---

3. Lee Chonghwa, *Motome no Seijigaku—kotoba—haimau shima* (Toward a politics of supplication—in search of words—islands that crawl and dance), Iwanami Shoten, 2004.

song are versatile, contagious, remain intact among other artistic forms, or rather are able to infiltrate and be incorporated with them. And because they have a rhythm that invites movement of the whole body they invoke a collective solidarity and empathy, and they empower. Because they are easy to remember they are able to instill within themselves complicated notions and the very core issues at hand.[4]

Grasping poetry and song as tools of memory which, because of their ability to "instill" those memories within themselves, can be seen as a "contagious ... movement of the whole body," and as "gesticulated words" capable of "giving us courage, and invoking a collective solidarity and empathy," Takahashi's words disclose to us an important opportunity for thought and praxis. It is precisely in its "gestural quality" that song and poetry may be able to "remain intact among other artistic forms, or rather able to infiltrate and be incorporated with them," and it is in this rearticulation that all art can be seen as "songs to live by." What is important is that memory becomes instilled within the depths of our body, and at the same time, that this bodily labor allows memory to slip into a disseminating circuit.

We encountered Ito Tari's performance, *I will not forget you* as one such attempt to make us relive this circuit, meeting the transformation of her body with our own bodies and foreseeing in this the time of our own transformation.[5] Through Takahashi Yūji's music, Nakaya Kōkichi's words become "songs that define [these words] as a vehicle of melody." As poetry and song flow into Ito Tari's body via this contagious circuit of song, they achieve transformation.

3. THE SOUND OF GESTICULATION

Ito Tari arrived at the auditorium early and stood stock still in front of the painting.

---

4. Takahashi Yūji, *Takahashi Yūji korekushion: 1970 Nendai* [The Takahashi Yūji Collection: 1970s] (Tokyo: Heibonsha Library, 2004), 287. The essay was first published in the journal *Ajia taido* 2 (1977).

5. Translator's Note. In these essays, we use *I will not forget you*, following the manner in which Ito has translated the title of her work, *Anata o wasurenai*, in previous English language contexts.

There was a tension in the way she stood that made it feel inappropriate to just start chit-chatting with her, so for a moment I stood quietly observing her from behind with one of the curators of the Sakima Art Museum, Uema Canae. After a while, however, turning around with a sigh, Ito Tari muttered, "What can I possibly do in front of a painting like this?"

The painting that she spoke of was Iri and Toshi Maruki's *Okinawasen no zu* (The Battle of Okinawa, 1984); a giant but intricately designed artwork that completely dominates a large room in the museum. I have seen this work many times myself. Each time I discover something new, and the painting itself has a transformative quality, a murkiness, as though it were breathing quietly and deeply, making one feel that it exists in a state of imperceptible flux. Confronted with the overwhelming power of The Battle of Okinawa panels, Ito Tari commits her body to a live art performance titled *I will not forget you*, even as she appears momentarily uncomfortable with enacting such an undertaking in a space dominated by this work.

But Tari, uncomfortable as she may have been, had already begun a profound dialogue with the painting. She asked Uema Canae a number of times about the wandering, fallen people in the panels; about those who killed and were killed in a massacre imposed on them by the Japanese military that would later be referred to as "mass suicide"; about the Okinawan civilians that had clearly been killed by the Japanese army; about the "comfort women" and soldiers indentured from Korea who were killed in Okinawa and continue to have "disappeared" into the abyss of the forgotten. It is perhaps at this point that her performance of *I will not forget you*, offered as an homage to the former "comfort woman" Kim Soon-duk, became a call of defiance against the act of forgetting, overlapping with the lamentations for the countless dead that are inextricably linked with the late Kim Soon-duk, and jolting the body of this lone artist into movement. This pain leaves deep traces within Ito Tari's performance itself, becoming a piercing noise that exudes from her body, passing to our own like a contagion.

I think it was when Ito Tari wove her way around us, walking at a very slow pace, moving in an arc toward the center of the room as we sat clutching our knees pensively, still not quite settled for the performance, that I was first struck by a voice that was not quite audible, like a quiet, urgent breathlessness. The thin black plastic film that clung to her body abruptly expanded and contracted like a balloon in various places on her body from the air that she blew into tubes. The fleshy boundary that swelled and deflated by means of these tubes made me think that something alien was being simultaneously injected and secreted by her morphing body, revealing a trail where she had flipped and turned her body. But none of the air that she so forcefully tried to blow into the space between her skin and the plastic managed to find a gap to fill and the air that burst forth from the tube made an intriguing noise which merged with the noise emitted from the monstrous, island-like balloons that heaved and sighed all over her body, at times bursting loudly.

Meanwhile her body was thrown down by some invisible force, wrenched to and fro on the floor. Each time her body was pinned down on that hard, polished floor, we found ourselves drawn in by each slap that reverberated around us, unable to do anything other than bear witness to the way in which that pain transformed into lamentation each time it coursed through her body.

All of these actions were performed under a strictly observed silence, as though it were some kind of terrible ceremony. This was of course clear proof of "the slippage in the production of meaning achieved through the exhaustive repetition of bodily gestures" that Ikeuchi Yasuko identifies as being a characteristic of Ito Tari's performances, and yet this dominant silence, insofar as its dominance was so overwhelming, continued insistently to give rise to the array of noises that emanated from her body.[6] These sounds—diffuse, discordant, and so far removed from any notion of scale and harmony—at times became urgent gasps for breath, revealing an exhaustion deep within the body, as well as a refusal that burst forth, perhaps thrust forth, from the depths of this very exhaustion. It was then that her body was pinned down, thrown around, pushed, and pulled by some other force. The pain it must have caused is inexpressible. In the midst of such violence being repeated on and by her body, such verbalization is both hindered and refused. It is in this way that the time of those bodies subjected to such unfathomable violence returns to us from the shadows of history. In this return it is difficult to discern whether the power that is being inflicted on her body is that of a violence that comes from outside, or the violence of an internal struggle that harasses her body as it continues to resist the violence of others. In any case, if anything is clear, it is that Ito Tari's own body is a corporeal abode forced to live in a time in which power seeks to exercise its will upon it.

At this point it seems impossible that Ito Tari's body remains under her own subjective control. Already it is transforming into a fragile assemblage of

---

6. Ikeuchi Yasuko, *Joyū no tanjō to shuen: Pafuōmansu to jendā* [The actress is born and dies: Performance and gender] (Tokyo: Heibonsha, 2008), 265, 266.

moving parts in which numerous bodies touch and connect excessively, tearing the boundaries between them and infringing upon each other. Her body can no longer maintain an interior self as something isolated from its outside thanks to its border of skin. Rather, in Ito Tari's *I will not forget you*, a power which bursts forth from within transforms her body into a foreign object which, as it interacts and merges with it, gives off the vital signs of life (of Eros), repeating the jostling and colliding between one body and another which invalidates the division between your body and my own. In other words, *I will not forget you* is a performance which resists this territorial bordering of the body, dismantles its realm of individuality and subjectivity, and attempts to strip this—"her own" body—from itself.

Here a question arises as to whether "performance" is in fact the word that best encapsulates this kind of bodily practice. If by "performance" we refer to an action through which the artist intends to communicate some kind of message or to undertake a kind of disturbance, then the body in *I will not forget you* appears to resist the very gaze that attempts to read from it any kind of intent or message. What do "you" think you are seeing right now? This is the question that is posed, quietly but persistently, at the same time that the question of what is happening within the body of this "I" that swears "I will not forget you" is also presented to us. I should hastily add that this question bears no relation to any subject or motif of "self-searching" but rather warns us, through a repetition in which this self-evident "self" is extracted from its very foundations, of the dangers inherent in consigning bodies to the shadows of history. Through the medium of Ito Tari's body, this danger is presented to us as the politics of those bodies which continue to exist in the present. The low, thudding noise that resonated through the room warned us all of the political nature of the body in crisis. We couldn't help but be seized by the trace of the "you" that lay in this noise.

This may well mean that the trace of a "you," which appears so suddenly to those who come into contact with a performance, like this, that foregrounds the body in crisis, is something that is largely unavoidable. This "you" appears within us, in a form that we didn't expect, through the circuit of Ito Tari's body.

This is conveyed to us unexpectedly—and completely unavoidably—through a repetitive action in which her heavy body picks up onions littered around her feet and commences to peel them. That odors impose themselves so insistently on our bodies may be because they convey to us the presence of a "you" that has already pervaded "my" body in the most material of ways. The odor of the onions imprints on the deepest recesses of the body that smells a "you" summoned from the shadows of history.

The persistent peeling of onions is repeated, suggesting a limitless retracing, a process without beginning or end, while the onions themselves also imply the impossibility of ever tracing back to the "center" of this stolen body. We might even suggest that this smell makes us aware of a violence inflicted on the body which continues to be eradicated from history; something which was taken away from "you," that "you" desperately need, but will never be returned. In making the return of this violence visible, Ito Tari's body—this body that is thrown around the floor even as it continues to grasp an onion—is at once prized, even burst open, only to be tightly closed up again as though in resistance. Every time this closed body is forced open, its limbs are thrust crookedly into the air.

In clarifying the deep wounds that were left by the sexual violence inflicted on the "comfort women," as well as the fissures borne by the body which must continue to experience the pain of those returning wounds, Ito Tari's body falls as it attempts to stand, and closes as soon as it has opened. If our bodies are indeed an opportunity for Asian politics to be reconsidered, then these compelling, bodily convulsions that reveal the otherness of the self cannot be understood as a mere instance of othering. Unless we understand the voiceless questions posed by the body we cannot hope to think politically about this place we call Asia.

What is happening with this body now? What kind of desires and uncertainties are being exercised within a power that transforms and harasses the body in this way? How are those bodies penetrated by this power possibly able to feel themselves? And how has this "you" lived as a body that represents a trace of this power, in a time and space distanced from history?

All of these questions are silently imbibed by the bodies of those who are confronted by *I will not forget you*. But these questions are not something which one can nonchalantly digest and consume. Many things are lacking, even here. How there is a "natural" unity that envelops the body, for example. A discrete distance that separates me from you. Those words that seem to give shape to our feelings. The whole system which makes me "me" and you "you." Is it a simple lack of all these things that allows a trace of "you" to irresistibly pierce my body as sound and smell so that I may live your body?

4. TOWARD AN UNEXPECTED ENCOUNTER

Of course, within Ito Tari's performance of *I will not forget you,* the body undoubtedly transforms into the site of struggle around a returning violence. When this happens, why must it be "I" that is subjected to the cacophony of noises and enveloped in the odors emanating from "you"? What is the response to a returning violence that ignores all the intentions and judgments made by this subject called "I," embroiling it, as it stands defenseless, into a circuit of contagion? It strikes me that it is Ito Tari's performing body which exposes me to this question; one which would find no place elsewhere.

However, it is clear that it is Ito Tari who is trying harder than anyone to relive this exposed body. It is in the reliving of a potentially problematic wish, such as the one in *I will not forget you,* that we find her performance, and this performance appears to us as something that bears no relation to her own intentions or to "our" interpretation. The body of Ito Tari as one performer is thrown into an unforeseeable multitude of contexts (historical, political, sexual, linguistic ...) and, in interacting with these many encounters, opens a horizon for a politics of the body which is able to cross into Asia's past and present. It is apparent that Ito Tari herself is someone who is cast out from this border known as "I" via the vessel of her own body, pushed toward an interaction with an unknown other. During this interaction her body wanders away from her, flowing into another space-time, spreading, exposing an unforeseeable politics of the body, and opening the way toward an almost entirely overturned meeting place for those whose encounters have been foreclosed by a history of division.

I can now vividly recall the moment which allowed me to so clearly foresee the horizon of the politics of the body which needs to come. I remain captured by that odd scene even now.

It was when Ito Tari was crouched, squirming as she peeled onions. As I allowed my eyes to drift to a spot slightly above her body—which was illuminated by a single beam of light in the dark auditorium—a huge dark shadow meandered from her body, repeatedly miming her gestures, before escaping into The Battle of Okinawa panels as if of its own accord. It passed over a woman involved in "group suicide," strung upside down with her throat slit, then crossed the flames, and headed toward the side of a group of Japanese soldiers massacring civilians. Is it possible that at that moment, in a manner that Ito Tari herself could not have envisioned, the "you," which through the vessel of Ito Tari's body was reliving the war that a former "comfort woman" had experienced, became a huge shadow that ended up superimposed onto a different war we call the Battle of Okinawa, so as to re-live the Battle of Okinawa as well? Did the dead depicted in the "Battle of Okinawa" panels also, through an unexpected encounter with "you," not end up living another war; one experienced by the former "comfort woman"?[7] In a space-time such as Okinawa that amalgamates and magnifies the warped colonial violence that has occurred in Asia, it is art that becomes the bridging point in an interaction that permits one to relive a war in which others have lived and died, and to becoming increasingly inundated within encounters between people who had been unable to meet in history. And of course it goes without saying that it is none other than this unexpected encounter which we are exposed to in art, and which we sense through the medium of our own bodies.

In this unexpected encounter that is achieved through art we have been able to rethink the Asian region as a communal place that differs from any kind of territorial concept. In it, we have been able to grasp, however fleetingly, a possibility of conceiving of politics not as a system of oppositions, or as a matter of representation, but as a physically intimate exercise. When we are able to discover contemporary Asia—an Asia in which today the bordering activity of division appears to have cut away the foundation of our lives in every possible realm, and to have institutionalized violence and engendered hate and apathy—within the alternative possibilities inherent in artistic practice, then the dead will return from the shadows of history, and the call and response between the living and the returned dead can begin in earnest.

If we now have the opportunity to conceive of an Asian politics with art as a bridging point, then this will almost certainly require us to envision a lived time shared by those who have been otherwise divided by a temporality known as "the past" and to then project this vision into the future. This strikes me as a problematic challenge; one in which a relation of call and response that had already been inaugurated in the past, but since erased from history, must somehow be reinitiated.

---

7. Translator's note: Here Shinjō seems to refer to the fact that Kim Sun-dŏk, who was sent to Shanghai and Nanjing, experienced the war at a different site from those victims of the Battle of Okinawa.

But can we not say that it is in such an entirely unforeseeable, unexpected encounter that this problematic challenge may be realized? Just as the words of a single youth who lost his life in Okinawa in 1966 and the "Japan" that he envisioned kick-started one musician's career and, transformed into the "poems and songs" of Takahashi's "Last Note," were reborn as "songs that define the gestures of word and rhythm as a vehicle of melody," so, too, do encounters appear and become relived. In these encounters, the "rain" that falls "far, far away" continues to summon the "you" that has died on the countless battlefields of Asia. Furthermore, when the time lived by one former "comfort woman" who has died is recalled again in the body of a performer who resists the act of forgetting, then the many people in the Battle of Okinawa panels who lost their lives in that conflict—and who appeared to be quietly standing watch from a silent space beside her—cross paths and become reacquainted with her in a shared time. In this connection between the reacquainted, an opportunity that we might call art itself is brought to the fore.

> They are versatile, contagious, remain intact among other artistic forms, or rather are able to infiltrate and be incorporated with them, and because they have a rhythm that invites the movement of the whole body they invoke a collective solidarity and empathy, and they empower. Because they are easy to remember they are able to instill within themselves complicated notions and the very core issues at hand.[8]

The nature of "poems and songs" that Takahashi Yūji identified allows us to recall that "sound" is a medium born when things are brought into contact with each other. And yet this "sound" must also resonate throughout the foundations of the art that links us one to another.

Art calls out and captures people within that resonance. In this resonance we are able to resist the political violence of division, and dream of a solidarity which connects us. There is a substantial foundation to be found in this kind of dreaming. When Takahashi Yūji's music calls the words of Nakaya Kōkichi—an Okinawan youth who died amid the failure of the "reversion to Japan" movement that he was dedicated to—back from the shadows of memory, and when Ito Tari's performances fight back against the violence of for-

---

8. Takahashi Yūji, *Takahashi Yūji korekushion: 1970 Nendai*, 287.

getting by moving closer to the memories of those in our mothers' generation who were once "comfort women," then art leads us to a circuit outside the closed realm of "our history." It leads us to shared existence with the Other who has been called back, allowing us to move forward in our search for a new politics, one that shares its existence with an Other that is yet to be known.

TRANSLATED BY ANDREW HARDING.

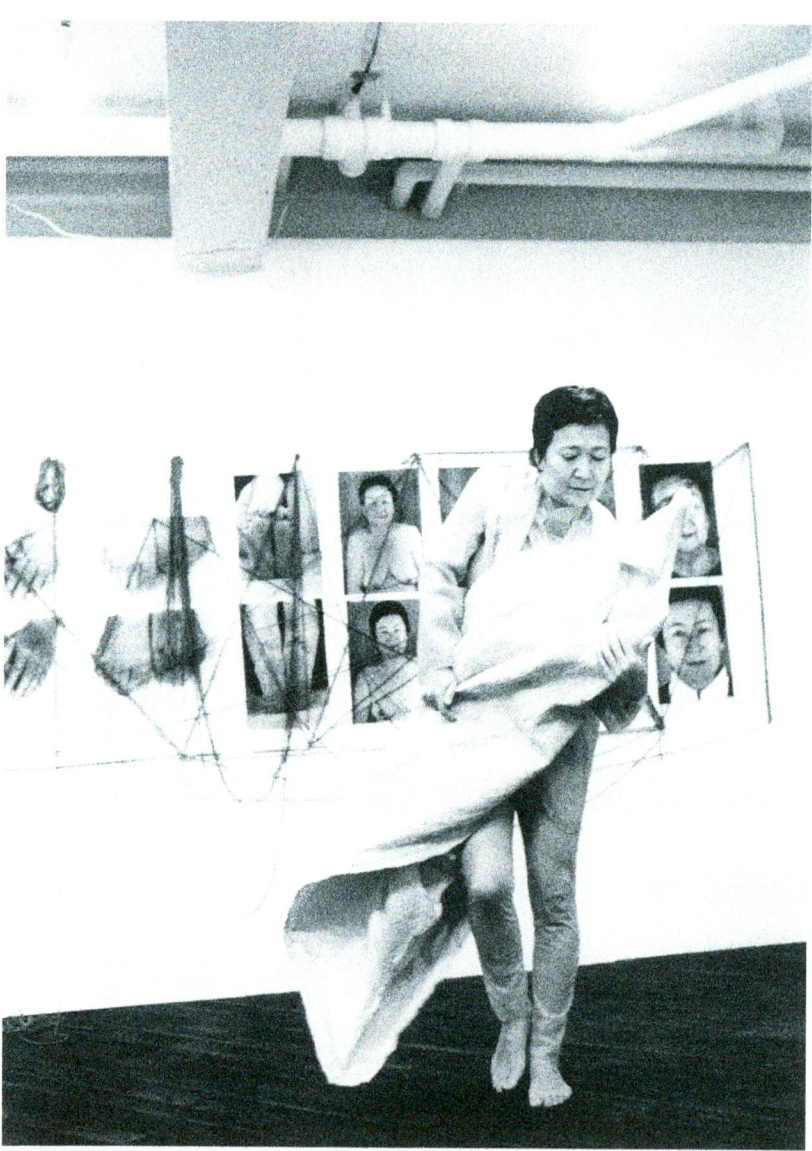

Ito Tari, *I will not forget you*, still photo from live-performance, Japan-Korea Art Relay, Seoul, 2009.

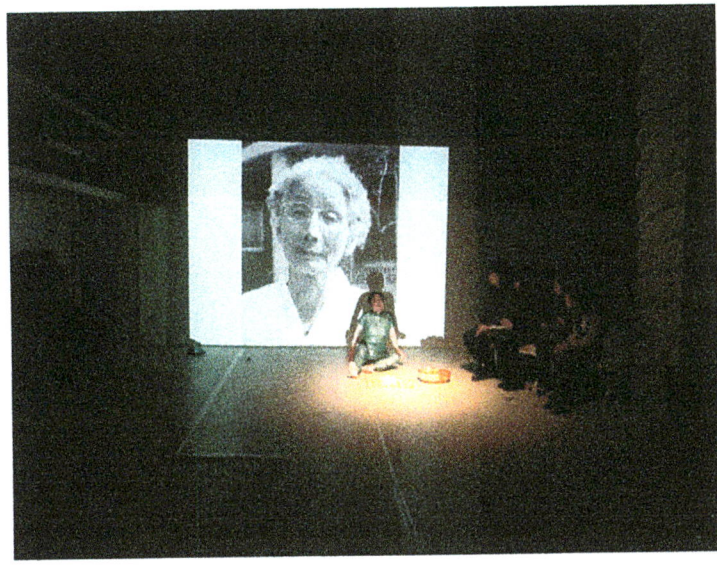

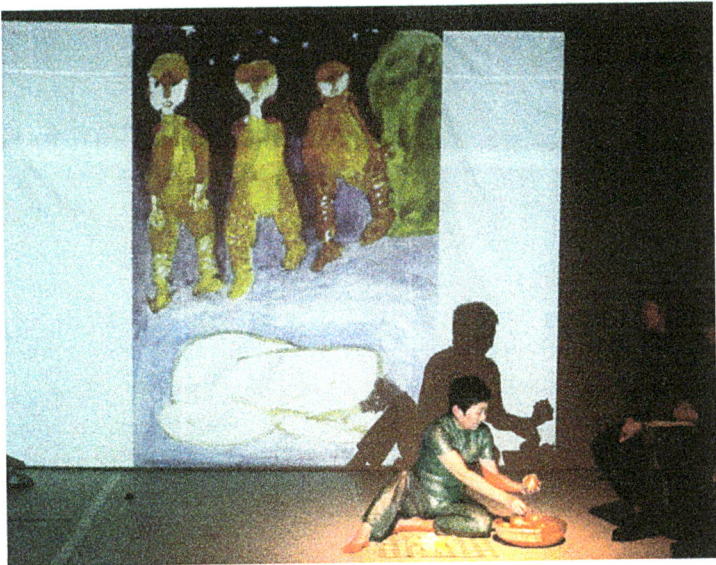

Ito Tari, still photo from live-performance, Japan-Korea Art Relay, Seoul, 2009.

CHAPTER 2

Deaths That Are Not Remembered

SATŌ IZUMI

B Y THE TIME you have noticed something and turned back to look, she has already entered the auditorium. How long has this person been walking, and when will she stop? Like a solitary wanderer whose points of departure and destination have long since been forgotten, she totters forward.

This is how Ito Tari began her performance, as we sat in clusters on the floor of the auditorium in the Sakima Art Museum. As she walked, taking breaths and footsteps that were almost inaudible, the whiteness of her bare feet lingered in our eyes.

This performance work by Ito titled *I will not forget you* is dedicated to Kim Soon-duk, a victim of the Japanese Imperial Army's "comfort women system." It was being performed in March 2007 in the Sakima Art Museum, located on what was formerly a corner of the Futenma Air Force base. The museum space was so quiet one could hear a pin drop. Yet, amid that quiet, the phantasmatic figures in Iri and Toshi Maruki's *The Battle of Okinawa*—displayed against one entire wall of the museum—seemed to emit groans and howls that shook the very earth itself.

While *I will not forget you* is by its very nature an intensely symbolic work that creates a new context for itself wherever it is performed, in a place like Okinawa this is particularly true, for there is no way the performance could

This is an excerpt from a longer essay with the same title by Satō Izumi in the original *Zanshō no oto* volume.

cordon off or delimit for itself a singular context there. This being the case, it was impossible to predict what emotions would be provoked in either artist or spectators when Ito's vision was projected back onto this site (at the Sakima Art Museum), itself shaped as a force field for war memories. For in Okinawa, too, there had been many Korean "comfort women." Assigned Japanese-style names like "Haruko" and "Suzuran," their real names were never recorded, and in the end not only their names but their very whereabouts and existences became lost before they could ever be remembered.

I will not forget you was first performed when WAM (the Women's Active Museum on War and Peace in Tokyo) sponsored an exhibit dealing with the topic of Korean "comfort women" left behind by the Japanese Imperial Army. The exhibit ran from April 29 to November 12, 2006. As it suggested, countless such women either lost their lives or were simply abandoned in battlefields where the Japanese army fought. One can only imagine what a long "postwar" these women lived through. In unfamiliar surroundings and unable to return to their places of birth, they had neither acquaintances, the financial means to keep themselves alive, nor knowledge of the Japanese language. Regardless of whether or not our feeble imaginations can fathom just how slowly those hours and days must have passed for them, the thought of what they must have experienced over those long years takes the breath away. Okinawa, too, was a site where "comfort women" were left behind.

For example, there was Beh Boungi, who was born in a small Korean village and lured into becoming a "comfort woman" for the Japanese Imperial Army, which then left her behind in an unfamiliar land.[9] Her story is told in Kawada Fumiko's report, *Renga no ie: Chōsen kara kita jūgun ianfu mondai* (The brick house: "Comfort women" from Korea, Chikuma Shobō, 1987). Kawada writes that "the country Boungi knew from the day she was born had always been a 'foreign country.'" She was born in a Korea already controlled by the colonial Japanese government, in which then ensued a fierce battle fought out between the Japanese and American armies. Following this,

---

9. Ito Tari always incorporates her "research" into her live art performance works, building on previous images and narratives. Her first trip to Okinawa was in 2007 to perform this work at the Asia, Politics, Art project workshop. On that trip she learned more from Shinjō Ikuo, Satō Izumi, and others about Beh Boungi and other military comfort women left in Okinawa. Seeing the U.S. Bases in Okinawa prompted her to do more research and she soon started incorporating information from the website of OWAAMV (Okinawan Women Act against Military Violence) into her works. In 2009 she went back to Okinawa to visit Tokashiki Island and other places where Beh Boungi lived. She started incorporating Beh Boungi's story into her live art performances as early as 2008.

Boungi found herself in an Okinawa under American occupation, where the land, the people, and the state that should have provided them with political representation were like foreign bodies layered one upon another. Raw violence welled up in the fault lines between these layers. Couldn't it be said, then, that Boungi had been "cast aside" even before she was left behind at Japan's defeat? And that throughout her life she had never freely chosen her own place to be? Boungi knew neither the Okinawan language, nor Japanese, nor English, and yet she seems to have also realized on some deep level that there was no "old home" to which she could return to remedy this lack.

Boungi had been sent with seven other young Korean women to Tokashiki Island, a base for the Imperial Army's suicide boats. As a "comfort woman" there, she witnessed Japan's defeat, at which point she was transferred to a detention center for civilians in Ishikawa. Once released from the center and literally "thrown out" into this unfamiliar land, she embarked on a way of life that almost defies comprehension. This was to spend the entirety of her first year wandering Okinawa on foot. Each day Boungi would walk until nightfall, seeking work in some bar in the barracks wherever she found herself, and leaving again at daybreak. Her lodgings changed every day, for she could not bear to spend longer than a day anywhere. Eventually Boungi found herself able to stay for a week, one month, or six months somewhere, but it was years before she settled down. What darkness she must have experienced in those days when something inside her made her pick up and leave the places she had walked to with great difficulty! Not only was Boungi a stateless person with no nation-state to be responsible for her, but—as if to eschew the very protection from the elements that might have been afforded by a roof and walls—she wandered barefoot, carrying in her hands the army-issued construction worker's rubber *tabi* that were her sole possession save for her bundled *furoshiki*. Boungi wandered in this manner for a year, as if retracing some fundamental mode of human existence—a life bare, without shelter, and not easily described. If asked why she was compelled to move from place to place, she herself was unable to answer, giving the impression that she had lost her mind. Yet perhaps this was because Boungi knew from experience a way of life in which safety involved restrictions, and protection could take the form of confinement.

... Ito Tari, having entered the auditorium so quietly, stops to gaze at the mural hanging on the wall at the front of the hall, as if seeking relief from the effort of walking. Yet one suspects that it is not even the scene from the Battle of Okinawa depicted there that she is looking at. Rather, Ito is immersing herself bodily in the deaths that were never recorded. Listening through her very skin to the fierce loneliness and overwhelming terrors that have accumulated in this silent room, she offers in exchange a weak, fragile body. Peeling the skin off an onion, she exposes a body that swells and then shrinks. Repeatedly banging the hard floor with her own body, she evokes tension and nervousness in the audience. The floor reverberates with the sensation of pain experienced by the flesh and bones of a human body so delicate it could not be expected to withstand the slightest force. Bare human existence makes the space around it resonate.

"I Will Not Forget You." Takazato Suzuyo, who discovered Beh Boungi hidden in an obscure location in Okinawa, has written in the book, *Okinawa no onnatachi: josei no jinken to kichi, guntai* (Women of Okinawa: The Military, bases, and human rights issues pertaining to women, Akashi Publishers, 1996) about how another victim of sexual violence she assisted reached out to her with the words, "Don't forget about me!" This woman, who had been raped by three U.S. soldiers at the age of twenty-one, suffered deep psychological repercussions in the wake of the event. She went from being a bar hostess to a nude dancer to a prostitute, and was visited, in the midst of her intolerable anguish, by delusions that people were accusing her of being a "filthy woman." "If a woman's life depends on her reputation," she charged, "then that is what I have lost." In her book, Takazato recalls how the woman called from the ward where she had been hospitalized; through the telephone receiver she heard the words, "I stopped being a human being when I was twenty-one. But I *am* human ... still ... don't forget about me!"

Now Tari-san walks with quiet steps through the groups of people sitting on the floor, stretching out her hands to them. I remember feeling a little nervous at that point, and I'm sure others were uncomfortable. Soni Kum alone had a broad smile on her face. She smiled without any reserve; she looked as if she fully expected the spirit of her own grandmother might be coming to visit her. In that moment I sensed the space between the living and the dead shift slightly. It was an overwhelming moment in the performance.

I will not forget you. Don't forget about me. Unspoken words, which could not possibly be summarized, commingled in the stillness of the auditorium. To be sure, this was a performance taking place before our very eyes. Yet it asked us to take a first step beyond the fixed distance that usually separates audience and performer.

TRANSLATED BY BRETT DE BARY.

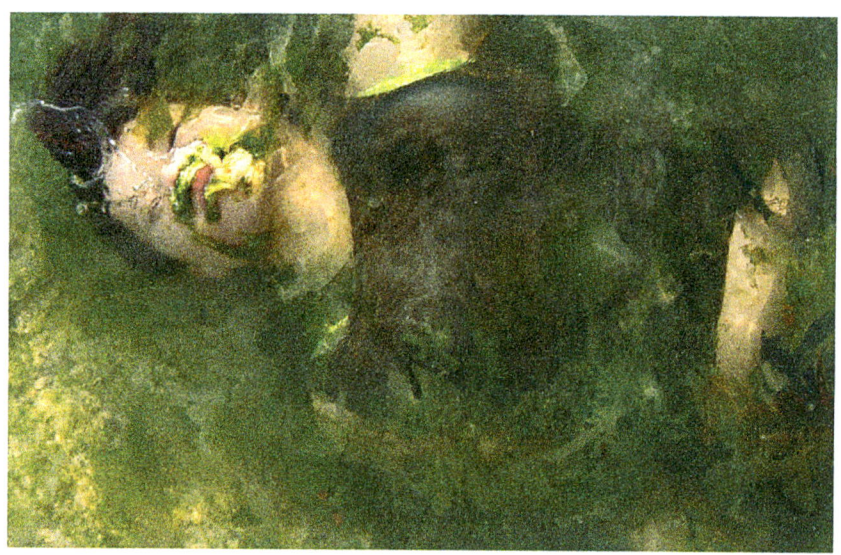

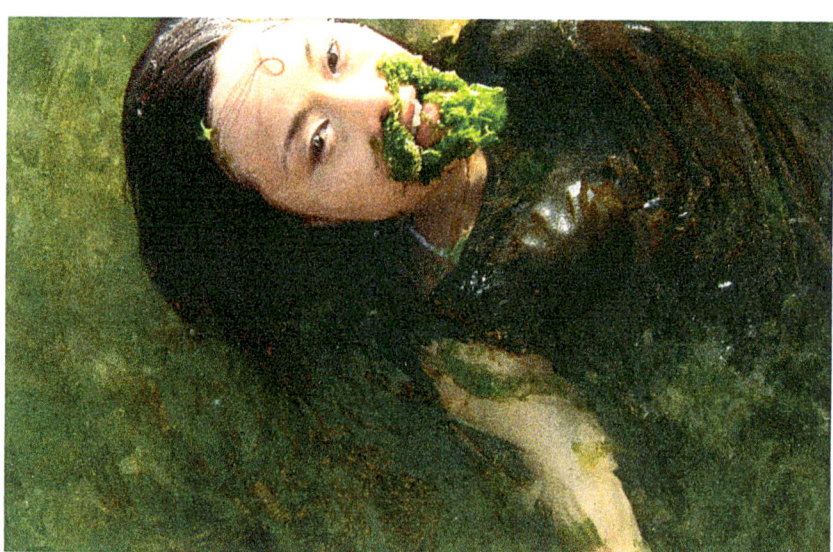

Yamashiro Chikako, *Seaweed Woman*, 8 still photos, with video (7 min 15 sec), 2008.

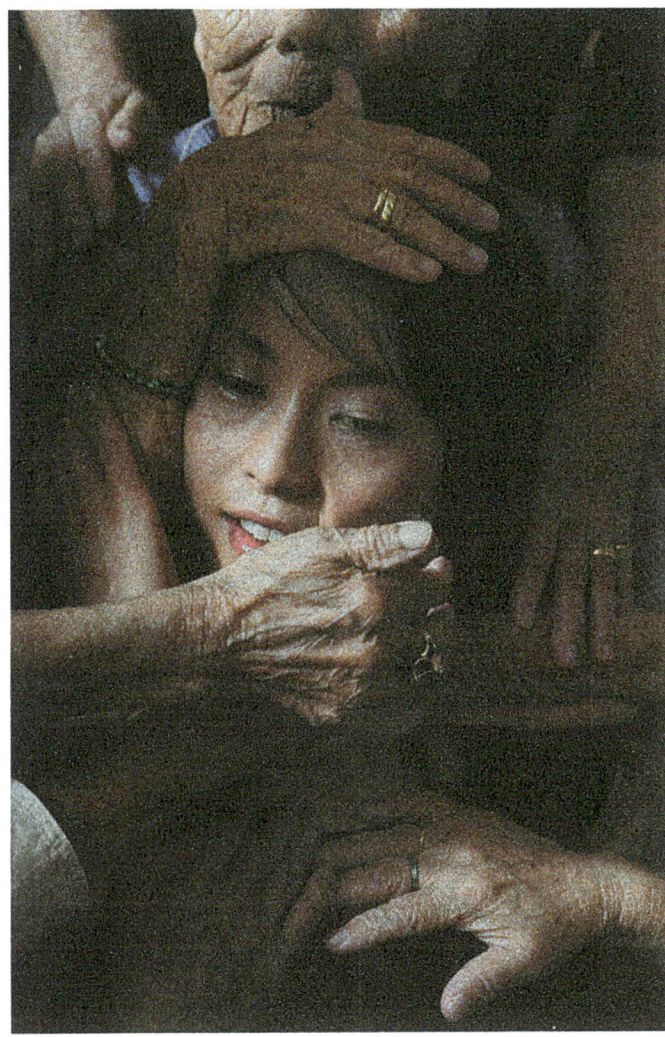

Yamashiro Chikako, *Virtual Inheritance*, photograph, 2008.

CHAPTER 3

Among Delicate Remnants

A *Tale of* Mokuninhama *or* Shore Connivance

(On Viewing Yamashiro Chikako's *Okinawa Complex Volume—
Shore of Ibano, Urasoe City*)

YANO KUMIKO

1. INTRODUCTION

WHAT IS THE difference between moving and not moving, flowing and not flowing? What is it that those on the side of movement and flow pretend not to see? Is the object of this "tacit tolerance" to be found with others or within ourselves?

A stranded boat out in the turquoise sea. A foreign object, static amid the shifting sky, sea, and waves. Blue sky, turquoise sea, and scraps of rusty iron. The tenderness that lies within them.

This was the first thing I thought of when I watched Yamashiro Chikako's film and its close-up of Ibano beach in Urasoe City. This beach, named Mokuninhama—that might be literally translated as "tacitly tolerated beach"—is surrounded by a coastline subsumed by a U.S. military base and on land reclaimed by public works projects. It is the only remaining natural beach in the area. A delicate remnant. Like a piece of tender flesh, left exposed to form the beach.

In the first scene, after the military base has been depicted through the four windows of a car passing at various speeds, the car stops, and the camera turns slowly toward the shore. Around the wire fence that surrounds the military base are discarded dressers, steel shelves, a station wagon, TVs, computers, beer bottles, buckets, and the effusion of garbage spilling from them. ... Not just industrial waste but everyday garbage also. An accumulation of things thrown away by ordinary folk. The distorted swellings of the world and society thrust upon a lonely remnant of nature. This alone would be a scene recognizable anywhere in contemporary society, but we also see a discarded boat or two. Unused, unwanted boats, discarded and with nowhere to go.

As the camera takes us past a sign that reads "BOAT DISPOSAL IN PROGRESS," the natural shoreline opens up before us. Small creatures crawl among the sand, pebbles, and shells. Puddles, old tires, scraps of metal. The water is stagnant, as if on the precipice of death. Here there is a small hut that seems to have been assembled from larger pieces of trash, next to which a number of small trucks are parked. There are dogs running around in this scene that, when I think about it, make me wonder where on earth they have come from. Are they stray dogs that have settled here? It is on such a beach that two men appear in turn in front of the camera to tell their, in many ways contrasting, stories.

2. THE MAN WHO FELT LIKE A "FOREIGN OBJECT"

Following a sound of unintelligible voices, the man's opening words—"It's kind of symbolic"—do not quite come across to the viewer as language. The *sound* certainly reaches us. There is also discernible a timbre. But there is a distance in the man's utterance, as though it is nothing more than sound. A voice, which recollects how he remains at odds with the environment, as though he faced real life with "his buttons done up all wrong." "The center of the world is me, after all," he says. His words seem to display a spirit of incomplete communication.

Here, Yamashiro inserts a device, perhaps to suggest that this is no ordinary interview. With the man's narration in the "background," a beach filmed in monochrome appears to us like the surface of another planet, scattered with boulders. The rocks even look like skulls. Small bugs or something or other crawl among them. In addition, an image of the "blue sky, turquoise sea, and one rod of scrap metal" is jostled in all directions. It's as if it's shaken by the "narration." In another scene, a sound effect that resembles the voice of an alien, among other things, is inserted.

A man appears. He wears a brown cap, an odd aloha shirt with a pattern of red flowers and white leaves on black cloth, and brown leather boots. He sits on a pile of concrete resembling the shell of a boat, looking like some kind of pseudo-Italian *Tora-san*, by the side of a puddle that draws an arc on the forgotten beach. It all feels very unreal. The man, who must be around fifty, appears to feel very strongly that he is a foreign object in this world. His speech, which he laces with themes of "subjectivity" and "identity" with a certain amount of verbosity and panache, laments the "sense of unease" he feels toward living and the "feeling of absence despite existing."

In a section where he is asked about "vicarious experiences," Yamashiro repeats the man's words, tracing over them in her own voice. A shadow formed from a strange repetition and its slight delay. This device, whereby the man's words are followed by those of Yamashiro, may not be an attempt to approach him as the "foreign substance," or as the Other, but rather a submission to the kind of oscillation that awakens the "foreign object"—the Other—within herself.

A question regarding "what he remembers" is thrown at a man sitting in the center of the image. The strange laugh with which he responds is painful for me to listen to. He says that he was once "heading toward violent impulses." Perhaps his feeling of dislocation is caused by that sort of daily struggle. In isolation, in ignorance, or perhaps simply in denial, words falter and violence implodes. Is this man's life still caught up in the emptiness of his memories of those days? In any case, his next muttering catches my ear.

No matter who you are, everyone's day-to-day life includes pain, worries, problems, and things that they need to deal with, but it always seems like other people have no problem in overcoming these hurdles at all, as though everybody else seems to get by somehow. This isn't really the case though. There's no such thing as a normal life, and while we may all have our ups and downs respectively, when there's no dialogue then other people might as well not exist, right? And if that's the case then there'll be no problems, nothing to be resolved, because there'll be no dialogue either. No dialogue means that others don't exist, and if others don't exist then it must mean that pain can't exist, right? And if pain doesn't exist then surely we reach a point where we aren't able to share a ... you know ... something that is "native" with one another?

Turquoise sea and scars. Here the artist turns the camera toward the sky, leaving the man in the corner of our vision. It is a sky that moves, with white clouds. ...

3. LANDFILL OVER "LIFE"

The interior is exposed and becomes a beach, and we zoom in on the human figures living on its skin. A contestation from the interior. Trash from other places—from parts where the flow of water has stopped because the surroundings have been reclaimed and built over—is piling up. From people who, even so, have no choice but to live by the sea.

The second person we see is a man whose connection to this coastline spans many years, who "trades information" about fishing and other various topics with other fishermen, and is well aware of circumstances from everyday, real-life experience. He is a stocky figure, suntanned and wearing a camouflage T-shirt and sandals. He is, perhaps, of an age similar to the first man. From his story of how this beach has changed, the reality of how these remains have been treated becomes clear. It seems that his own life, too, has been wounded in a different way, as though it has been stripped of its "here-and-now."

Here, the narration takes place inside the beach hut. Yamashiro steps into the "reality" of the hut's interior, appearing on screen with her friend. The scene is set for the two of them to listen to the tale of this man of the sea. Another man, a friend, comes in and offers them beer and snacks. They sit on a sofa that may once have been trash, in a hut dotted with "furniture" that may once also have been trash, somehow appearing to connect the world on the inside with the one on the outside. And so the interview proceeds. In an arrangement whereby Yamashiro listens to what is being said as an outsider, as a guest, the viewer is also taught by this "man of the sea," forced to take notice. The man's voice, which appears to tremble somewhat in the opening shots, soon strikes me as increasingly frank, but in a way that doesn't cause him to raise his voice in the slightest.

Until a decade ago the sea around that beach was far more beautiful than it is now and full to the brim with fish and seaweed. It was a place that supported people's livelihoods, as well as a place of rest. Of course, it was a part of a limited segment of the sea with a "restricted water zone" imposed by the

American military, but it hadn't been polluted yet. Then "Irijima" on the west coast was reclaimed and built over in the name of economic stimulus; the water flow changed, and all the River Ajagawa trash flowed straight into this small bay. What's more, until 9/11 there were lively events like *tsukimi-kai* (moon-viewing parties) held by the "corporate contractor bosses," who "accepted the contracts on public works and jobs relating to the military," where hundreds of people would attend, including politicians and the like. Back then the people who turned up also cleaned the beach. After that, however, it was a place that came to be forgotten.

"Has the landscape changed?" asks Yamashiro, to which the man starts to answer in hushed tones.

Well, the sea is polluted. ... You can tell, even without diving. Basically, it's dirty. It's not that the flow of water itself is dirtier than it was. It was clean a long time ago. If you set up a fishing rod at this river dike you used to be able to catch hundreds of fish. ... It was clean until ten years ago. After they built over Irijima all the trash from Ajagawa drifted over here. ... There's fewer octopus. There was a lot of octopus but now you can't catch any. ... See those stranded boats over there? Up until they were abandoned there were all sorts of things. ... If only they hadn't buried the coastline. ... What I can say about these land reclamation projects is that they can't compare with the economic benefits that we got from the sea. ... I think it's accurate to say that public works and the sea are not something that can be weighed against each other. ... The people that used to cast nets and dive to gather seaweed. ... Whatever happens, Okinawa shouldn't bury the sea. ... Yes, it would be fine if they could reclaim the land and fix everything so that we could catch fish like we used to. But once the environment is destroyed you can't fish anymore. ... If we leave the sea alone then it can be used by our grandchildren's generation and into eternity. We sea people don't mess up the sea. Of course it'll get dirty with what we're doing now because there's no more water getting in. This goes beyond the sea's self-cleansing power. ... Everywhere is filled in, everywhere but here. ... It's boring! When you can't catch fish. When you can't catch a fish in the sea and have a beer.

We learn from this conversation that, although this beach had never been designated for any specific purpose, it gradually became surrounded on all sides by the military base, with the upshot being that the land was then reclaimed as part of public works projects designated for commercial purposes. Then garbage from elsewhere began to pile up. A stagnation and slow death occurred in the places where water stopped flowing. That this small natural beach, where people were once able to breathe freely, was turned upside down and discarded as a "foreign body" is too painful to bear, a land reclamation that "does construction in the sea," causing the loss of not just modest, everyday life, but also of hopes and of reasons for living. To "stop flowing" is to block the natural circuitry, wounding people's lives. It is the pain of delicate remnants.

From the "reality" of the small hut, the camera shifts once again toward the sea, catching the figures of people entering the sea silently to fish. The dogs frolic at the water's edge.

4. TO ENTER, TO JOSTLE, TO MOVE

Those who turn their attention to the silent anger of the beach and the particular lives of those who live by it realize that they in turn are themselves foreign objects to them. But the moment we become aware of that sensation that the parts of us that are able to feel are becoming fewer, are hardening, are stagnating, and the pain is building up, that is when we must act.

We must commence action to regain a "flow" while avoiding the violence of "self-cleansing" or of "cleansing others."

For those people who go into the sea, the people who fish silently, the people who come home after fishing, it is the camera that is seen as a "foreign object"—it's in observing this that I am suddenly made aware. Then I wonder, can I really say that I am what is moving in this scene? Like the airplanes and freight ships that occasionally appear on screen, perhaps I, as a viewer, am just "passing through," pretending not to see these remnants. We are simply the side that believes we are the ones moving, flowing.

The suspicious look that a man flashes toward the camera as he returns from the sea is clearly a critical one. For him, Yamashiro is also an outsider. Having found and entered this Mokuninhama, in what ways has she intervened?

I felt that the devices and tricks which I alluded to in this short essay—that is, the oscillation that Yamashiro applies to "the story of Mokuninhama"—form an action that attempts to bring change to this location by means of art. The oscillation that attempts to recover "flow," on the one hand, shows Yamashiro's irritation toward the environment that surrounds these people, while on the other it displays a hope for change. Yamashiro's method is not to close in on the Mokuninhama, but is self-conscious of its distance in relation to the people who live in this environment. The frustrations that we, forced into a corner, have toward "nature." We have a sense of being right on the brink.

Even so, I would assume that it was not just I who felt somehow reassured when I saw those people by the sea. This is the basic power in "movement": to jostle and awaken the remaining tender parts within and restore the space to move. To distance oneself slightly. To move from there. I wonder if it is too optimistic to believe that if these kinds of gestures increase in number, something might just change.

TRANSLATED BY ANDREW HARDING AND RYAN BUYCO.

CHAPTER 4

Specters of East Asia

Okinawa, Taiwan, and Korea

CHOI JINSEOK

INTRODUCTION

Among a cluster of underground air-raid shelters that made up the former Okinawa Army Hospital in Haebaru, in the city of Naha, is a cave where the character for the Korean surname "Kang" has been carved three times into the ceiling. As the Battle of Okinawa raged, workers and patients at the former hospital had fled the center of the city, moving repeatedly until they finally arrived at Haebaru's underground shelters. Here, wounded soldiers received surgery and medical treatment alongside military porters working with pickaxes to hew out a tunnel about 6 feet high and 230 feet in length.

I came upon the place where the name "Kang" had been engraved, after walking alone through pitch darkness, about midway through the tunnel. The characters had been carved, it appeared, by a *chōsenjin* soldier hospitalized for some kind of injury to his lungs.[1] Judging from their position on the

---

We acknowledge the help of Christopher Ahn, Ikeuchi Yasuko, and Mizutamari Mayumi in providing explanations for the varied uses of the terms *zainichi* and *chōsenjin* in this text.

1. Translator's note: Throughout this translation we will use the romanized *chōsenjin* and Chōsen whenever these terms appear, either written in kanji or katakana in Choi's essay. This method of translation has been chosen both to demonstrate, and accord with, the argument developed by Choi in the course of the essay, which calls attention to the historical specificity of the word Chōsen, as used by the Japanese colonial regime (1910–1945) to refer to the entirety of its colony on the Korean Peninsula, inclusive of areas partitioned into North and South at the end of the Korean War in 1953. As Choi points out later in this essay, residents of the Korean

ceiling, I could surmise that the soldier had carved them while lying on the upper bunk of a makeshift hospital bed inside the tunnel. Perhaps, trying to escape the flames of war, the soldier had fled until his physical strength was depleted, and had carved these characters with the foreknowledge that he would die there in the underground shelter. Although it was clear that the three characters had been produced by the hand of the same person, the size and depth to which each one had been carved were different. In their differences, they seemed like a record of the last days of someone striving desperately to leave behind some trace of his existence, while dying in a distant place called Okinawa. One could say I had come across his grave.

What could that soldier possibly have felt as he carved the three characters of the name "Kang" here, in a distant land, I wondered. Whatever his feelings were, they defied my imagination. Yet as someone living in the present, I felt obliged to use at least the physical sensations I was experiencing here to understand, to a small extent, the unimaginable. To meet a "faraway death" means to carve your own name in stone three times, with diminishing levels of strength. And, lest we forget, to meet a faraway death can also mean to die with no grave at all, without even being able to carve one's name in stone.[2]

---

peninsula who were subject to forced mobilization as porters for the Japanese Imperial Army or laborers for mining, dam building, and other work in Japan, were called *chōsenjin* by the Japanese, although they themselves most probably would have continued to refer to themselves by the Korean-language term *joseon saram*. Throughout the postwar period, the terms *chōsenjin* and Chōsen have continued to be used in Japan. For example, although the political entity called Chōsen is now defunct, it is listed as a "nationality" (*chōsenseki*) on the Alien Registration Cards of those who remain stateless, i.e., those who did not declare South Korean, or any other, citizenship after the conclusion of the South Korea–Japan Basic Relations Treaty in 1965. While the terms Chōsen and *chōsenjin* both continue to carry some discriminatory overtones, in recent years both have been reclaimed by activists and progressive scholars. In the pages that follow, Choi argues that those "Koreans" who lived and died under Japanese colonialism should be referred to by the term *chōsenjin*, rather than the sanitized *kankokujin* (referring only to citizens of today's Republic of South Korea) or even *zainichi kankoku/chōsenjin* that some have chosen as a more politically acceptable term today. Thus the memory of the suffering of *chōsenjin* under Japanese colonialism will not be erased. At the same time, as we will see later, Choi envisions that a reclaimed *chōsenjin* could be used as an umbrella term to bring together those in Japan who are now fragmented by loyalties to either South Korea (Kankoku) or North Korea (still often referred to in Japanese as Chōsen).

2. Choi, like Lee Chonghwa in her introductory *taidan* with Takahashi Yūji, makes the trope of "faraway death" central to the rhetoric of this essay. Like Lee, he uses the archaic term *kakushi* (客死), literally, "to die while traveling" or "to die while a guest," whose ideographs do not rely on a distinction between "foreign" and "native." The term also evokes the ethical question of how to deal with anonymous or unmourned deaths.

1. MY EXPERIENCE IN TAIPEI

I went to Taipei in January 2007. At that time, I visited the now closed coal mine–turned-sightseeing area in Jingtong in the Pingxi area near Taipei. While there I had the opportunity to listen to the local people talk about the mine.

Jingtong Mine, which had thrived in the 1920s, allegedly hired Japanese engineers together with Taiwanese, indigenous, and *chōsenjin* miners. It goes without saying that these four groups of workers were not treated on an equal level but had been organized around a clear-cut hierarchy. In the ranking of Japanese, Taiwanese, indigenous people, and *chōsenjin*, the *chōsenjin* occupied the lowest place. Below the Taiwanese were the indigenous people, and then, below them, were the *chōsenjin*. It is not hard to imagine that, based on the hierarchy existing between the empire and colony and among colonized territories themselves, day-to-day practices of discrimination took place in the mine, as the violence of colonial oppression was transferred from one group to another. This situation must have intensified under the extreme conditions of war.

The mine is now a small museum called the Jingtong Coal Mine Museum, where historical records of the Jingtong mine such as chronological records and photographs have been retained. I found, however, absolutely no records relating to *chōsenjin* miners. Not only were the records therefore incomplete, but in general materials concerning the Japanese colonial period were displayed in the museum quite haphazardly, memorializing only those aspects of Taiwan's mines that put Taiwan's mining industry generally in a good light.

Preserved in the area surrounding the coal mine was also the dormitory for the Japanese engineers who had worked there. The actual dormitories of the Taiwanese, indigenous, and *chōsenjin* miners had long since disappeared, but their former locations and names bluntly conveyed a hierarchy with Japanese at the top. For instance, if we consider the names of the dormitories, we find that the dormitory where the Japanese engineers lived was called Kōgu, or Imperial Palace. This dormitory took the form of a traditional Japanese home, and the building has been carefully preserved to maintain the look of the times. Even now, it retains its name from the colonial period, and is being used as a teahouse called Kōgu. In fact, when I went inside to have coffee I felt as if I had slipped back in time to the colonial period; time seemed to flow differently inside and outside the building. Ironically, I had never experienced such a feeling in Japan. I had the sense that for the first time here in Taiwan I was encountering the refinement of a traditional Japanese home. Shamisen music played inside the teahouse, sounding more Japanese than any music that I had heard in Japan, while its interior had been decorated with a stronger sense of Japaneseness than anything one could find in Japan today, giving me a very strange impression. Here there seemed to exist a Japan that was more Japanese than Japan—a case of "reverse Orientalism"? According to the brochure for those who visited the teahouse, the dormitory for the Japanese engineers faced the Imperial Palace in Tokyo, symbolizing that their hearts were turned in the direction of Mount Fuji and their homeland. Indeed, in those days, ordinary people were not allowed to approach the Japanese engineers' dormitory.

Let me return to the matter of the dormitories' names. The dormitory housing the Taiwanese miners was given the name Tokyo, and the one where the indigenous miners stayed was called Hokkaido. Did this signal that Hokkaido, although on a lower rung than Tokyo in the order of buildings, was highest among all of imperial Japan's colonies? The dormitories themselves were no longer standing, but here and there in the streets of Pingxi one could find signs saying "Tokyo" and "Hokkaido." Although the signs designated tourist inns, they gave me a sense that the memory of those places still lives on in the area today, even if in the form of a nostalgia from which the bitter memories of the colonial past have been excised.

But what about the *chōsenjin* miners who were lowest in status? Based on the ranking among Japan's colonies at the time, one might think a dormitory called Ryukyu would be appropriate for them. But the *chōsenjin* miners' dormitory was not even adorned with a name like Ryukyu. Sadly enough, it had no name whatsoever. Moreover, one could figure out approximately where the dormitories called Tokyo and Hokkaido were located, but I was told no one knew where the *chōsenjin* miners had lived. I hope to learn more about this mine in the future. But upon hearing that the building for the *chōsenjin* miners had never been given a name, and that its whereabouts were completely unknown, I was quite overcome. "So that was the status of Chōsen ..." I thought, staring off into the distance.

I remember my experience in Taiwan vividly, to this day. I wonder if this is because I had already visited Okinawa before going to Taiwan. The air in Taiwan feels very much like the air in Okinawa. Geographically the two islands are close and belong to the same archipelago, so it is not surprising that they share similarities. The humid, subtropical air and soil feel the same in both places, and the attitude to life Okinawans call *chirudai* seems to link them in my mind. But what inextricably links the two places for me is the fact that *chōsenjin* died, away from home, in both places. *Chōsenjin* were killed during the Battle of Okinawa not just by Japanese, but also by Okinawans. Still today, beneath the runway of Kadena Airforce Base, lie the remains of *chōsenjin* porters who served as forced laborers for the Japanese Army. Their bones can still be found there.

For me, this connection between *chōsenjin* who met faraway deaths in Taiwan and Okinawa prompts thoughts of East Asia, Japan, Okinawa, Taiwan. This is an East Asia that rests on the sacrifice of the *chōsenjin* dead. It is an Asia that has already internalized these *chōsenjin* dead as Other. By this I mean that they no longer have any visible presence in East Asia. Unmourned and out of sight, the *chōsenjin* dead swarm over Japanese, Okinawan, and Taiwanese land. They cannot be seen, yet they have never disappeared. I think of light and shadow. In terms of such a metaphor, one could say the *chōsenjin* dead are East Asia's shadows. A person surrounded by light cannot see that which is in the shadows. From the shadows, however, it is possible to make out that which is in the light as well as that which is in the deepest of shadows. An East Asia imagined by those who remain blind to the *chōsenjin* dead will not be capable of dismantling "modernity," "nationality," and "the state," and will merely repeat the violence inherent within them.

2. DWELLING WITH THE DEAD

In the Jeju Island Uprising, as well as in the civil war which arose from its escalation—the Korean War—people of Korean ethnicity slaughtered each other in the cruelest ways humanly possible, committing horrors even hell couldn't conceive of. This phrase, "horrors even hell couldn't conceive of" are the words of the elderly Yang We-hon in the documentary *Ama no ryan san* (Grandma Yang the diving woman), directed by Haramura Seiki in 2004. In this film, which frames the awe-inspiring life of an elderly woman born on Jeju Island, who survived the uprising by escaping to Osaka as a stowaway, Yang responds to the interviewer's questions as to what the massacre was like with this phrase, and a pained expression. "Horrors even hell couldn't conceive of." Could humans know anything more tragic than what played out here?

Yet it is safe to say that among Japanese today—whether it is because the

Korean War is only remembered for the economic boom the military procurements industry created for Japan, or simply because the war has been cleansed from memory—it is entirely unknown that these massacres and the war that followed can be precisely traced to Japanese colonial policies. Antagonism between the cunningly utilized pro-Japanese landowners and police, and the people of Chōsen whom they had continuously harmed and exploited, lay at the very root of what caused these events, including those prompted by revenge, that preceded and succeeded it.

In addition to such preexisting internal conflicts within communities and villages, after the liberation from Japanese rule, there was also the confrontation between the Soviet Union (which thoroughly promoted land reform and punished the pro-Japanese collaborators in North Korea) and the United States (which in governing South Korea took full advantage of the negative legacies left by the Japanese colonial government, such as the Governor-General's Office and former pro-Japanese collaborators), in other words, the structure of the Cold War. Veiled within that structure, conflicts within the Korean Peninsula grew increasingly severe, until the Jeju Uprising of 1948 occurred, leading eventually to the Korean War, which was actually a civil war. The wartime situation changed at a dizzying pace, and every time it did so, the battlefront would be moved, so that revengeful massacres of increasing brutality were carried out over and over again.

Also, although a majority of the massacres of civilians in the Korean War were perpetrated by the South Korean army, we should remember that this army was an institution originally organized by pro-Japanese collaborators. These were people fully steeped in the militarist mentality of the Japanese army and its brutal ways. Throughout the Korean War, the army officers and police openly carried Japanese swords, which they used in the massacres of civilians. As the Korean sociologist Kim Dong-choon astutely grasped, "If we consider the fact that it was the pro-Japanese forces, cornered in a moment of crisis, who played a leading role in these massacres, following practices inculcated in them by the Japanese Imperial Forces, it is also possible to see the mass killings that took place during the Korean War as a direct legacy of the Japanese colonial rule."[3] If we do not grasp these continuities with Japanese colonial rule, and only take into account the confrontation between the

---

3. Kim Dong-choon, *Chōsen sensō: Hinan, senryō, gyakusatsu* [A social history of the Korean War: Displacement, occupation, massacre], trans. into Japanese by Kim Mihye, Choi Deokhyo, Cho Kyong-hee, and Chong Yong-hwan (Tokyo: Heibonsha, 2008), 236.

United States and the Soviet Union, we will not be able to understand why this sort of massacre took place, and why the tragic "horrors even hell couldn't conceive of" came to unfold. It goes without saying that the civil war we call the Korean War, and its massacres, cannot be seen as "someone else's business" by the Japanese. The Japanese were involved in those deaths.

The Korean War has not yet come to a conclusion; the Korean Peninsula still carries the scars of those massacres. It is the same as with Okinawa, which still carries the scars left by the mass suicides that happened during the Battle of Okinawa. Even sixty years is not enough. The Korean War has not ended. The Battle of Okinawa has not ended. In a situation in which it is still not possible to solve the issue of pro-Japanese collaboration in South Korea, and in which the perpetrators of those massacres, as well as their surviving families and subordinates, continue to be in positions of power, our social structure remains incapable of punishing the perpetrators.

As is well known, Japan remains unwilling as a state to face the history of Okinawa's mass suicides. But the situation in Okinawa is even more complex. That is to say, not only do Okinawans carry the all-too-enormous scars of the violence committed against them that was worse than anything "hell could conceive of" but they also retain similar memories of violence they themselves committed against former colonies, chiefly Chōsen.

Nevertheless, the relationship between Okinawans and *chōsenjin* should not be regarded as a dichotomy of perpetrators and victims. Should we speak in these terms, the existence of the dead will slip from view. This is because the violence perpetrated by imperial Japan and its mainland population was completely different in kind and quality from the violence perpetrated by Okinawans in Okinawa. Before displacing it elsewhere, we need to unravel this vortex of oppression and violence that existed between the colonies of Okinawa and Chōsen. Moreover, we need to properly grieve for those *chōsenjin* who met faraway deaths in a land called Okinawa. What this would involve in concrete terms is to uncover the true circumstances surrounding their deaths, as would be the case with unearthing the dead who lie under the runway of the Kadena Military Base.

I catch my breath when some Okinawan friends, recalling the violence of the war, talk about the damage done to *chōsenjin* as if they themselves had been the perpetrators. This is extremely painful to hear. It is, of course, of primary importance to speak about these issues, but won't the practice of Okinawans continually speaking about them from the standpoint of the perpetrators become dangerously commonplace? And doesn't speaking from the point of view of the "perpetrators" force Okinawans to expel those other deaths, of Okinawans, that have long been internalized and held within? In other words, if this narrative of "perpetrators" and "victims" does indeed become a pattern, won't we simply be dealing with abstractions? Perhaps this is the pitfall of any account that tries to be conscientious. But in this particular case, I think we can better understand the situation in Okinawa by considering how the history of violence toward *chōsenjin* is remembered in Japan.

One often sees on cenotaphs or in the archives of coal mines and dams in Japan the statement, "The number of forced laborers from Kankoku/Chōsen who died in Japan in the line of duty is still unknown." The *chōsenjin* dead, their number, even their names, remain unclear, and at the present time in Japan the impetus to find this information is lacking. What this tells us is that, at the time that these dams and mines were in operation, Japanese did not actually consider *chōsenjin* to be human beings. Occupying the very bottom rung on the social hierarchy, *chōsenjin* were not only made to work in the most degrading and dangerous of environments. Even when they died trying to perform these tasks, they were not treated as human beings. When the Japanese proprietors of the coal mines and dams had trouble disposing of the corpses, many bodies were simply burned or thrown away on the spot. Thus it has come to be that their number and their names went unrecorded. The word "discrimination" alone simply cannot describe a violence like this, which transcends our imagination. And if the word "violence" is premised on an understanding that it is something done to humans, then not even that word will do. If I may repeat myself: the Japanese did not treat *chōsenjin* as human beings.

It is a common practice in today's Japan to refer to those who lived on the Korean Peninsula in the colonial era before it was divided into North and South, and before the Democratic Republic of Korea was established, as *kankokujin* or *kankoku/chōsenjin*. This, however, is clearly a historically erroneous appellation, a form of arrogance of the living who try to impose their will on the dead. The polite term for "person" (*kata*) is also often used these days, as when the expression "*Chōsen no kata*" is used in place of *chōsenjin*. However, this politically correct mode of address is also a kind of hypocrisy, since it disguises the facts and obfuscates that history in which *chōsenjin* were not treated as human beings. While this way of speaking occurs when Japanese attempt to refer to the victimhood of *chōsenjin* from the position of the perpetrator, it results in an erasure of the dead. It is a kind of remembering-while-forgetting that, by dint of repetition, turns the existence of the dead into

an abstraction, forces the dead to return to silence, and has meant that a palpable sensation of confronting those from the former colony who lost their
lives has been lost. But if it is true that the very ground we are standing on
contains—detectible to the naked eye—the bones of those who were abandoned, whose ground is it? We need to exercise our imaginations at least to this
extent. We need to understand that this earth we now inhabit, before being a
possession of the living, belongs to the dead. Isn't this what is required of us?
An ability to imagine the dead that is basic to our very existence as humans?

The Truth Commission on Forced Mobilization under Japanese Imperialism (established in South Korea in 2005 through the Special Law Supporting Fact-Finding on Forced Mobilization under Japanese Imperialism) is
now carrying out the national project of having the remains of *chōsenjin*
forced laborers returned to South Korea.[4] Even today these remains are scattered on the grounds of temples near mines and dams throughout Japan.
Some Japanese, whether out of pangs of conscience or a fear of being cursed,
saw to it that such remains were at least delivered to a temple. The South
Korean government is now committed to having them transported home. Of
course, since this is in every respect an undertaking of the South Korean
government, set forth within the framework of the nation-state, it has inherent limitations. Investigations will be carried out only in Japan (the territory
of the former colonizer) and not in Taiwan or Okinawa. There is also the risk
that the South Korean state will intervene in this history and use it for its
own purposes. Nevertheless, it is a significant effort. It is especially so when
we consider that contemporary South Korea has trodden a long path, from
military dictatorship to democracy, in order to reach this point where it can
come to terms with its past as its democracy matures. It is also significant
when we take into account the fact that South Korea still cannot act independently of the U.S.- and Japan-led anti-Communist bloc in East Asia, starting
first and foremost with the provisions of the peace treaty concluded with

---

4. Translator's note: The South Korean government of Roh Mo-hyun established the Truth
and Reconciliation Commission in 2003 to investigate human rights abuses and civilian massacres that occurred in Korea from the colonial period through the overthrow of the military
dictatorship by the *minjung* movement in 2003. The Truth Commission on Forced Mobilization
under Japanese Imperialism started its visits to former worksites throughout Japan in April
2005, against the background of state-level negotiations over the repatriation of the remains of
conscripts known to be retained in Japan. With much of its work uncompleted, the Truth and
Reconciliation Commission and other groups linked to it were disbanded by the Lee Myung-
bak administration when the commission's first mandate expired in 2010.

Japan during the quagmire of the Vietnam War, which was facilitated by South Korea's complicity with Japan and the United States in waging that war. And when we consider that the Cold War (and the Cold War era that posed so many obstacles for South Korea) has still not ended in East Asia, we could even say that the South Korean government has been prompt in moving to undertake this project. Why then, we might ask, has Japanese society remained unresponsive to, disinterested in, and ignorant of this project? These are, bear in mind, the very same Japanese who were inflamed over the kidnappings of Japanese citizens by North Korea. I hardly consider the repatriation project something of no concern to Japan.

A friend who is involved in the activities of the Truth Commission on Forced Mobilization told me this story: There are cases in which family members who are sent the remains of the deceased, once the whereabouts of the body have been discovered and the circumstances of death clarified, burst into tears and grieve, even after sixty years have passed. Yet in addition to that long-neglected grief, which indeed had already started to wither away, these survivors experience a second grief. This is the grief that occurs when they discover that the remains that are delivered are not bones but ashes. Normally, cremation does not take place in Korean culture. This is also the case in Okinawa, where, unlike Japan, burial is done rather than cremation. Because burial is a Korean tradition, survivors who receive cremated remains of the deceased experience a second grief. What could it be like to experience this second grief, after the passage of sixty years' time?

Let us return the discussion to Okinawa. The Okinawan view of the relation between life and death is something like "dwelling together with the dead," as I understand it. As a matter of daily experience, the dead and the living dwell together. One can immediately tell that similar views of life and death have been held in Okinawa and Chōsen by looking at the shapes of the graves: we find burial mounds on the Korean peninsula, and turtleback tombs in Okinawa. In both places, graves are a ceremonial space where the dead and the living mingle—in a Korean cultural sensibility, the grave was a wide-open space or a yard, or *madang*. For instance, the series of artworks by Yamashiro Chikako that use the turtleback tomb as a stage seek to evoke the essence of such tombs, which are rooted in the Okinawan idea of "dwelling together with the dead." In the video art performance "Okinawa Complex" (2007), which was staged in a garden with a turtleback tomb, the legs of the performer appear from amid a bed of foliage, slowly opening and closing in a repeated pattern. The beautiful lines of her legs are themselves almost like flowers reaching up to heaven from the surface of the gravesite. They seem to waft pleasantly in the wind. Through the repetition of this exercise, a festive space opens up, in which the living and the dead mingle, so that the appearance of the tomb site is gradually transformed in a richly humorous manner. Looking at the intense, almost poisonous shadows, lights, and colors that appear one by one in this piece, the spectator begins to have a languid feeling, the feeling of *chirudai*.

"Dwelling together with the dead." Here in Okinawa—a force field richly expressive of this view of life and death—should it not be possible to maintain the presence of the *chōsenjin* dead, too, as a sensation, even as an internalized Other, that is held and confronted within? I am not speaking of the dead as an idea here. Rather, I speak of the dead as existences upon which we can train our gaze precisely as what is unseen, yet has not disappeared from this world. I want to believe that the sensation of these graves, and the view of life and death prevalent in Okinawa, have the power to dismantle even the pressures of Japanese and American imperialism that have so far held Okinawans and *chōsenjin* apart.

3. UNDOING/RESOLVING *HAN*

To the Spirits of Our Brothers and Sisters who Perished on this Island[5]

Why has this island become silent?
Why is it that it no longer tries to speak
Of the sorrow of the women
Of what happened to our brothers and sisters of the Korean Peninsula?

Oh, older brothers who were abducted, torn from your families
Who breathed your last in the suffocating heat of ships' hulls
Whose hands and feet were blown off in this land of Okinawa
Whose souls were trampled upon!

---

5. "Undoing/Resolving *Han*" is a translation of the subtitle: 恨を解く、恨解き. The concept conveyed by the character 恨 in this section's subtitle can mean "grudge" or "resentment" in Japanese, while in Korean it can also refer to "bonding based on suffering and hardship." *Furigana* beside the second part of the title (恨解き) give it the gloss ハンプリ to evoke "*hanpuri*," the Korean pronunciation for "loosening the bonds of suffering."

The war has ended, time has passed,
Yet the sound of soldiers' boots never fades from this island
Stolen land, vanished villages, the cries of women, all continue
The hearts of the people are still parched.

Oh, older brothers,
Unmourned to this day, buried in the crevices of these limestone cliffs
Are your bones, bones, bones
Even they cannot return to the grave mounds of your home-towns
Our older brothers!

We, Okinawans,
Bow our heads, brothers and sisters,
Before the spirits of you who were trampled underfoot by soldiers' boots
And left lying there.

We bow our heads before our sisters,
Who were violated as sex slaves by the Japanese army
Before our brothers, who became its victims as military porters
We believe that, before long, the hardened pods of the *tesangu* will burst
    open
And the seeds, scattered across the sea we share, will blossom as flowers.

Oh, brothers and sisters,
Never ceasing to tell of the hardships you experienced
We will banish war and armies from this earth
To your spirits, to you, who perished in this land
We vow it.

This poem is carved on the stone, Monument to Han, located in Yomitan
Village in Senaha, Okinawa. Erected to memorialize *chōsenjin* military porters
who died in Okinawa during the war, its unveiling ceremony took place on
May 13, 2006. The monument stands in a deserted spot atop a small hill,
looking out over the beautiful sea that borders Yomitan Village. Standing in
front of it, surrounded by massive Ryukyuan limestone cliffs, one feels a wind
that seems to have blown directly across the ocean from the Korean Peninsula.

In May 2008, I had the good fortune of visiting the Monument to Han,
guided by Asato Eiko and Murayama Tomoko, who had played key roles in
its construction. Asato Eiko is the person who had carved the inscription

above into the stone. She informed me that the large Ryukyu limestone formations into which the monument had been set were themselves composed of bone—fossilized coral, to be exact. The Monument to Han itself, that is, rests within a massive bone.

Asato's inscription embodies the sentiments of those Okinawans involved in building the Monument to Han, and their determination to mourn the deceased *chōsenjin*. Implicit in this gaze of Asato, who in addressing the porters and women who were forcibly made into sex slaves as "older brothers," "older sisters," or "brothers and sisters" treats them as an inner presence or literally "family," are what I might call the first stirrings of a new relationship between Okinawa and Korea. It is a new relationship that could become a means of working though *han*, which is the duty of future generations.

The Korean word *han* refers to a sadness that throbs, that has congealed and hardened; and also to something that "loosens" it. In the Korean expression "undoing *han*" (*hanpuri*), *han* refers to a congealed feeling that loosens and hardens again, loosens and hardens again—to a process of rumination that is repeated over and over. *Han* never disappears. It does not disappear, but *hanpuri* can also allow one to carry on with living—and without *hanpuri* one will become physically debilitated. *Hanpuri*, that is, could be called the very activity of human life itself. Nevertheless, the depths of *han* being what they are, it will be difficult to undo the *han* of those dead who have been neglected for over sixty years. Rather, we should try to keep them company as long as we live.

That the Okinawan people have a connection to those killed in the Korean War should be a principle that sustains the antibase struggle in Okinawa, and can be a continuing intellectual resource for that struggle. Moreover, the antibase struggle is, properly speaking, a way of mourning the faraway deaths of *chōsenjin* who died in Okinawa during the Pacific War. This is the sense of the words carved by Asato Eiko: "Oh, brothers and sisters, never ceasing to tell of the hardships you experienced, We will banish war and armies from this earth, To your spirits, to you, who perished in this land, We vow it." This vow, our determination in the here and now, can be the beginning of a rebirth of the bond between Okinawa and Chōsen.

4. BEYOND THE "ANTI-REVERSION THEORY" OF THE 1970S

When I first read Arakawa Akira's essay, "Hanfukkiron" (Anti-reversion theory), developed around the time of Okinawa's reversion to Japan, I found it to be a form of thinking that was full of resonance for *chōsenjin* in Japan. "Anti-reversion Theory" has something universal about it that could be directly connected with the present historical situation of those who are called *zainichi chōsenjin*. Most especially, up until recently I have read "Anti-reversion Theory" as something concerning me (although I realize I may have misread many points). The work has the power to appeal to the singular existence. When encountering its words, I was able to grasp and historicize something I, too, had been subjected to in Japanese society: for Arakawa understands the violence of reversion as a form of assimilation—a form of "becoming Japanese." Reading the essay, I had felt in the tangible presence of a continuing history, the violence of a past and present in which reversion also constitutes the form of assimilation known as "becoming Japanese." In that violence that connects Okinawans and *chōsenjin* with each other—the violence of reversion as a form of the same assimilation that has been borne by both groups—I felt I could discern how certain structures of Japan had come into being.

What is noteworthy about "Anti-reversion Theory" is that it is not simply a criticism of the nation, but rather that it takes up the problem of the state as a question of "totality versus singularity." In other words, "Anti-reversion Theory," while thoroughly basing itself on the perspective of the singular existence, takes aim at the totality, as a theoretical praxis critical of assimilation. In the essay "Okinawa as 'Unpropitious Space' of Antistatism," Arakawa draws on his own editor's foreword to the special issue of *Shin Okinawa Bungaku* (New Okinawan literature) published a year earlier, to define anti-reversion theory as "a matter that has to do with to what extent I, as a singularity, am involved with 'Japan as a state.'" And he writes, "Insofar as this is a problem of singularity versus totality, it is not a question to be raised about others but directed inward, to the self."[6] Continuing, Arakawa writes of "Anti-reversion Theory":

> Thus, in the case of "Anti-reversion Theory" I am in no way referring to the institutional and territorial reconsolidation of a Japan and Okinawa that have been divided, which would be an external phenomenon. I am pointing to what might be called a spontaneous ac-

---

6. This essay, "'Han kokka no kyōku' to shite no Okinawa," was included in the book *Han kokka no kyōku* [The unpropitious space of antistatism] (Shakai Hyōronsha, 1971). Arakawa was editor of the special edition on the antireversion debate compiled by the quarterly magazine *Shin Okinawa Bungaku* [New Okinawa literature] 18 (December 1970).

tivity of thought whereby Okinawans, willingly and on their own, allow themselves to be subsumed by the state. In this sense, I would have no objection to referring to "Anti-reversion Theory" as a spiritual inclination, on the level of the singular, to thoroughly and continuously reject fusion with the state. To reformulate it even further, let me say that anti-reversion equals "Antistate" and "Antination." It is a manifesto directed inward, whereby I ceaselessly position myself as a person without nationality.[7]

Moreover, "Anti-reversion Theory," insofar as it manifests a "spiritual inclination, on the level of the singular, to thoroughly and continuously reject fusion with the state," is a critique of assimilation, or a critique of colonialism as a whole. Herein lies the universality of Arakawa's theory, and the power of his writing to appeal to the singular. This is certainly an unforgettable work. But going beyond its theoretical argument, what is even more unforgettable is the way in which the very idea of anti-reversion theory is fraught with black humor. There's a kind of virulent laughter in the work. I smile wryly, especially when reading descriptions such as the one below:

> That is to say that, as I have stressed repeatedly thus far, it is by unrestrainedly flaunting Okinawa's geographical and historical heterogeneity and its "otherness" that we can begin to grasp their potential. In other words, it is only when Okinawa puts forward everything that is decidedly different and "other" about itself that Okinawans will be able to both relativize and see in their own minds the "state," which is at one and the same time an actually existing organ of repression and an uncanny, bewitching monster that defines our lives as a whole.
>
> When this happens, we will be able to clearly put into perspective for the first time that the "state," or "Japan as state," is not simply an ideological concept, but instead is a lived sensation. Then, we will be at last able to liberate ourselves from the value systems of the nation, as well as from the curse of having our own lives defined in response to those values. For the first time, "Japan as state" will appear before us Okinawans in concrete form as something to be rejected.
>
> It is truly only in that moment of realization, when "the state" takes shape before us as something to be rejected, that our existence

---

7. Arakawa, "'Han kokka no kyōku' to shite no Okinawa," 304.

(the existence of Okinawa itself) will become a poisonous arrow shot deep inside "Japan as state," a kind of extremely malignant tumor. Like gangrene, Okinawa can become a region that has the potential to implode the very idea of "Japan as state," rotting it from the inside out. Okinawa's historical and geographical situation for this very reason endows it with the good fortune of being an existence to be envied by every other region of Japan. In no way should we allow this privilege to be "detoxified" by an unquestioning espousal of the ideology of "reversion," which is in fact a will toward assimilation.[8]

If I may put it this way, we see here in Arakawa's "Anti-reversion Theory" a kind of black humor that contains a virulent laughter that is also a curse directed toward the nation of Japan. As a *chōsenjin* who has been "resident in Japan" (*zainichi*) since my birth in the year after Okinawa's reversion, I must say I was bodily susceptible to infection by this curse. I could think of no greater pleasure. But I now realize it is not enough to simply define the virulent laughter that suffuses "Anti-reversion Theory" as black humor. To do this causes another feeling inherent in the work to drop out of sight. Although it is something that I have come to understand only recently, I would define that feeling—if I were to link it to Okinawan sensibilities—as *chirudai*. Here I would like to quote the words of the producer Nakazato Isao, referring to *chirudai*. Attempting to conceptualize the *chirudai* that is richly put into an image in the work of filmmaker Takamine Gō, Nakazato defines Okinawan *chirudai* as "a subtropical remainder/surplus that cannot be forcefully subsumed by the narrative of the nation and its people." He writes:

> *Chirudai* is an Okinawan expression that can mean "to be out of it" or "to become sick of it," or "vacantly." As such, *chirudai* could be understood as that unproductive idleness often associated with countries of the South. But Takamine's work instills into it a second dimension that lacks these negative connotations. For him, *chirudai* is "a natural phenomenon that is rooted in the land and the blood of Okinawa, from which the Uchinanchu cannot possibly escape, whether they wish to or not—one might say it is the very physical

---

8. Arakawa Akira, *Shinpan: Hankokka no kyōku: Okinawa, jiritsu e no shiten* [New edition: The unpropitious space of antistatism—a perspective on Okinawa and independence] (Tokyo: Shakai Hyōronsha, 1996), 136–137.

constitution of Okinawa." If I were to make bold to reformulate this in my own words, I would say that *chirudai* is the subtropical remainder/surplus that cannot be forcefully subsumed by the narrative of the nation and its people. In other words, *chirudai* is not only something like the "Okinawan constitution" but can also be the means of producing a heterogeneous image that counters the patriarchal nature of the national narrative.[9]

Let me suggest that the feeling of *chirudai* that Nakazato conceptualizes here (so splendidly it takes one's breath away) is similar to the feeling that forms the basic undercurrent of Arakawa's "Anti-reversion Theory." Let me suggest that we can sense that same feeling in the words, so typical of Arakawa's manner of expression, used to describe the state of mind of those people who, in living out the philosophy of anti-reversion theory, live as "people without a country" or "stateless persons." Arakawa writes, "The weapons of those who live as stateless persons are the philosophies of 'having no homeland' and of 'idleness.' Such ideas are like gangrene to the hypertrophic nation. We do not need to be impatient at all."[10] Moreover, today, a full thirty-four years after reversion, Arakawa still links anti-reversion theory—as a philosophy spun out of *chirudai* in precisely this idle, "no need to be impatient at all" way—to the vision expressed in Lu Xun's "My Old Home": "For actually the earth had no roads to begin with, but when many men pass one way, a road is made."[11]

Of course, we must acknowledge that, regardless of the existence of Arakawa's "Anti-reversion Theory," Okinawa thereafter reverted and continues to revert to Japan, as it is absorbed into Japan's economy and politics. Moreover, at the present time, when we are experiencing both a "Korean Wave" boom and an Okinawan boom in Japan, Okinawa is undergoing a kind of cultural absorption under the auspices of a touristic, Orientalist gaze. Films made by the director Nakae Yūji might be seen as an example of this tendency.[12] And

---

9. Nakazato Isao, *Okinawa: Imeeji no ejji* [Okinawa: The edge of the image] (Tokyo: Miraisha, 2007), 244.

10. Arakawa, *Shinpan: Hankokka no kyōku: Okinawa, jiritsu e no shiten*.

11. The words of Lu Xun are from "My Old Home," in *Selected Stories of Lu Xun*, trans. Yang Hsien-ji and Gladys Yang (Beijing, 1972), 63–64.

12. For a discussion of the ways in which Japanese notions of Okinawa can be seen in the films about Okinawa produced by director Nakae Yūji, see Ōmine Sawa's essay "Uragaesu koto, omotegaesu koto: 1999 nen ikō no Okinawa no hyōshō" [Inside out and outside in: Representations of Okinawa after 1999], in *Okinawa Eigaron* [Okinawan cinema], ed. Yomota Inuhiko and Ōmine Sawa (Tokyo: Sakuhinsha, 2008), and the transcription, in the same collection, of the

yet one wonders. Do these developments mean that anti-reversion theory has come to an end, or become outmoded? I can hardly think so. Rather, anti-reversion theory remains unassimilable by "Japan as state," and as such it continues to curse that state. It is "that subtropical surplus/remainder that cannot be forcibly subsumed by the narrative of the nation and its people: *chirudai.*" If I think of Japan surrounded by an East Asia that includes Okinawa and Chōsen, or take a bird's-eye view of a shabby Japan that is rotting from within because of the gangrene inside it, I feel convinced of this. And I am convinced that now, more than ever, "Anti-reversion theory" is not old, but very new.

Nevertheless, I feel there is something missing in "Anti-reversion Theory." We need to write its "sequel" at the present time. I would therefore like to offer a critical rereading of the text, as a way of repaying my debt to it and expressing the highest form of respect to its author. I see my criticisms as a way of perpetuating its legacy.

To put it bluntly, what is missing from "Anti-reversion Theory" is a gaze toward the Other who dwells within. This is the result of a kind of dualism that an argument "against" something can fall into, and insofar as "Anti-reversion Theory" adheres to such a dualism, it will not be able to maintain a gaze toward the Other within. Arakawa's argument needs to look forward. It goes without saying that at the time it was written Okinawa was directly confronting all-too-suffocating, gigantic pressures from Japan and the United States and did not, perhaps, have the luxury of anything other than dualistic thinking. But insofar as it lacks a gaze toward the Other within, even an Okinawa that resists reversion will be entangled in the logic of "modernity," "the nation," and "the state." Let me offer a reading of Arakawa's essay "Modern Okinawa and Korea," published in the winter issue of *Sanzenri Quarterly* in 1978, as a text that is suggestive of this problem.

Arakawa does not take up Chōsen directly in this article, published six years after Okinawa's reversion to Japan, but he does allude to relations between Okinawa and the Joseon Dynasty in the premodern and modern periods. Given his stance in opposition to reversion, it is perhaps to be expected that Arakawa expresses criticism of certain developments that followed upon reversion, and took place against the backdrop of a collusive relationship

---

panel discussion on this topic convened at the symposium Okinawa kara sekai o miru (Seeing the world from Okinawa), held at Meiji Gakuin University in June 2007.

between the Japanese and South Korean governments: for example, the establishment of a "Japan-South Korea Friendship Association in Okinawa Prefecture," and the ongoing introduction, without heed for the sacrifices of the South Korean people, of South Korean laborers and South Korean physicians to help in the spheres of industrial and cultural production, or health and welfare, in Okinawa.

In the course of his argument, touching on the relationship between Okinawa and the Korean Peninsula in the modern period, Arakawa criticizes a form of discrimination that has existed in Okinawa, arguing that "Okinawans have rarely grasped how foolish they have been in choosing a narrow-minded way of life, whereby everything has been channeled into 'becoming Japanese' rather than becoming a good friend for those on the Korean Peninsula, let alone other neighboring peoples." As Arakawa describes, the detrimental influence of Okinawans' desire to become Japanese under the authoritarian *kōminka* (Japanization or assimilation) policies of the Japanese empire, meant that modern Okinawans deeply despised and vehemently rejected any association with others who had been discriminated against and oppressed by Japan (such as the Ainu, those on the Korean Peninsula, and Taiwanese), feeling that the greatest hardship was for their "Japaneseness" to be questioned. However, we should bear in mind that the same discriminatory views were also present in the colony of Chōsen, and even, one would presume, in Taiwan and among the Ainu. As a result of the Japanese empire's oppressive policies, the modes of interaction that had existed among regions in East Asia prior to modernity, as well as the ability of other East Asians to imagine a resistance to imperial Japan, were completely undone. It was precisely this division of East Asia that proved to be imperial Japan's cunningly cruel design. Even today, under the pressure of Japanese/American imperialism, East Asia has yet to overcome its division.

This brings me back to my main point. In his essay, Arakawa criticizes a modern Okinawa that marched toward assimilation with blind faith (produced by its lack of a meaningful relationship with the modern Korean Peninsula), and he also speaks of the necessity to restore the memory of the interactions between premodern Okinawa, the Korean Peninsula, and Asia as an alternative path. Memory of premodern East Asia, in other words, offers for Arakawa an opportunity to do away with modern Okinawan discrimination and to "restore a rich openness" to postreversion Okinawa. He writes:

It is my sense that, were we to unearth and reaffirm within mainstream culture the thriving interaction that originally existed between
the people of the Korean Peninsula, China, and the peoples of the
regions in the South Pacific, our spirit would without doubt reclaim
a rich openness for itself. With modernity, the Okinawan spirit has
atrophied all too much due to the detrimental influence of its assimilation goals. Okinawa has been an imitator, chasing after the distorted spirit of a modern Japan that does not feel the pain of others
as its own.[13]

I empathize with Arakawa's perspective. Particularly, I feel that interaction
between Okinawa and Jeju Island should be reestablished. As is apparent in
the similarities between their intonation of words and their readings of Chinese ideographs, exchange between Okinawa and Jeju Island was once abun-
dant. They are both islands that experienced similar tragedies, where "acts
that even hell couldn't conceive of" were committed under the pressure of
Japanese/American imperialism. The Battle of Okinawa should be understood more broadly and placed within its East Asian context, with its connections to the Jeju Uprising recognized. Only then will our historical awareness become richer, and will we attain a perspective that can structurally
account for why such tragedies occurred.

However, I also feel that the renewal of a relationship between Okinawa
and the Korean Peninsula, before being based on any history of premodern
interactions, should begin with a restoration to memory of *chōsenjin* in the
Battle of Okinawa. Any recollection of a premodern relationship that fails to
acknowledge this modern event will surely be limited to the conceptual level.
In the essay I have been discussing, it is true that Arakawa does touch on
modern Chōsen. But his gaze is on Chōsen as if it were something exterior
to Okinawa, with no inner connection to it. This is because Arakawa does
not touch on the bitter memories evoked by the presence of *chōsenjin* as an
internal Other within Okinawa. In Arakawa's gaze, the palpable sensation of
chōsenjin as an internal Other of Okinawa is lacking. Can we not say that this
remains a problematic aspect of anti-reversion thought as a whole? For, insofar as it is based on the binary logic of "anti"—in other words, as long as the
fragmented "Okinawa" that returns to Japan is not in its turn fragmented—it

13. Arakawa Akira, "Kindai Okinawa to *Chōsen*" [Modern Okinawa and Chōsen] published
in *Kikan Sanzenri* [Sanzenri Quarterly] (Winter 1978): 165.

cannot perceive Chōsen as an internal other. Herein we find the limits of the anti-reversion theory of the 1970s.

There is a scene described by the critic Okamoto Keitoku that I have not been able to forget. In his memoirs of the Battle of Okinawa, in the essay "Gūkan" (Random thoughts) published the year before he died, Okamoto unexpectedly makes a reference to the presence of Koreans:

> What the Japanese army called "provisions" were kept in storage in the neighborhood of a linen factory on the island of Miyako, along with the army's military equipment. Sometimes I caught sight of *chōsenjin* military porters sneaking in to eat the raw rice grains, which made them sick to their stomachs. If discovered, they were severely beaten. All around the factory one could see trails of their shit, containing the grains of raw rice they could not digest. Looking back on it, it is clear there were many dramas unfolding around these *chōsenjin*, having to do not only with food but with the discrimination they faced. But, at the time, these things were totally beyond our ken.[14]

The kinds of scenes Okamoto witnessed were not restricted to Miyako Island. At the height of the Battle of Okinawa, they occurred throughout the various islands where *chōsenjin* military porters were deployed. As the surviving elders, or *halaboji*, who had served as porters to the Japanese army repeatedly recall when they tell us about that time, "The Japanese did not treat *chōsenjin* as human beings."[15] One survivor of the battle on Aka Island spoke of his memory (although it is a piece of history that can barely be conveyed in words) of Japanese soldiers executing twelve *chōsenjin* military porters for plucking rice plants on civilian agricultural lands and putting them in their pockets. Other porters were forced to dig a hole and bury the bodies. One can imagine that, in an atmosphere where not treating *chōsenjin* as humans prevailed, such executions must have taken place on other islands as the battle raged.

What could have possibly gone through the minds of the porters who were severely beaten for furtively stealing food? Were they, in fact, able to be

14. Okamoto Keitoku, "Gūkan, 42" [Random thoughts, 42], *Keeshi Kaze* 4, no. 7 (June 2005), in Okamoto Keitoku, *"Okinawa" ni ikiru shisō—Okamoto Keitoku hihyōshū* [A philosophy of living in Okinawa: Critical writings by Okamoto Keitoku] (Tokyo: Miraisha, 2007), 248.

15. The Korean word *halaboji* (grandfather) is a respectful way of addressing older men.

angry? If it is possible that—under the most extreme conditions in the Battle of Okinawa, and in that moment of execution and at that site—those who had not been treated as human beings were not even allowed to feel anger, then that pent-up anger of the dead who were executed, that festering *han* which has never been released is ours to revive and reflect on anew in the here and now. It needs to be expressed, as part of new politics that would overthrow the memory politics that consigns to oblivion *chōsenjin* who met faraway deaths throughout East Asia.

Okamoto Keitoku—I deeply admire how, in the days before his death, he took a moment to remember the *chōsenjin* who were in the Battle of Okinawa. It is essential for us to understand how meaningful this was. In the few sentences of that one passage, it seems to me that Okamoto, as his own body declined, foresaw how he could express a new kind of encounter with Chōsen by thoroughly dismantling his own Okinawan identity. It is even possible he had already achieved such a reencounter. Not through ideas, but through his bodily sensations. Through the smell, the color ... the streaks of shit on the earth with their raw, undigested rice. If it is possible, at the risk of impropriety, to pick up on those bodily sensations, let me propose that Okinawa exists on top of the shit of dead *chōsenjin* and, in this sense, Okinawa *is* Chōsen.

It seems to me that a gaze that regards the *chōsenjin* dead in Okinawa carries out a further dismantling of the "Okinawa" already dismantled by anti-reversion theory and takes us beyond it. Isn't another revolution of the spirit demanded of us here today?

5. FROM "MINORITY" TO "MULTIPLICITY"

We are all familiar with the word "minority." I have been called that in Japanese society and have defined myself that way. Before I ever faced the world, the sign "minority" had been prepared for me, since—whether it was being used by people trying to reclaim the human rights of minorities, or by those seeking to consume minorities—this discourse flooded, and continues to flood, our environment. However, when I consider it now, I have been trapped in the cage of that word "minority," which pared down my existence and imaginative power. As long as I allowed myself to be trapped by the term—was it for the sake of restricting my existence within a binary relationship that simply defined it as the opposite of "Japanese" or "the majority"?— I was unable to conceive of those *chōsenjin* who met faraway deaths in East

Asia. It also now seems to me that, despite the fact that I am a scholar of modern Korean literature and an activist engaged with postcolonial theory, I had allowed myself inadvertently to be lulled into occupying the position of the minority, subsumed into a system that had come to be controlled and consumed by the majority. This constraint, which enfolded me like a fate, is the very essence of politics and the political.

I will therefore refer to myself not as a "minority," but as "multiplicity."[16] Thinking of myself this way, I am ready to take revenge against the term "minority." "Multiplicity" is not the logic of numbers that dictate who are the "minority" and "majority," but a way of being, grounded in the magnitude of the existence of the Other that one internalizes. "Multiplicity" is the shadow one encounters when delving into and dismantling the self. To what extent can one dismantle the self and exist along with its shadows? "Multiplicity" is a way of thinking based on such a "dwelling together with the dead"; it is a will to express that which, although invisible to the eyes, will never disappear. I am not the minority, but multiplicity. On the basis of a "coming right of self-determination" I invoked at an earlier conference on anti-reversion theory convened here in Okinawa, I named myself in this way.[17] Moreover, I, as multiplicity, am addressing one more multiplicity. That is Mr. Arakawa Akira, who eventually embraced a self who was once "one of the enthusiastic advocates of reversion, whose eyes had been clouded by the grand proposal of reversion to the 'fatherland,' " as an Other within.

"I am afraid of the Japanese people. As an Okinawan, I am extremely afraid of them."[18] These words of Mr. Arakawa in his interview in the quarterly magazine *Zenya* are very striking and have remained with me to this day. Precisely because they were the words of someone who had committed him-

---

16. The word "multiplicity" (*tasū*) was my stage name in the play *Hengen kasabutajō* (Shape-shifting scabrous castle) performed by the troupe Yasen no Tsuki Haibiitsu in Tokyo and Beijing in 2007, and is a poetic expression that the play passed on to me. It is a word connected in my mind to the playwright and actor Sakurai Daizō, as well as to the troupe that performed the play. And it is without doubt a word I myself came to embody as an actor in that troupe. Whenever I weave that word into my critical writing, I think of it as a kind of translation of the play and also an expression of my esteem for it.

17. "I am not a minority, but multiplicity." This is something I determined for myself when I participated as a panelist in the symposium on antireversion theory, titled Maakarawajiiga?! Kitarubeki jiko ketteiken no tame ni (Where will the anger come from? Towards a right of self-determination to come) held at the Sakima Art Museum in Okinawa on May 18, 2008.

18. Arakawa Akira, "Hanfukkiron to dōka hihan—shokuminchika no seishin kakumei toshite ikkikan" [Antireversion debate and the critique of assimilation—on a spiritual revolution under colonialism], *Zenya* 9 (Fall 2006), 300.

self to a life of anti-reversion that was already being spent in splendid isolation and surrounded by misunderstanding; Arakawa's sensation of "fear" seemed to me deeply philosophical. I was lucky enough to be present at the time of this interview. Mr. Arakawa said those words not overdramatically, but frankly without hesitation.

I can understand his feeling. Living in Japan on October 2, 2006, after North Korea had carried out its atomic tests, I began, for the first time, to feel the bodily "fear of being stabbed in the back." This was an event that changed my sense of history in a revolutionary way: in that instant I encountered the colonial Korea which was referred to in Japanese as Chōsen. And, although this might sound like a strange way of putting it, I could feel a bodily connection in that moment to the *chōsenjin* who had been attacked from behind by Japanese carrying bamboo spears at the time of the Great Kanto Earthquake—who had been stabbed and met their "faraway deaths" there. Or, at the very least, what was brought home to me at that moment was that nothing had changed in Japanese society since that time.

That truly painful, fearsome feeling that one could be attacked from behind is something I no longer harbor. I think this is because I have taken up the outlook of "dwelling with" those dead who perished far from home, and I have come to feel myself embraced by them, to use the words of Sakurai Daizō of the tent-theater troupe Yasen no Tsuki Haibītsu. Within their embrace, I (and many other "I"s) are not "minorities." We are multiplicity. This was the hope I was able to express and gradually embody while performing as an actor with that troupe, and standing with my feet planted on the earth beneath tents I had erected with my own hands.

Today, East Asia has become a vivid sensation for me, almost as though those *chōsenjin* who died in Japan, Okinawa, and Taiwan were calling out to me. I have an intense desire to know more about the circumstances of their deaths. What, I wonder, were the expressions in the eyes of *chōsenjin* who were stabbed to death with bamboo spears by Okinawans during the Battle of Okinawa? What did they see in that very moment? Moreover, this involves my facing an internal Other as well. His name is Saitō Hiroshi, and he is myself at the time when I adopted a Japanese name.

To explain—during my primary and middle school years, I went by the name Sai, the Japanese reading of my Korean name. Many *zainichi chōsenjin* lived in the ward of Adachi, in Tokyo, where I was raised, and people from Jeju Island were especially numerous. However, since most of them used Japanese names in their public lives, and because it is difficult to distinguish *zainichi chōsenjin* by their appearance, not knowing who was who was a routine matter at the time. By disappearing into the homogeneous and transparent atmosphere of Japanese society, we ended up supporting that homogeneity and transparency—or, more precisely, we were forced to support it.

During this period, because I had always been the only *zainichi chōsenjin* in my classes at school (although I later learned, through rumors that circulated after graduation, that some others had been so as well), a massive inferiority complex gripped my spirit. I was unbearably ashamed, not only because I was not Japanese, but also because I was the only person with such a strange name. Although I never experienced the blatant discrimination endured by previous generations of *chōsenjin*, Japanese society at the time continued to be pervaded by an atmosphere that foisted "Japaneseness" on all its citizens, and as a child I was especially sensitive to that. The result was that I blindly believed in those days that if I could only become Japanese, I could be freed from my inferiority complexes and live a normal life. I settled on a Japanese name (Saitō Hiroshi) for myself when I entered high school, and ended up going through school under this name. Having at last become Japanese through my own doing, I could not at that point even fathom living my life as Choi Jin Seok.

For a while, perhaps for half a year, everything seemed rosy. But I was unable to completely repress the feeling that somehow or other I was living a lie. There were even times when, gripped by the illusion that everyone around me must surely have known that I was actually a *chōsenjin*, I could not get myself to go to school. Those were dark, bleak days. In fact, even now I find it difficult to recall this time in my life.

However, after graduating from high school, I came to the realization that I could no longer go on as Saitō Hiroshi, and that I could no longer think of myself as Japanese. Rather, the next step was to become South Korean. And so I studied abroad in South Korea for a year, and desperately studied the language. I had become a fervent nationalist by the time I returned and entered university in Japan, introducing myself using my actual birth name. I became "Choi Jinseok, South Korean." But that phase did not last long either, because I could not adapt to being South Korean so suddenly. Either way of identifying myself seemed impossible, and as one might imagine, those, too, were dark days.

Just at the point when I had almost given up on trying to decide what to do with myself, a realization hit me like a bolt from the sky. I had wanted to become Japanese, and then to become South Korean. Either way, I realized,

I was on a path that left me harboring an unrequited desire to be part of a nation-state. It was at this very time that I had a similarly profound encounter with literature. From that moment on, I was finally released from the spell I had long been under. I gradually began turning my gaze, instead, toward the history of the Japanese colony Chōsen; toward the history of the Korean War; and toward the forgotten *chōsenjin* who had perished in Japan. At last, I had gotten my mind around the idea that I was, indeed, a *chōsenjin*.

This became a process of inner dismantling for me, a spiritual revolution. Once I embarked on it, my life changed and became directed toward my own liberation. It was also a path of forgetting "Saitō Hiroshi" and separating myself from him. As I struggled to face my contradictions, "Saitō Hiroshi" came to feel like a foreign body I was harboring, with whom I could never be at peace. Now, however, I think of it thus: I have internalized "Saitō Hiroshi" as just one of the dead I harbor within me. The idea of "Saitō Hiroshi"—even his name—is a testament to that lonely time in my life when I lived rather desperately. I had been thinking that forgetting him would enable me to live, but I now wonder if his presence, as one of the dead within me, has not actually been what has kept me going. It seems it is my turn to accept him. This is how I will exist from this point on. I (together with many other "I"s) am not a minority, but a multiplicity.

6. TO CONCLUDE

Surely now is the time for all those who are called *zainichi* to begin to talk with each other about *who* are the *chōsenjin*, and to bring to bear on that question all the tension of our bodies that are in the here and now. As a beginning—and regardless of whether one is a *zainichi* with South Korean citizenship, a *zainichi* with Japanese citizenship, a *zainichi* registered as a Chōsen national, or a *zainichi* who is absolutely unable to talk about these matters because the words with which to do so have been stolen—as a beginning, we *zainichi* who are wavering in various crevices, having been scattered, strewn, and divided by the violence of colonial assimilation, should now once and for all, confront the gaze of the poet Kim Shi-jong, who scrutinizes "the shadowy term"—*chōsenjin* used with negative overtones—together with the word *zainichi chōsenjin*, a word which might function as a common denominator for all of us. The hope of *zainichi* truly lies in the rereading of these words at the present moment. Kim has put it like this:

Speaking as one called *zainichi*, my impulse would be to take the term *chōsenjin* (チョウセンジン), the shadowy term that has even become a kind of code for *zainichi* (i.e., with the meaning "born in Japan")—and revive in it the very resonances that it shares with the written word *chōsenjin* (朝鮮人) as a call for pride, friendship, and love. As fellow members of the same ethnicity (at least insofar as some of us with South Korean citizenship are designated *zainichi chōsenjin*, while others who retained their prewar colonial designation are also called *zainichi*), we belong to the "sum of a sum total," which we must retrieve from the midst of our shared *zainichi* existence.[19]

To echo the words of Kim Shi-jong, I also believe that anyone who feels their self-esteem as "Korean" (朝鮮人) has been damaged should seek to recover it in the sound's consonance with *chōsenjin* (チョウセンジン), and that is precisely within these overlapping resonances that we can move forward together. My registration card denotes me as a person "of Chōsen nationality" or *chōsenseki* (朝鮮籍), insofar as I am registered in the category of *zainichi chōsenjin*. Following Kim Shi-jong's notion, then, it is within that "sum" of the "sum total" of the *zainichi* population that can be called *zainichi chōsenjin* that I wish to locate myself ... and also to find something that lies beyond that. This is because, insofar as *zainichi* refers to those "in Japan," *zainichi* identity cannot be absolute. *Chōsenjin* do not necessarily exist only within Japan. They are also in Okinawa, Taiwan, and Korea. Only when *zainichi* who live in Japan can feel how they are connected to the bodies of those *chōsenjin* who met faraway deaths in East Asia can they, together with other *zainichi*, transcend the designation *zainichi*. It is at this point that another

---

19. Kim Shi-jong, "'Zainichi' no hazama de" [In the crevices of "zainichi"], in *Heibonsha raiburari* (Tokyo: Heibonsha, 2001), 457. Translator's note: In our reading, when Kim Shi-jong refers to the way the terms *chōsenjin* and *zainichi* have become almost interchangeable, he does so as a poet who is himself called *zainichi*. Although he has lived in Japan for over sixty years, Kim Shi-jong was born on Jeju Island and holds South Korean citizenship. He searches for a way to give both the terms *zainichi* and *chōsenjin* new meanings which might overcome the divisions arising out of the different terms and categories by which the fragmented *zainichi* community is now known. Moreover, Choi here uses the ideograph 朝鮮人 for *chōsenjin* by contrast to the prior katakana spelling of チョウセンジン (also read *chōsenjin*) to suggest that the discriminatory nuances that still cluster like shadows around the word might be replaced by a literal reading of it as "people of Chōsen," in the same way that an American in Japanese is *Amerikajin* or a Canadian *Kanadajin*.

word will come to meet us. I would like to think of this as a transition from *chōsenjin* to *joseon saram*. ...

Joseon saram. In the Korean language, *Joseon* refers to Chōsen and *saram* to 人 or "person," that is, *joseon saram* means a "a person of Chōsen."[20] It is a word every *zainichi* knows, and that no one except a *zainichi* would know. The young people of the generation after my own already find themselves in the same condition as the youth of present-day Okinawa. Youth who cannot speak the Okinawan language (*uchinānguchi*) are in a similar position to *zainichi* who did not go to an ethnic school and therefore cannot speak Korean. Every *zainichi*, however, even those who did not go to ethnic schools, recognizes the word *Joseon*. This is in much the same way that anyone who is Okinawan—young or old, man or woman—knows the word *uchinānchu*. The reason the words *joseon saram* and *uchinānchu* will not disappear is because they are the names for our very being.

I cannot help at this point but add that the word *saram* in Korean means "person," but the word "love," pronounced *saran*, is written the same way. In other words, in the Korean language, *saram* and *saran*, "people" and "love," are homonyms, etymologically related, and similarly written. (Is it not splendid to think of "people" and "love" as having the same sound?) Therefore, I would like to impress on your minds this way of referring to the people of Chōsen, as *joseon saram*, which ends with the same sound as "love." I would like to impress this upon you for a Korea to come.

In the near future, under the tide of present-day neoliberalism, it is likely that U.S.–North Korean relations will be restored, the Korean War will be formally concluded, and that, as diplomatic relations between North Korea and Japan are resumed, the Korean Peninsula will be reunified by forces of neoliberalism without any voices of protest being raised. It is not hard to imagine the desperate situation that will present itself at that point. The rich but untouched natural resources of the People's Republic of North Korea, together with its highly skilled, low-waged labor force, will be wantonly exploited. These tendencies are already visible on the economic level, but it is easy to foresee a situation in which the advances of American and Chinese industry will be followed by moves forward on the part of Japan, which will then result in the development of North Korean industry in a delayed fashion. Under such conditions, it is probable that the same types of disparities

---

20. The Korean peninsula was unified under the Joseon Dynasty from 1392 until the time of its annexation by Japan in 1910.

and discrimination that exist between the former East and West Germany will be produced in Korea. This would certainly confront us with a deeply hopeless scene. Yet even a state of despair need not mean the end of the world. Despair can be converted into the energy that will change the world; it is capable of serving as a force field for political expression.

A reunification of the Korean peninsula would effectively mean the end of the Cold War in East Asia. When this happens, all kinds of records and remembrances that we who live on one side of the Cold War divide have never come into contact with will emerge from the other side. The archives of land reform, for example. In these we may expect to encounter issues similar to those raised by the so-called Tibetan Uprising. But when the Tibetan problem is taken up, no reference is ever made to the archives of the land reform carried out by the Communist Party after entering Tibet and taking power, when land monopolized by Buddhist temples was forcibly taken away from them and distributed to Tibet's enslaved and completely landless population. Nor, when demands are made for "human rights" or to "Free Tibet," is the question ever raised of why it was monks who were the central force in that movement and exactly what kind of "freedom" they were demanding. These questions cannot be grasped by applying ready-made epistemologies from our side of the Cold War divide, an approach that simply results in further obfuscation of problems in the capitalist sphere. What exactly does "modernity" mean for China, and for Tibet? As the Chinese scholar Sun Ge astutely points out, this is where the essence of the Tibet problem lies. We should not see it as merely posing a problem for others, but as "an epistemological challenge posed to all of us by the contemporary histories we are living through."[21]

Once reunification occurs, and we are faced with the society and politics of a People's Democratic Republic of Korea, which has its own archives of land reform, together with the scars of the Korean War and a history of continued struggle against American imperialism, it seems likely that a similar epistemological challenge will emerge, requiring the fundamental questioning of "modernity"—a problem which cannot become apparent by applying only the ready-made concepts of "freedom" and "human rights." We can expect such challenges to accompany us as we find ourselves swept across to the other side of the Cold War. And to the extent that the violence of neoliberal-

---

21. Sun Ge, "'Sōgō shakai' chūgoku ni mukiau tame ni" [Toward encountering China as a "synthetic society"], *Gendai shisō* 30, no. 9 (2008): 54–58.

ism is likely to become more apparent once reunification takes place, challenging questions will inevitably be raised about whether capitalism, progressing under neoliberal economic principles, is an economic system that can really offer "equality," along with "freedom," and what "freedom" actually consists of. Surely the aporia of "freedom" and "equality" (with "freedom" pursued by the capitalist world but unachieved by the socialist world, and "equality" pursued by the socialist world but unachieved by the capitalist world) will remain as a weighty "epistemological challenge" that the world has still not resolved. Indeed, it is just possible that the revival of Japanese interest in the proletarian author Kobayashi Takiji's *Crab Cannery Ship* is an indication that capitalism is already being challenged in this way. It is being challenged by a young underclass who have been passed the buck of neoliberalism's contradictions, and by alienated members of multiplicit(ies) who have been withdrawing themselves from the world. At any rate, it is perhaps because the concepts of "winners" and "losers," and the smokescreen of "personal responsibility," no longer hold sway among these groups that these challenges are being raised.

Furthermore, there is even now something of great importance that concerns every person—as well as the "people" as a whole—who have been affected by the Cold War.[22] That is, the coming of the dead. When the Korean Peninsula becomes unified, the reality of the damage done to the North during the Korean War will become ever more real, and materialize before us. And when that time comes, we shall finally, as a collectivity, be able to mourn those who died during that war. Indeed, the *madang* awaits us where we may resolve the *han* of those dead and loosen its bonds. The Cold War began because of the division of the Korean Peninsula during the Korean War, and that war has continued to determine what life is like in the societies that were involved. In that sense, it is not just those on the Korean peninsula, but every person (and the "people" as a whole) who has been affected by the Korean War and the Cold War who are inevitably summoned to this *madang*. At such a time, it should follow as a matter of course that all core U.S. archives that pertain to the substantive supervision of the war by the United States, as well as to the process of its intervention, and especially facts related to the time immediately before and after the outbreak of the war, be declassified.

---

22. Translators' note: When Choi places "peoples as a whole" in apposition to the plural of "persons" (人々), he uses the character 人民 to clarify that he does not mean "nation" or "people" in the nationalistic sense.

Then, for the first time, we may be able to investigate the true nature of the Cold War, to finally understand what U.S. imperialism in East Asia consisted of, and thus to piece together a more genuinely synthetic perspective on the Cold War.

But let me now shift attention away from the question of what historical and political paradigms will be at stake when reunification occurs, to the question of what reunification will mean concretely, as an event that takes place on the level of everyday life. I think it will mean the arrival of *joseon saram*. The people of the Democratic Republic of Korea—its artists, its researchers—will appear before us. The day when they will join us under our theater tents, in research groups, symposia, assemblies, and drinking parties, will arrive. Who knows what name the Korean Peninsula will bear by that time? But whatever that name is, it will not change the fact that all those who join us will be *joseon saram*. In the near future, *joseon saram* will be among us. This is why I would like to impress that term on the minds of all of you who are here today.

Whether we think of them as part of our past or present histories, we must engrave in our minds what is conveyed by the term *joseon saram*. I have introduced the term because those who died in East Asia before 1945 did not think of themselves as *chōsenjin* when they were recruited as forced laborers, or when they died far away. Since we can surmise that few could speak Japanese as well as they could speak their mother tongue, it is likely that they would have referred to themselves with the words "Naneun joseon saram iya," whether at the time when they arrived in Japan or at the time when they perished abroad. That is, the dead we bear within us were *joseon saram* before they were *chōsenjin*. I would like you to remember the term. Try murmuring it—you can pronounce it either as *joseon saram* or *joseon saran*—just once when you have a quiet moment to yourself.

COLLABORATIVELY TRANSLATED BY RYAN BUYCO, BRETT DE BARY, ANDREW HARDING, MIYAKO HAYAKAWA, HIRANO ORIBE, KEIJI KUNIGAMI, JILLIAN MARSHALL, ANDREA MENDOZA, AND PAUL MCQUADE.

CHAPTER 5

The Angels of History in Okinawa

On Takemine Gō and Higa Toyomitsu

HIGASHI TAKUMA

Though I don't count myself as a mystic, I find it arrogant when someone sums up the human world according to terms that are understandable only to humans.

—TAKAMINE GŌ

When I stepped out into the sacred garden, fascinated by these older women's sacred songs, I found myself illuminated by moonlight that was not really there.

—HIGA TOYOMITSU, *Hikaru Nanamui no kamigami*
(The luminous gods of Nanamui, 2001)

The angel resembles all human beings to whom I bade farewell. Moreover, it resembles things. The angel resides in the things that I no longer claim as my own.

—WALTER BENJAMIN, "Agesilaus Santander," 1933

The longer version of this essay was collected in the volume *Zanshō no Oto: "Ajia, Seiji, Aato" no Mirai e*, edited by Lee Chonghwa (Tokyo: Iwanami Shoten, 2009). This English translation appeared in the journal *ACT: Art, Critique, Theory* and has been reproduced with the kind permission of the volume's editors.

CONDITION GREEN IN OMOROMACHI, OKINAWA

I visited the exhibit The Trajectory of Okinawan Culture: 1872–2007 at the Okinawa Prefectural Museum and Museum of Art, a complex containing an art museum and a history/natural history museum that opened as the forty-seventh and hence last prefectural museum of Japan in November 2007. One of the aims of my visit was to see Takamine Gō's *Wild Wumak Okinawan* (Wild boys of Okinawa), a documentary film about Condition Green, Okinawa's legendary rock band from the 1970s known for their daily live performances for the American soldiers stationed on the island. The members of Condition Green made frequent appearances in Takamine's films as important cast members.

Although I will not go into the details of the complex cultural and political circumstances that surrounded the establishment of the museum complex, these issues were frequently debated at the symposiums held for the inaugural exhibition of photography titled *Photography Year Zero: Okinawa*. I only want to mention here that the two museums sit on top of the former sites of U.S. bases, which prior to that had been among the fiercest combat zones during the Battle of Okinawa. Today, the whole area is known ironically as Omoromachi—named after the best-known work of classic Okinawan literature, *Omorososhi*. I say "ironic," because the place, more than anything, looks like an exhibition area for large corporations and businesses from mainland Japan. What also struck me then was the disparity between the innovative display of works (including Takamine's films) and corresponding curatorial willingness to push beyond the traditional boundaries of art displayed by the Museum of Art, and the Prefectural Museum's decision to display archaeological artifacts related to so-called Minatogawa Man.

While some archaeologists and anthropologists argue that Minatogawa Man represents the ancestors of the Jōmon and Yayoi peoples, since they inhabited both mainland Japan and Okinawa, such positing of a common root for the Japanese and the Okinawans is imbued with politics. While I myself was not able to visit the exhibit, the TV documentary made by NHK frequently referred to Minatogawa People as "our ancestors." Obviously, I have difficulty understanding what the term "our" means in such a context.

My own personal experience with Takamine's film, which deals with Condition Green in such a politically charged cultural milieu, attests to the ways in which his films always contain chaotic moments of critique. This film does not even appear on Takamine's filmography published in "Documentary Box #22," a pamphlet that was put together by the Yamagata International Documentary Film Festival. The film, which I assume was made as a supplement to Takamine's *Okinawan Chirudai* (Sacred slowness of Okinawa), features Kacchan, a leading member of Condition Green, who exudes an extraordinary presence. The film offers depictions of the band's dynamic performances in the U.S. base town of Kōza in the 1970s in which the members set fire to snakes and tore them up on the stage, drank alcoholic beverages from a pair of boots, and forced the audience to drink likewise. Kacchan and others' performances on the beach actually parodied discourses such as the one about Minatogawa People that are still deployed to construct the image of primordial Okinawans from which today's more "modern" Japanese somehow descended.

Cuban American artist Coco Fusco and Mexican American artist Guillermo Gomez-Peña once displayed themselves as indigenous American people in various museums and thus mobilized cultural stereotypes for the sake of subverting them. The work by Fusco and Gomez-Peña resonates with Okinawan playwright Chinen Seishin's play, *Jinruikan* (The house of peoples) that critiques the Japanese government's exhibition of colonized Okinawans at the 1903 World Exposition in Osaka. Similar incidents are littered across the history of Japan and Okinawa and indicate the problem that has yet to be overcome today. The bodies and the gestures of the members of Condition Green thirty years ago in Takamine's film critically intervened into the archaeological and anthropological episteme that reduces Okinawan bodies to objects of knowledge in prefectural museums.

SONG/BODY: SPIRITUALITY IN TAKAMINE GŌ

Many spectators say that Takamine's films are beyond comprehension. Once, at a symposium about the above-mentioned play *Jinruikan*, Takamine himself proposed the phrase "dewdrops of incomprehensibility" to describe his own works. But what does it mean when one says a particular film is beyond comprehension? From the outset, I argue that there is a subtle yet important difference between the ways in which films by Godard and Resnais, for example, challenge our comfortable levels of apprehension and the ways in which Takamine's works—often categorized under the rubric of "Okinawan Cinema"—defy our understanding.

What is unconsciously implied by the charge of incomprehensibility is perhaps the consumerist dissatisfaction with the fact that certain audiences cannot understand these films by Takamine, which refuse to posit Okinawa—Japan's South—as a place of brightness and happiness. There is such a gap between the Okinawa as posited in Takamine's own phrase "Okinawan Cinema," and the conceptualization of Okinawa in the minds of mainstream consumers. To be sure, such a gap arises from the latter's lack of knowledge about the local culture, society, and history of Okinawa, and could certainly influence the ways in which one interprets and receives his films. However, the fact that many consumers utter the phrase "beyond comprehension" even before critically reflecting upon their own lack of knowledge about Okinawa already displays the unconscious desire that is projected upon this island. What looms in the background is also a quasi-religious, yet nonetheless innocent, longing for the films they see and music they hear to be "comprehensible." Such naive faith in culture and the paradisiacal world they expect from "the South" can easily form a relation of complicity.

Moreover, that complicity can incite conformist sentiment among the filmmakers in Okinawa, as exemplified in the case of Nakae Yūji, whose films exemplify the desire to be "comprehended" by mainland Japanese consumers.

There is also another way in which the very "incomprehensibility" of films like Takamine's can be inducted into the canon. We need to be wary of the tendency to use the term "magical realism"—originally developed to promote a certain type of Latin American literature—to describe Takamine's films, as such a term only makes literary and filmic works marketable by demarcating the categories in which they could circulate as commodities. Incomprehensibility, in the same fashion, comes to designate a specific style of cultural products in commodity culture. How do the films by Takamine refuse these modes of comprehension and the desires harbored by some marginalized artists to be comprehended? This essay aims to offer some thoughts about his films, while critically avoiding the desire to comprehend his works and relegate them to a compartmentalized subgenre of cinema.

First, one must pay attention to the presence of the actors that appear, not as personas but as bodies, in Takamine's films. Such attention is perhaps more important than sophisticated analyses of the narrative structures or cinematographic characteristics of the films. The bodies in Takamine's films bear what I would tentatively call "spirituality" or "sacredness." That is, Takamine's films provide a stage on which bodies are neither alive nor dead, but rather manifest their liminal status in various guises: they appear as the bodies of the dead, or spirits, or gods. At other times, these figures incessantly go back and forth between the categories of life and death. The protagonists of his narrative feature films *Untamagiru* (Chivalrous robber of Untama Woods, 1989) and *Mugen Ryukyu/Tsuru-Henry* (1998) are bodies that "cannot die" and, as such, overlap, in the view of Takamine the director, with the status of Okinawa in history. Though *Okinawan Dream Show* (1974) can be classified as a documentary film, similar spiritual forces permeate this work. *Okinawan Chirudai* (1979) also defies the critic's desire for classification. I, for one, still cannot say with confidence whether the characters in this film are alive or dead.

In narrative features such as *Paradaisu byū* (Paradise view, 1986) and *Untamagiru*—two films that, according to the critic Nakazato Isao, constitute the hallmark of New Okinawan Cinema—the impossibility of demarcating between the dead and the living, and the sacred and the secular, is further pronounced. While, in *Untamagiru*, the protagonist robber Untamagiru exemplifies the figure who cannot die, its female characters possess strong spiritual and emotional dimensions that are central to the narrative of the film. In *Paradise View*, the members of the Okinawa Independence Party enact a traffic or symbiosis between seemingly binary categories at the borderline. Or, to put this more accurately, instead of a borderline that neatly separates one subjectivity from another, Okinawa in these films offers multiple planes of "borderland" (to use Gloria Anzaldua's term) that define the island to be constitutively plural and open.

Such an Okinawa begins to manifest its spatial and temporal extensions in later films such as *Tsuru-Henry*, a work that features multiple internal films within itself and includes footages of non-Okinawan locations. In *Mugen Ryukyu: Okinawa shimauta Pari no sora ni hibiku* (Mugen Ryukyu: Okinawa Island songs echoing in the Parisian sky, 2003), an internal TV documentary about the Okinawan singer Oshiro Misako is interspersed with segments from another film within the film, *Tsuruhen*, and the two films within the film seem mutually indistinguishable. In the two works that constitute the *Mugen Ryukyu* series, the female singer Tsuru (Oshiro Misako) occupies the so-called Elephant's Cage—a U.S. military communication facility in Okinawa—as well as the Eiffel Tower, transmitting her songs and stories. In these films, a distinction between the character Tsuru and the singer Oshiro Misako is very hard to maintain. Oshiro/Tsuru in these films appears as the privileged bearer of the spectral/sacred qualities I have described above that are vividly manifested in this cinematic space.

I myself first encountered Takamine's films when both *Paradise View* and

Untamagiru opened at theaters in Tokyo. After I became a professional music critic, films such as *Kadekaru Rinshō: Uta to katari* (Kadekaru Rinshō: Songs and stories, 1994, a documentary about Okinawan musician Kadekaru Rinshō), and *Tsuru-Henry* left strong impressions on me. As I began to write occasional reviews and criticism of Takamine's films, I always experienced the simple pleasure of viewing these works. However, each viewing experience led to new discoveries, each of which seemed different. Why did such discoveries occur? There must have been multiple folds contributing to the intensity of this pleasure for me.

OKINAWA, WALTER BENJAMIN, AND IMMORTALITY IN TAKAMINE'S FILMS

There are several reasons why I want to juxtapose the writings of Walter Benjamin and the works of Takamine that revolve around the theme of death. Benjamin, as critic and philosopher, has written pieces such as "Critique of Violence," "The Work of Art in the Age of Mechanical Reproduction," "Theses on the Philosophy of History," "The Task of the Translator," and *The Arcades Project*. These works thematize issues important to our contemporary concerns. For example, violence, artworks in the mediatized world, history, translation, and the flaneur are all matters that remain crucial for those who work in contemporary thought and art in Japan. At the same time, Benjamin's works amalgamate Marxism and Jewish mysticism, and exhibit both erudite analyses and illuminating presentiments.

One of the first references to Benjamin in Okinawan cinema is the citation of a passage from the Japanese translation of "Critique of Violence" in the film *Yasashii Nihonjin* (The gentle Japanese, 1971), directed by Higashi Yōichi. Released in the time between the Kōza Riots against the U.S. occupation in 1970 and Okinawa's "reversion" to mainland Japan in 1972, the film features a protagonist who has survived the mass suicide of Okinawan people at the end of the Pacific War and now lives in Tokyo. It includes the following citation from Benjamin: "All mythical, lawmaking violence, which we may call executive, is pernicious. Pernicious, too, is the law-preserving, administrative violence that serves it."[1] Such a citation allows us to imagine how Benjamin was read under those historical circumstances.

---

1. Walter Benjamin, *Reflections: Essays, Aphorisms, Autobiographical Writings*, ed. Peter Demetz (New York: Schocken, 1986), 300.

In 2004, a U.S. military helicopter crashed into the campus of Okinawa International University, leading to the U.S. military forces' occupation of the campus for a period of time. It was then that "Critique of Violence" was heavily read and discussed again in Okinawa, due in part to the reintroduction of Benjamin through the works of Giorgio Agamben. Many intellectuals reflected upon the im/possibility of what Benjamin calls "the general strike" in such a political situation.

Although I do recognize very much the importance of Benjamin in such a specifically Okinawan context, I would also like to consider the relationship between Benjamin and Takamine in a way that sheds a slightly different light upon the same problem of the critique of violence in Okinawa. More precisely, I would like to see Takamine's films as particular instantiations of the Benjaminian "angel of history." This is the figure of the angel that comes to life in the following context in the "Theses on the Philosophy of History."

> The tradition of the oppressed teaches us that the "state of emergency" in which we live is not the exception but the rule. We must attain to a conception of history that is in keeping with this insight. Then we shall clearly realize that it is our task to bring about a real state of emergency, and this will improve our position in the struggle against Fascism. One reason why Fascism has a chance is that in the name of progress its opponents treat it as a historical norm. The current amazement that the thing we are experiencing is "still" possible in the twentieth century is *not* philosophical. This amazement is not the beginning of knowledge—unless it is the knowledge that the view of history which gives rise to it is untenable.[2]

Takamine Gō defines his own films as "anti-Japanese films," when they present bodies that cannot die, an Okinawa that cannot consign itself to death. The body consciously refuses to belong to Japan, or it does not collectively self-determine its being part of Japan. I do not have to reexamine here in detail the uncanny overlap within the Japanese term *jiketsu* (自決) of two seemingly opposing meanings: "self-determination of the people" and "collective decision to commit suicide." But the important fact is that the decision not to die or the inability to die is tantamount to the refusal to be-

---

2. Walter Benjamin, "Theses on the Philosophy of History," in *Illuminations: Essays and Reflections*, ed. Hannah Arendt, trans. Harry Zohn (New York: Schocken, 1969), 257.

come Japanese. Moreover, the very inability to die also means a refusal to lead a normal life as such and instead to reimagine a body of alternative history.

The spectral body in Takamine's films becomes paradoxically animated in approaching death. It is also a sexual body whose flesh itself marks an undeterminable zone between life and death (as exemplified in the women's bodies that appear in *Paradise View* and *Untamagiru*, and those of the band members of Condition Green and the singer Oshiro Misako).

In relation to Anzaldua's conceptualization of "the borderland," Sugiura Tsutomu warns against the privileging of hybridity and syncretism at a specifically bounded location. As Sugiura continues, the borderland names "an identity that necessarily includes and is permeated with pain, death, and alterity" beyond "the framework of humanity, rationality, and logics formed by 'the west,' which is inherently a hybrid construct." What is important in that context is to inherit the "spiritualized knowledge" as discussed by Michel Foucault that, according to Sugiura, instantiates the kind of "politics based upon conflicts between multiple differences (instead of institutionalized standards), emotions (rather than sanitized social conditions), openness (rather than defense), materiality (instead of abstraction), and intersubjectivity (instead of individualism)."[3]

The so-called incomprehensibility in Takamine's films perhaps lies in such resonance between the "spiritualized knowledge" of the borderland and the historical materialism of Benjamin. As Sugiura mentions in his essay "Spirits and Women," such spiritualized knowledge informed a powerful tendency within the minority movements in the United States of the 1980s. In Okinawa, such a force has been reconceptualized as the new forms of community formation and worship that are nonetheless specific to the island.

IN "THE LANDSCAPES WE CANNOT HELP SHOOTING"

It is perhaps necessary to examine the works and activities of the photographer Higa Toyomitsu, who was born in 1950 and more or less belongs to the same generation as Takamine, who was born in 1948. Higa has been known for his works of photography, as well as for a series of documentary films he has produced with the fellow members of the Ryukyu Archipelago Docu-

---

3. See the essays by Sugiura Tsutomu, *Rei to onnatachi* [Spirits and women], in *Mirai*, vols. 479–488 (Tokyo: Miraisha, 2005–2007). The essays are also collected in Sugiura Tsutomu, *Rei to onnatachi* (Tokyo: Insukuriputo, 2009).

mentary Society. When I first saw *Nanamui*, a documentary film about the religious rituals held exclusively by the women of Miyako Island, I had a strange rumination about what Walter Benjamin might have seen if he had been given a chance to cross over the French-Spanish border and somehow found himself in Okinawa during the 1940s. I justify such a rumination of mine as born out of a desire to juxtapose the sacred and the spiritual in East Asian shamanisms and Benjamin's own methodology of the angel of history.

Furthermore, Higa's photography and films make us recall *Divine Horseman* (1985) by Maya Deren, which records the rituals of voodoo as they were practiced in the 1930s. Like Deren, who was born in Ukraine and arrived in Haiti via the United States, it might not have been so impossible after all for Benjamin (who was Deren's contemporary) to somehow arrive at Miyako via somewhere else, despite his original intention to escape to the United States. Imagining such idiosyncratic cultural histories is a necessary part of making up for the dearth of studies that juxtapose, for example, American intellectuals' approach to the Caribbean Islands (as exemplified by Zora Neal Hurston and Alan Lomax), and Japanese intellectuals' relationship with Okinawa in a period when local gods began to disappear from the world map through systemic colonial policies. To undertake such idiosyncratic cultural histories is to ask, therefore, "What alternative histories could these local gods have led?"

Higa was admitted to the Department of Arts and Craft at the University of the Ryukyus in 1970 and immediately began taking photographs as a member of the university photography club. His photographs from the period—some of which document the Kōza Riot and have been preserved at the Okinawa City Museum of Regional History—have been included in his monograph, *Akai gōya: Higa Toyomitsu shashinshū* (Red bitter melon: Photography of Higa Toyomitsu, 1970–1972). As noted on the front flap of the book, the monograph is suffused with what Higa calls "landscapes we could not help shooting, regardless of whether we wanted to do it nor not."[4] It is these landscapes that moved the young photographer, who could not help producing a number of blurry photographs that recorded the extraordinary tension and energy of the era.

His subsequent work, *Atsuki hibi in Kyanpu Hansen* (Hot days in Camp Hansen) was made in collaboration with photographer Ishikawa Mao and

---

4. Higa Toyomitsu, *Akai gōya: Higa Toyomitsu shashinshū* [Red bitter melon: Photography of Higa Toyomitsu, 1970–1972] (Okinawa: Yumeaaru Shuppansha, 2004).

published in 1982, although it was later banned for various unfortunate reasons.[5] The book's photographs show images of women, men, and children in the red-light district that sprawled out around the U.S. Marine Force's Camp Hansen in the town of Kin. Ishikawa recalls the period during which the work was shot:

> Even today, I cannot keep myself from dancing and singing to tunes like the Stylistics' "You Are Everything" or "From the Mountain," and the Eagles' "Hotel California," as they blast from my car stereo. I do hate the music by Kiss played in a bar owned by white people, though. Soul music of the 1970s is part of my body, you know.[6]

Higa is now one of the central members of the Ryukyu Archipelago Documentary Society, along with the local ethnologist Murakami Tomoe. Their six-hour work, *Shimakutuba ni kataru ikusayo* (*War Stories Told in Shima Kutuba*) (2003), and *Nanamui* (2003) exude a presence that resists compact summary. While the former documents local people's stories of the Battle of Okinawa, narrated in languages indigenous to the neighborhoods they grew up in, the latter records the religious rituals on Miyako Island. However, both works foreground the materiality of sounds, words, and voices and invite a comparison with materialist practices of Takamine and Benjamin. While my own summaries of these films might make them appear to be products of a nostalgic gaze toward now-lost objects and cultures of the past, the strength of the words, sounds, and songs in the films exposes an actuality that grips the spectators viewing them in the present. We see community here, not as something that once existed in the past, but something with an intensity that is to come.

The use of local languages in *War Stories Told in Shima Kutuba* overwhelms the viewer, while the voices and facial expressions that accompany the intimate language of each neighborhood breathe with lives of their own. Most Japanese viewers, who do not even understand the standardized Okinawan language, cannot comprehend these multiple neighborhood dialects without laboriously following their translations. However, we need to once again scrutinize what is meant by the term "comprehension" as it relates to

---

5. Higa Toyomitsu and Ishikawa Mao, *Atsuki hibi in Kyanpu Hansen* [Hot days in Camp Hansen] (Okinawa: A-man Shuppansha, 1982).

6. Ishikawa Mao, *Okinawa Souru* [Okinawa soul] (Tokyo: Ohta Press, 2002).

our experience of viewing the work. In contrast to the typical notion of comprehension, which reduces it to the recognition of linguistic messages translated into standard Japanese, comprehension in this film occurs as the viewer articulates her or his reading of the captions, while watching the facial expressions on the screen and attentively listening to the modulations and breathing of speaking voices. Thus, the spectators are drawn to historical memories as they arise in the present tense. *War stories told in Shima Kutuba* has multiple folds, within which multiple whispers of the speakers' bodies are manifested.

While the experience of the Battle of Okinawa shares some characteristics with the experiences of the atomic bombings of Hiroshima and Nagasaki (in the sense that in both the civilian population and their urban living environment as a whole became the targets of destruction), Okinawa's war experience is qualitatively different from those of Hiroshima and Nagasaki. Atomic bombing obliterates a city in a flash and brings about an indescribable scene of suffering, but the Battle of Okinawa was a ground battle that continued for a prolonged period of time. It unfolded as the U.S. military's overwhelming presence gradually came to dominate Japanese troops who, in turn, imposed a series of discriminatory orders upon the local Okinawans. When speakers in *War Stories Told in Shima Kutuba* tell of their experiences of having lost children, parents, relatives, and friends, they effectively summon the bodies of these dead in the very words they use and from their own whispering skins.

WHISPERINGS OF BEING-WITH

Nanamui is a documentary film that records the ritual practices that have been passed down from the women of one generation to another on the island of Miyako. The sight of women in white garments, performing their rituals as sunlight filters through forest leaves and creates a contrast between darkness and light, is striking. The songs for the gods these women sing not only differ greatly from Okinawan music as we know it stereotypically, but emanate something at once fragile and sublime that takes the breath away. But the film is not only notable for these climactic scenes. It also carefully documents the everyday events in which the women prepare for the rituals and practice their music. This continuity between the quotidian and the sacred gives new significance to the rituals. *Nanamui* documents rituals that are practiced exclusively by women, and exhibits what I would call multiple whisperings of "being-with." In this six-hour video work that shows an intimate network of women preparing for the ritual festival (in the neighborhood of Nishihara in the city of Hirara, on Miyako Island), we encounter the whisperings of the body in a specific locality that are somewhat similar to those we heard in *War Stories Told in Shima Kutuba*. While it is certainly true that the presentation of the women's voices in polyphony constitutes the climax of this work, we are also drawn, even at the preparatory stages, to their facial expressions that exude something like the joy of living. The work gains in actuality precisely because its presentation of such supple joy in quotidian settings sets it apart from typically ethnographic works that train their gaze on the details of religious rituals. The actuality of the ritual in *Nanamui* is not that of a tradition that has been frozen in the past. Rather, it is an event that goes through its own process of becoming. While the ritual itself has a long tradition that has not been disclosed to the public for many years, we can see—in the ensemble of images and sounds that capture lived experiences like deeply held private secrets—a future-oriented work of imagination and construction.

Nanamui is also a document of individual women, their collective, and their families, whose mutual ties do not revolve around labor and production, but are made by something rather idle and insignificant according to modern standards. These ties bring them together as intimate strangers. Despite their thematic differences, both *Nanamui* and *War Stories Told in Shima Kutuba* deal with something that emerges from relationships, places, and languages, and thus posits a continuity between memory and the everyday. People appear in both films as intimate strangers who at once extend, but also form an alternative to, the institution of family. It is too facile to call them village relationships. These intimate relationships arise as a process of becoming through the use of these languages and ritual practices.

ANGELS OF HISTORY IN OKINAWA

We need to be reminded here that these documentaries dealing with local languages and rituals are far removed from the stereotypical images assigned to the otherwise emblematic figures of locality. This is characteristic of both Higa's and Takamine's works, which engage in certain *presentations* that occur across the documentary/fiction divide. If local languages and rituals constitute a *location* where these people weave their livelihoods, we need to juxtapose them with the critical conceptualization of location offered by Caren Kaplan:

> Location is not a productive concept when it is seen as reflective of authentic identities that are to be reestablished and reconfirmed. ... Discourses on location can also be mobilized to naturalize borders and binary distinction between the center and the periphery under the disguises of beauty, nostalgia, and fabricated similarities. Such discourses of location can be an agent of appropriation, or problematically construe equality when materialist history exposes inequality. Instead, the concept of location must be used to put into question the stereotypical images that have been uncritically accepted. These images have been the remnants of colonialist discourses and other structural inequalities of modernity.[7]

Kaplan's proposal and warning are directed toward critics and scholars. However, the acute aesthetic styles of Higa and the various concepts and techniques Takamine employs in filming practices deftly and effectively avoid the risk Kaplan mentions. Such critical filmmaking is enabled not only by visually instantiating the so-called *machibui* (chaos) of Okinawa and sympathetically identifying with the speakers of the island's local languages and the practitioners of the rituals. These practices also enact what Kaplan in the above-mentioned book calls "the practice in and against the local," by achieving movements that are far removed from the act of identification. In the depth and openness of the relationships that may initially seem like an extension of the family, these works disclose an area that cannot be subsumed by either the family or the nation.

This is perhaps why Takamine's films at times achieve commercial success but are also strongly rejected by viewers in Okinawa. Takamine's career progressed from earlier works such as *Sanshingwa* (Dear photograph) to *Okinawan Dream Show* and *Okinawan Chirudai*, and then extended from *Paradise View* and *Untamagiru* to *Mugen Ryukyu/Tsuru-Henry*. Toyomitsu Higa, on the other hand, pursued a path that included his photographic project

---

7. Caren Kaplan, *Questions of Travel: Postmodern Discourses of Displacement* (Durham, NC: Duke University Press, 1996), 187. Higashi's citation is from the Japanese translation *Idō no jidai*, trans. Murayama Kiyohiko (Tokyo: Miraisha, 2003).

on Camp Hansen and documentary films such as *Nanamui*. Having never crossed paths in the course of all these years, the two filmmakers documented what they saw, heard, touched, smelled, and ate in the midst of the landscape, which "they could not help shooting." These elements constitute *mabui* and *machibui* (soul and chaos in the Okinawan language) of the island.

Walter Benjamin's "Angel of History" was written under the immense influence of a painting by Paul Klee. The angel, who faces the past while his wings are driven by the wind of modernity toward the future, is someone who predicts the future but does not fall prey to the progressivist notion of history. Drawing upon Benjamin's conceptualization of the angel, Massimmo Cacciari argues that the angel is the figure that "says what it needs to say" and "says what the words themselves are in the process of becoming." As Cacciari adds, the angel is also a narrow path and a gate.[8] Takamine's films and Higa's documentary works multiply such paths and gates. In the "dewdrops of incomprehensibility" live the angels.

TRANSLATED BY INOUE MAYUMO.

---

8. See Cacciari's discussion of Benjamin's angel in Massimo Cacciari, *The Necessary Angel* (Albany: State University of New York Press, 2001).

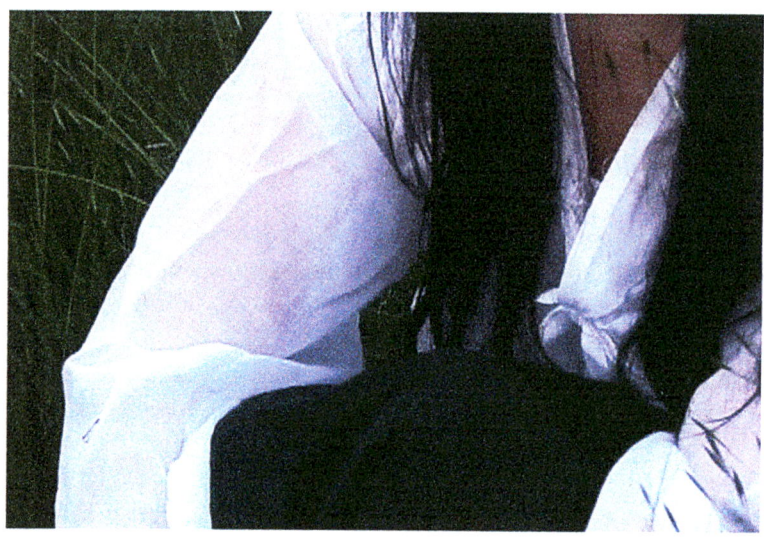

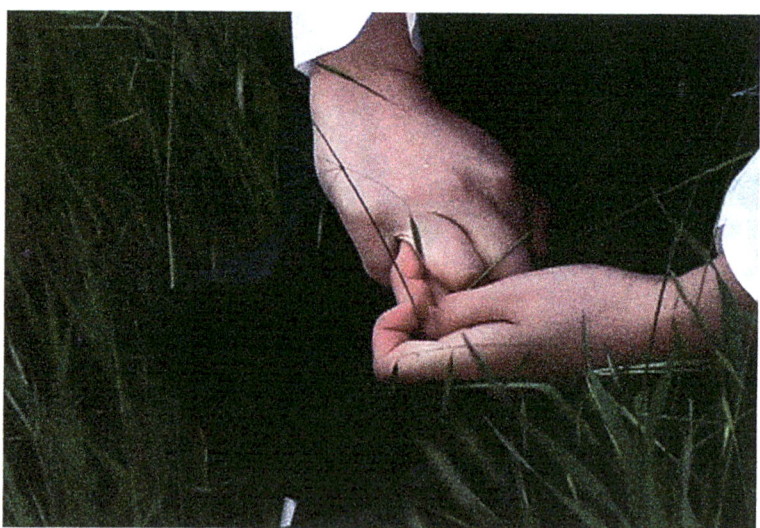

Soni Kum, "Subway, I Plant Myself," 2004, 5 min.

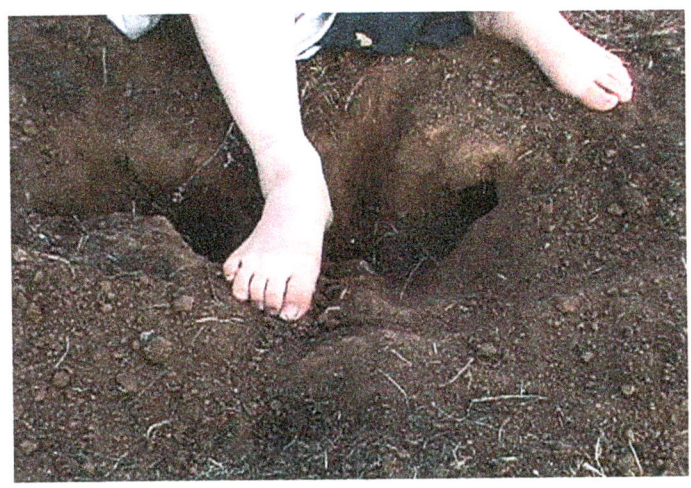

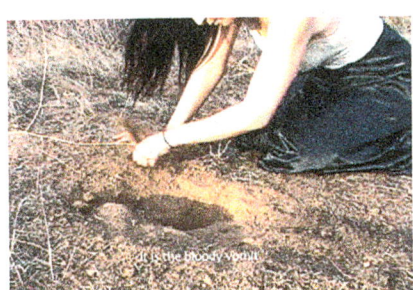

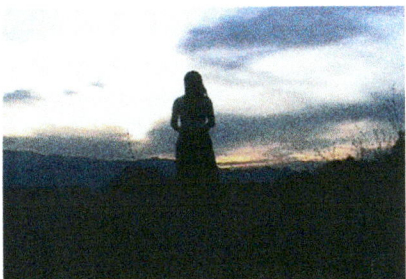

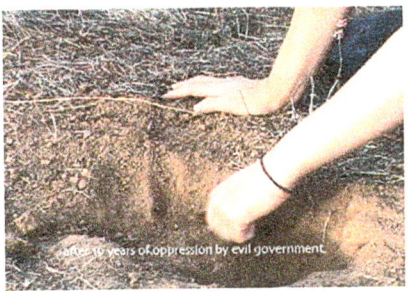

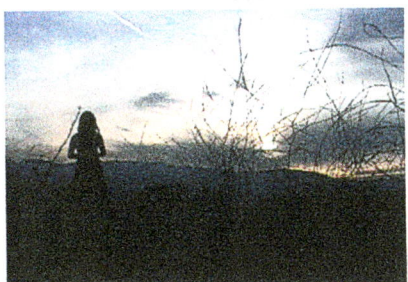

Soni Kum, *Beast of Me*, video, 18 min.

Chapter 6

Her Narration and Body

On Soni Kum's Film Work

IKEUCHI YASUKO

INTRODUCTION: WHY THE TITLE *BEAST OF ME?*

While attending the 2006 winter symposium titled Film/Women/Power: Gender and Visuality[1] held at the International Institute of Language and Culture Studies of Ritsumeikan University, I was introduced by Lee Chonghwa, one of the commentators at the symposium, to a video work named *Beast of Me* (2005) made by Soni Kum, a young, third-generation Korean video producer living in Japan who is also a performance artist.[2] At that time, due to the tight schedule, I was only able to see the first half (about 10 min-

The author is grateful to Soni Kum for her answers to my numerous questions about her work as well as the valuable data and information that I have received from her during the process of writing this essay. I have also obtained important data and information from Yang Insil, a scholar of representations of *zainichi* Koreans.

1. This symposium was held by the International Institute of Language and Culture Studies at Ritsumeikan University on February 21, 2006. The presenters were Takemura Kazuko, Saitō Ayako, and Ikeuchi Yasuko. Lee Chonghwa and Tazaki Hideaki were the commentators. It was published in *Ritsumeikan Gengo Bunka Kenkyū* [Ritsumeikan Studies in Language and Culture] 18, no. 2 (November 2006), 1–57.

2. Soni Kum is a third-generation *zainichi* Korean born in Tokyo. After she finished her high school education at a Korean ethnic school (also often known as "North Korean" schools in Japan), she eneterd a Japanese university. Upon graduation, she went to study at CalArts in Los Angeles from 2002 to 2005, and received her MFA degree from the School of Film/Video. Kum started producing and performing in video and film works while studying at CalArts. *Beast of Me* was exhibited at Sweeney Gallery at the University of California at Riverside, which was opened in March 2005 while she was studying in the U.S., and later it became her graduation project. Her original plan was to make *Foreign Sky*, a work that she started earlier in her gradu-

utes) of *Beast of Me*. But this video piece, together with Lee's comments, impressed the participants of the symposium with its vivid images.

I have been told that the source of the title *Beast of Me* is a poem by the Korean poet, Yu Chihwan, which is quoted by one of the characters in Oshima Nagisa's film, *Death by Hanging* (*Kōshikei*, 1968).[3] Interestingly enough, when Kum first watched the film, she was not in Japan but in Los Angeles, studying at CalArts (California Institute of the Arts). This was in 2002, at a screening of several Japanese film "classics" that had been selected by Susan Sontag as part of a project for the Los Angeles County Museum of Art. In other words, Kum's selection of a title grew out of a chance encounter with words by the Korean poet Yu Chihwan, cited in the film *Death by Hanging*, which she saw while studying abroad in America. "Beast of me," then, is a phrase Kum encountered as a translation of a translation. Because she was watching the film in America, the phrase from the original Korean-language poem, recited in Japanese translation as *kemono to narite* in Oshima's film, appeared in the English-language subtitles as "beast of me."

Let me briefly suggest what I see as the implications of the history of translation and retranslation of this poem for Kum's work.[4] In the movie *Death by Hanging*, a passage from Yu Chihwan's poem, translated into Japanese, is quoted by the young *zainichi* woman called Sister, played by Koyama Akiko.

> Owareta kain no gotoku
> *Kare ga* oeru kanashimi wa, hisashikarisedo
> Ikan zo, kono kannan o, kemono to naritemo, taezaramu[5]

---

ation project, but eventually *Foreign Sky* was finished around July 2005. The two films were done in the same period and are closely related in terms of theme and form.

3. The following is information about Yu Chihwan (1908–1967) the author received from Yang Insil in a private letter dated May 4, 2008: "Yu has been the subject of recent debates about Japanese collaborators, but generally he is not considered to have been a pro-Japanese person. He had been active as a poet since 1931, and had spent time studying in Japan. But in the history of Korean poetry Yu was known as a poet of modernity who belonged to the so-called Life School. In general, his poetry is appreciated for its strong national consciousness and demonstrating awareness of essential questions about life."

4. Translator's note: This sentence has been added to the English translation, with Professor Ikeuchi's permission, to emphasize the interpretive importance of the question of translation for this part of her argument.

5. Author's emphasis on masculine pronoun *kare*. That the source of the poetic phrase cited in Kum's video work was Nagisa Oshima's film, and its subtitles, I learned in an interview with Soni Kum on August 26, 2008. For the filmscript of *Death by Hanging*, please see *Sekai no eiga*

An English translation of the passage appears in the English subtitles:

> Like Cain, long pursued
> *His* sadness is profound
> Even though it makes a beast of me
> I will endure this suffering.[6]

Seen retrospectively in its own historical context, Yu Chihwan's poem was first written in Korea when it was a prewar colony of the Japanese empire. It was then translated and edited by Kim So'un (1907–1981) and put in his *Chōsen shishū—chichiiro no kumo* (Collection of Korean poetry: Milk-white cloud), published by Kawade Shobō Press in Tokyo in 1940. This collection of poetry, edited and translated into precise, succinct Japanese, was also welcomed and praised by many poets and writers in the Japanese empire at the time. Critical responses of Japanese poets and writers, however, were utterly lacking in awareness of the difficult struggle of those colonized writers whose language had been taken away from them. For example, in his essay "Words to Welcome Korean Poets to the World of Poetical Writing in the Mainland," the noted novelist Satō Haruo, who had access to the first version of *Milk-White Cloud*, wrote that only if Korean poets could produce high-quality poetry by abandoning their practice of using "an old language that is

---

sakka 6: Oshima Nagisa (Film Writers of the World 6—Oshima Nagisa) (Kinema Junpōsha Press, September 1970), 187. What is not mentioned in this compilation, however, is that the translation of Yu's poem used in Oshima's film was taken from *Tsumi to shi to ai to* [Crime, death, and love], ed. Bok Sunam (San'ichi Shobō Press, 1963).

6. Author's emphasis. Translator's note: An alternative English translation of the same poem in Japanese might be "Like the banished Cain / He has borne this suffering from of old / How, even if he were to become a beast / Will he endure it?" In this alternative reading of the Japanese verse, the final line poses the rhetorical question "*how* will he endure this suffering?" and implies the suffering probably cannot be endured. This interpretation is closer to the interpretation by Kim So-un, which follows. We would also note that Ikeuchi's use of italics in the examples she cites calls attention to the varied ways in which the pronouns used in the original Korean poem have been translated and inflected in differing historical and political contexts. That is, translators have exploited the ways in which the Korean pronoun *jeohui* (저희) found in these lines can range in meaning from first-person plural to third-person plural and can be differently inflected for gender. Ikeuchi suggests how the very languages used in Kum's video resonate with traces of Korea's colonial history, refracted, in turn, through *zainichi* experience in Japan through the postwar. By turning to the English "beast of me," Kum appropriates the pronouns in Yu's poem for yet new referents: the bodies and stories of women (including the Bok Sunam "invisibilized" in Oshima's film). The translators are thankful to Ikeuchi Yasuko, Meredith McKinney, and to Watanabe Naoki's correspondence with Junliang Huang for illuminating these matters.

facing extinction" as if it were the language of everyday life would their works have lasting value.[7] This statement, although probably meant to encourage Korean poets in their efforts, "is such a cruel claim it makes one want to avert one's eyes," as the critic Hosomi Kazuyuki stated in 2004.[8]

After the war, the same collection of poetry was published simply as *Collection of Korean Poetry* by Iwanami Bunko in 1954. In that book, we find the same work by Yu Chihwan titled "Ode," but interpreted differently in Kim So'un's translation.[9]

> Owareta kain no gotoku
> *Karera ga* oeru kanashimi wa, hisashikarisedo
> Ikan zo, kono kannan o, kemono to naritemo, taezaramu[10]

> Like the banished Cain,
> *They* have borne this suffering from of old
> How, even if it were to make beasts of them,
> Will they endure it?

Recently this *Chōsen shishū* [Collection of Korean Poetry] was translated yet again by the *zainichi* poet Kim Shi-jong, over sixty years after Kim So'un's translation. While showing respect for Kim So'un's work, Kim Shi-jong described his own process of retranslation as a struggle against "Japanese-style lyricism." Consider the different translation of the passage originally written

---

7. *Chōsen shishū* [Collection of Korean Poetry], ed. Satō Haruo and Kim So'un, trans. Kim So'un (Tokyo: Iwanami Shoten Press, 1954), 225–228. In this edition the phrase in Satō's title, "the world of poetical writing in the mainland" is changed to "the world of poetical writing in Japan."

8. This is Hosomi Kazuyuki's comment on Satō Haruo's words mentioned earlier. It was presented in the lecture, "The Future of Japanese Language, the Future of Poetry" (November 14, 2003), third in the fourteenth series of lectures, titled "Korean Diaspora: Interwoven Multiexpressions," held at the International Institute of Language and Culture Studies of Ritsumeikan University, and published in *Language and Culture Studies at Ritsumeikan University* 16, no. 1 (June 2004), 50. The presenters were Kim Shi-jong and Hosomi Kazuyuki, while the commentator was Fujii Takeshi.

9. Translator's note: Ikeuchi's italics below emphasize that, although the 1954 version is by the same translator, Kim So'un, he has changed the singular pronoun "his" to the plural "their." Also, henceforth, we depart from the English translation given in the English subtitles to Oshima's film to more accurately reflect our own reading of the Japanese verses.

10. *Chōsen shishū*, 199, author's emphasis.

in Korean by Yu Chihwan in Kim Shi-jong's *Saiyaku: Chōsen shishū* (Retranslation: Collection of Korean poetry, 2007):

Owareta kain no yō ni
Temae-domo hisashii aida kurai kanashimi ni kogarete wa itemo
Ikade kono kannan o kemono ni sareta tote taeenai koto ga arimashō ya[11]

Like the banished Cain
We have struggled from of old with a dark suffering
How, even if the burden were to make beasts of us,
Is there any way we will not endure it?

In this retranslation of Yu Chihwan's poem, the isolated subject who endures suffering like a beast shifts from the "*kare* (he)" or "*karera* (they)," in Kim So'un's versions, to "*temaedomo* (we)." Compared to the *kare* or *karera* that experience suffering—both of these male pronouns convey a heroic tone—the term *temaedomo* can actually be said to convey modesty on the part of the speaker. At the same time, it is a word that implies a plural "we" that is somehow resilient, that resonates without lyricism. In Kim Shi-jong's translation of Yu's poem, we sense the emergence/appearance of a new subject. We can see how the profoundly alienated subject of Yu's poem might have been referred to in the first-person pural in the original Korean.[12]

So far I have traced the derivation of the title of Soni Kum's work, but this tracing alone brings us to such a complicated situation of language that it cannot be grasped through an explanation that simply centers on the phrase "beast of me" as an English translation of *kemono to naritemo*. Moreover, we cannot help but take into account the complicated situation of language that Kum herself faces today at many moments, from moments in her everyday life to moments in her production of artworks. Kum was born and grew up in Japan, went to Korean ethnic schools to learn Korean, and thus

---

11. In *Retranslation: Collection of Korean Poetry*, trans. Kim Shi-jong (Tokyo: Iwanami Shoten, 2007), 206, we find the poem attributed to "Yu Chihwan (pseudonym 'Cheungma,' 1908–1967). Yu published his first collection, *Poetry by Cheungma* in 1939, and the second, *Book of Life*, in 1947. Yu served as the president of the Young Literati Association after the August 15th liberation of Korea, and became a leading figure of the anti-communist national literature movement." *Ode* can be found on pages 211–213 of the book, and the cited phrase on pages 211–212.

12. As we explain in n. 9, the Korean pronoun *jeohui/jeodeul* (저희) found in these lines can range in meaning from first-person plural to third-person singular or plural.

became bilingual. But in addition to that, while studying in the United States, she expressed the titles, concepts, and narratives of her film works and performances in English, making her trilingual in that sense. Considering Kum's complicated linguistic situation, one might well hesitate before simply translating the English title of her work into Japanese.

However, if we do want to translate the title of Kum's video work into Japanese, we might then have to raise again the question of the politics of translation, since the phrase in her title had already been translated in the 1940s from the Korean poem into Japanese as *kemono to naritemo*. This translation was, as I mentioned above, born out of the historical context of Japanese colonial control of Korea. Needless to say, this historical context does not pose a problem that can simply be solved by refusing to translate Kum's title into Japanese. If we were to take into account Kim Shi-jong's own recollections of the end of the war, when at the age of seventeen he studied "a Korean that was facing the sad fate of extinction" as if he were "literally clawing at a wall," while continuing to write poems in Japanese—something Hosomi has defined as an "acute" or "decisive experience of translation"—we might find it more meaningful to ask how we ourselves, who take for granted our lives within a dominant language, might ever experience something like "acute" or "decisive" translation.[13]

Another question I will go on to explore in this essay is the following: when Soni Kum in this work shifts the referents of Yu Chihwan's verse from the masculine *kare* (he) or *karera* (they), to a feminine *watashi* (I) or *kanojo-tachi* (they), what kind of subject, what kind of story, and what kind of body are brought into view?

Let me begin to discuss this matter by noting that the film *Death by Hanging* has had peculiar significance for Kum, as suggested by the fact that Oshima's images are also cited in her longer documentary film *Foreign Sky* (2005), made around the same time as *Beast of Me* (2005). At this point, therefore, I would like to approach Kum's work through a kind of detour, by constructing an interface between the filmic text of Oshima Nagisa's *Death by Hanging* and another text that has remained largely invisible, although it was crucial to the composition of Oshima's film.

---

13. Kim Shi-jong, Note 6, *Ritsumeikan Gengo Bunka Kenkyū* [Ritsumeikan Studies in Language and Culture] 16, no. 1 (June 2004), 60, 62. The concepts of "acute" and "decisive" translation are introduced by Hosomi Kazumi in the same volume, 67–68.

1. THE TEXT/CONTEXT OF THE FILM *DEATH BY HANGING*

Death by Hanging (1968) is a film that takes as its subject matter the Ri Chin'u Incident, in which the *zainichi* Korean youth Ri Chin'u was arrested in 1958 for the alleged crimes of rape and murder, and executed in 1962.[14] As many have described it, the film *Death by Hanging* presents a logical argument that carries a specific message, convicting the state for crimes of murder in carrying out capital punishment and waging war. By taking up the historical case of the *zainichi* Korean youth Ri Chin'u's death sentence and execution, the film offers a radical perspective on the way the logic of the Japanese nation-state even in postwar times has maintained prewar imperialist and colonialist ideas and frameworks deeply embedded in itself.

In the film, Ri Chin'u is represented as the condemned character R. All the characters bear titles like Detention Director, Education Officer, Prison Chaplain, Chief of Security, Doctor, Public Prosecutor, Prosecutor's Officer, and Woman, none of which constitutes a proper name. By thus removing individuality from the characters to highlight executioners' roles as functionaries supporting the organs of the state, Oshima transforms the film into an allegorical drama about the nation-state's power to kill. Interestingly enough, a "woman" whom R calls Sister (Onē-san) appears in a traditional Korean *chima jeogori* dress, and is made into a striking symbol of overlapping gendered and ethnic difference. However, since Sister appears in an imaginary scene at the execution chamber, as a ghostly existence who can only be seen by R and certain of the executioners, I would hold that the surrealistic quality of her existence, which has been rendered (in)visible, confirms the allegorical nature of this film.

Death by Hanging is a highly provocative film—steeped in the radical

---

14. What is known as the Ri Chin'u Incident refers to both the murder at the Komatsugawa High School on April 20, 1958, of a twenty-three-year-old cafeteria worker called Tanaka Setsuko (known at the time as the Female Cafeteria Worker Murder Incident) and the killing of a sixteen-year-old part-time student named Ohta Yoshie at the same school on August 17, 1958, of the same year (known as the Komatsugawa High School Female Student Murder). Ri Chin'u was arrested on September 1, 1958, and sentenced to death at his first trial, February 12, 1959. Ri's appeal on February 28, 1959, was rejected by the Tokyo District Court. His second appeal on January 10 in the next year was also rejected by the Supreme Court on August 17, 1961, and he was sentenced to death. Voices advocating for commutation of Ri's death sentence, as well as efforts to request a pardon and save his life were dismissed, and the *zainichi* Korean Ri was executed on November 16, 1962. (He was sixteen at the time of the incidents and twenty-two years old when he was executed.) Ri's story was taken up by the playwright Kinoshita Junji, and the writers Ooka Shōhei and Ōe Kenzaburō.

thoughts and representational strategies of Oshima and his collaborators—which initally astonishes spectators with its shocking opening scene. Guided by the camera's eye that looks down from the sky at a Japanese execution chamber, we go directly to the site of the execution, and witness the moment when the body of the condemned, with his eyes covered and the noose around his neck, is suspended in the air. Even more shocking is the very surrealistic sequence in which the body of the condemned R, who is supposed to have been executed, repels the execution and comes back to life again, although in an amnesiac state.

In the scenes that follow this, the propositions "R DOES NOT ACCEPT BEING R," "R ACKNOWLEDGES THE EXISTENCE OF R AS A STRANGER," "R TRIES TO BE R," "R WAS PROVEN TO BE A KOREAN," "R FINALLY BECOMES R," "R ACCEPTS BEING R FOR THE SAKE OF ALL Rs" are presented on the screen with each cut to a new scene. Through this mechanism, the constructed-ness of these scenes is brought to our attention, and the realistic flow of the movie's narrative is interrupted. Moreover, the confounded executioners, who are directly confronted by the failure of the execution, and their chaotic behavior, make for excellent comedy with powerfully estranging effects. In order to complete the execution, they need to restore to R his consciousness of being R by acting in his stead and investigating the empirical evidence of his motivations and criminal behavior based on the court verdict used to convict him. But such a theater of the absurd that reverses their roles produces a satire laden with black humor.

A target of especially drastic irony is the party held by the prison officials following the crime scene inspection and the execution. A reversal of the plot is inserted, in which an executioner, in order to re-present the rape scene committed by the condemned, commits sexual crime as if he were having a daydream. The ritual purification banquet after the execution, too, transmutes into an orgy for the executioners, thus revealing the sexual desire that is latent in the homosocial community of men who support the state at these outermost margins.[15]

Among the critical writings that analyze the film's "erotic" politicality is a unique essay written by the French critic Pascal Bonitzer. Limiting the politicality of *Death by Hanging* to the sphere of the erotic, Bonitzer pays atten-

---

15. Although parodying the homosocial relationship is a representational strategy on Oshima's part, I cannot help but believe that Oshima's grotesque and exaggerated depictions of homosociality are suffused with homophobic feelings.

tion to the form of the execution and the representation of the ritual of
hanging in the film. As he writes,

> The eroticism of the film lies not just in the ritual that climaxes in the
> cruel, decisive rigidity of the person who was hung, a ritual the film's
> linear plot and "chapters" present with such intense "objectivity." The
> noose used for the hanging is itself erotic. This empty object—such
> emptiness haunts the film—is, in its shape as an "O," made for the
> purpose of being filled and tied up. The action of tightening it auto-
> matically creates an association between the pleasure of the executed
> and death. *The empty noose is a kind of symbolic existence that organizes
> the film's content and is pulled tight around it; it is the space of lack (and
> thus desire) and the space of the sign. As a gaping orifice, it is the space of
> difference (i.e., of the dead), and a symbol.*[16]

Bonitzer dissociates *Death by Hanging* from representations that question
concepts such as nation and ethnicity, and asserts that Oshima's film is "not
passionate because it brings up issues such as capital punishment, racial discrimination, and the guilt of Japanese imperialism." His critique is interesting because while paying attention to the narrativity of Oshima's film, he also
presents a structuralist and semiotic interpretation of the film's symbolism in
terms of relations between "signifier" and "signified." It is undeniable that if
we pay attention to the narrative aspect of Oshima's images, we can read the
pleasure of death, and the erotic as excess, into the empty hole of the noose
used in the execution. However, analysis of the relationship between *signifi-
ant* and *signifié* should not be limited to just that.

As I have also mentioned earlier, what Oshima depicts with all his pas-
sion in this film are the disputation, bodily gestures, and "lewd" dances that
burst forth during the male homosocial ritual—the party following the execution, which Oshima parodies as the feast of a male community who share

---

16. Author's emphasis. Pascal Bonitzer's research on *Death by Hanging* (published in the
Oshima Special Issue of *Les Cahiers du cinéma*, March 1970 on pages 155 and 156) is introduced by Yamamoto Kikuo in his article "Kaigai in okeru Oshima Nagisa hyōka" [Overseas
critiques of Nagisa Oshima], in *Sekai no eiga sakka 6: Oshima Nagisa* [Film writers of the world
6—Oshima Nagisa] (Tokyo: Kinema Junpōsha Press, September 1970), 135–158. Bonitzer's
arguments cited here are from Yamamoto's article. However, Yamamoto spells Bonitzer's name
as Bontsue rather than Bonizeiru in Japanese.

the logic and ideology of Japanese imperialism, of racial discrimination, and war and capital punishment as legitimized by the state. I am thus drawn to propose the following rewriting, borrowing Bonitzer's outstanding analytical terminology but at the same time countering his critical discourse that restricts the politicality of *Death by Hanging* to an erotic one:

> The hole of the "empty noose" that is used for the execution is the "state," the symbolic existence that is both sustained by this male homosocial community but that also organizes them and tightens itself around them. It is the "space of lack (and thus desire)" and the space of the "sign." As a "gaping orifice," it is the space of difference (i.e., of the dead), and a symbol, which subsumes (while also excluding) those who are designated non-"citizens."

What makes this interpretation tenable, I think, is that it is not only the empty hole of the noose, but, even more so, the empty circle of the Japanese national flag that appears from time to time as a signifier that compels our attention in this film. In light of this, we can only conclude that the signified here is the state, that "site of lack (and desire)" whose gaping orifice can be seen here and there in the film.

In Japan as well, *Death by Hanging* has been recognized as a unique film, and has been discussed from different angles by film critics. A special issue titled *Oshima Nagisa Kōshikei ron* (Essays on Oshima Nagisa's *Death by Hanging*) was published by *Eiga Geijutsu* in March 1968. There Haniya Yutaka positively evaluates the rigorous architecture of the "multifaceted structure of logic" presented in the film, while giving attention to its "seemingly meaningless shots." He states:

> I am not sure if this is just because I'm a person who likes rivers, but I was filled with a sense of freshness whenever I encountered seemingly meaningless shots, like the scene of the river bridge where the young man R is running after the prison officers, or the shot from the riverbank where a motorboat cuts across the screen that shimmers in black and white. From my spot in the preview room, it occurred to me that in that area through which the glittering river ran there must have been many such scenes—seemingly meaningless, yet filled with the meaning of great life itself—random scenes of life capable of

countering the oppressiveness of that single room, furnished with its execution stand, that is the organ of the state.[17]

I count myself among those who are charmed by the shots of the river that alternate with the absurdist crime inspection scenes in the movie. In the same vein, there is the following commentary by Iijima Kōichi:

> In the first half, the movie unfolds as a parody that mocks the side of prosecutors and executioners in the execution chamber. But shortly after, it switches to the crime inspection scenes, set in the outdoor space along the banks of the Sumida River. Then, again, it shifts to the young man R's cramped apartment, where a family drama commences. Amid its slapstick humor, from time to time a window opens, letting in a breeze that creates a feeling of something I might even call "transparent melancholy." Is it a feeling borne out of Oshima's sympathy for the persecuted Korean? These gently lapping waves of melancholy, which (because of the comedic setup) simply never degenerate into bathos, waft in like the breeze blowing in from the river. From the screen I can smell the Sumida River.[18]

Not only the images that belong to the structure of logic, but also the images in the "seemingly meaningless shots" that are not directly connected with it, create something enormously attractive in this film. The smell of the Arakawa River banks, the wind that blows in from them, the sun reflected by the surface of the river, as well as the shots of the Korean community that lives beside it—all these shots are cut out from scenery that richly emanates the "meaning of great life itself" in the era of the 1960s when the film was made.

There is another impressive image in the river, in which R and Sister appear riding a bicycle valiantly along the Arakawa River shore. This dreamlike scene is inserted among scenes of the party being carried on by the homosocial community of executioners. In the scene the romping couple are seen falling from the bicycle and rolling endlessly down the slopes of the river-

---

17. Haniya Yutaka, "Shinjitsu no tamensei" [The multiplicity of reality], in *Eiga Geijutsu Tokushūgo: Oshima Nagisa Kōshikeiron* (Film art special issue: Essays on Oshima Nagisa's *Death By Hanging*), (Tokyo: Eiga Geijutsu, March, 1968), 28, author's emphasis.

18. Iijima Kōichi, "Kigeki *Kōshikei* ni mirareru hibō to yume" [Extravagant hope and dream seen in the comedy *Death by Hanging*], in ibid., 31.

bank. Moreover, a long shot of the two embracing each other on a raft that floats in the middle of the river, their figures illuminated by the sunset in the background—leaves an indelible impression. It is a scene of the imaginary love between the two, and Oshima named it "the sunset full of heavenly grace."[19] As I will discuss later, Soni Kum cites this imaginary scene in her video work repeatedly.

However, whereas Shibusawa Tatsuhiko in the same issue expressed doubts about the way "an argument about the nation-state" and "the metaphysics of love" are brought together in this film,[20] Yajima Midori, on the contrary, criticized the connections made between them as too weak.

> It is not only in the prison named the "state" that people become objects of surveillance. Sometimes it is the family, the morality of civilized society, or the affect named "love," that, as a smaller state inside the state, or as small *states within us*, monitors us. To struggle against the inner state is different from struggling against some external state. For relations between men and women become entangled with these struggles. Sexuality, too, cannot be disconnected from *the inner state*. ... The sex scenes in Oshima's work are always the same— they are like painful collisions experienced by men and women attempting to have sex for the first time.
>
> The love between R and Sister in *Death by Hanging* ends where it should be able to get started, and hence never makes it to the point where it can be connected to a passionate pursuit of the question of *the inner state*. ...
>
> If Oshima is indeed interested in calling into question *the inner state* of human beings, I would hope that he would stop assigning women nothing but second-class roles as saviors of men in his films, and start to look into them much more deeply.[21]

---

19. Oshima Nagisa, *Oshima Nagisa 1968* (Tokyo: Seidosha Press, 2004), 200. Another excerpt: "The reason I inserted a scene full of love and heavenly grace there is because I thought R would have been too pathetic if there was no such thing at all. R was supposed to be living a life in which he could experience that kind of love, but he didn't, and he was executed before he could. I must have inserted the scene of the sunset full of heavenly grace in order to emphasize that. Inserting the scene gave the film consistency, and has contributed to my longevity as a director (laughter). But you can't fill a film up with too many scenes like that or it becomes saccharine" (201).

20. Ibid., 28–30.

21. Yajima Midori, "Umibe no yume wa yume no mata yume—Matsuda Masao, Oshima

As we can see, Yajima Midori's perspective problematizes the invisible power operating in our daily lives through which inner state and nation-state are bound together, especially within gender relations. She criticizes Oshima's *Death by Hanging* for its lack of a deep grasp of that kind of "inner state," which leads to its restricting women's roles to secondary roles as saviors of men. With regard to the representation of the *zainichi* Korean female in *Death by Hanging*, Iijima Kōichi also comments, "Played by Koyama Akiko, the Korean woman called 'Sister' is highly ideological, stereotyped, and lacking insight into others."[22]

As mentioned earlier, although Sister is notable in the film as a representation in which gender and ethnic difference intersect, she is set up as an imaginary existence invisible to anyone except R and some of the executioners. Fantasy can act as a multivalent representation of something transcending reality, and in this film, we have fantasies as intimate dialogic space that exists between these two characters, invisible to the executioners, as well as of their bicycle trip along the riverbank, and the "sunset full of heavenly grace."

However, if we take into account the text on which Oshima's film was actually based—that is, the letters exchanged between the imprisoned young man, Ri Chin'u, who was facing the death sentence, and the *zainichi* woman Bok Sunam, who was involved in supporting both Ri himself and the efforts to have his sentence commuted—we come to see a certain limitation in the way their relationship is portrayed in the film.[23] At the same time, the issue goes beyond being a simple matter of Oshima's rather limited representation of this relationship, and, while being closely related to the "male chauvinism" that Yajima points out, involves some other problems.[24] The question I my-

---

Nagisa no josei besshi o o ni" [A dream of the seashore is a dream within a dream: On Matsuda Masao's and Oshima Nagisa's male chauvinism], *Eiga geijutsu*, June 1968, 48–49, author's emphasis. The passage was written as a critique of Oshima's *Kaettekita yopparai* [The drunk comes home].

22. Iijima, "Kigeki *Kōshikei* ni mirareru hibō to yume," 31.

23. Bok, *Tsumi to shi to ai to*. From the mid-1960s, Bok Sunam devoted herself to transcribing the oral histories of Korean victims of the Hiroshima A-bomb and Korean laborers who worked in the mines of Kyushu. In addition, she investigated the traces of Korean military porters and comfort women in Okinawa. Her documentary titled *Ariran no uta, Okinawa kara no shōgen* [The song of Arirang: Testimony from Okinawa] was released in 1991, and has been featured at the Yamagata International Documentary Film Festival and elsewhere.

24. Using the term "male chauvinism," Yajima criticized the solidarity of the male community of the Sōzōsha Film Company, which was in control of providing for its own needs in every area, ranging from production to direction, scenario writing, actors and actresses, and film critics. To this charge, Oshima responded, "Yajima just hated Sōzōsha. And she acted afraid of

self want to take up has to do with another topology related to the presentation of the condemned R and Sister that Oshima has made (in)visible in his film. For there is a gap between the superb representation of "the self" that Ri Chin'u and Bok Sunam have woven together, and the allegorical representation of *zainichi* Koreans in this film. I think this gap is also suggestive of ways in which the allegorical representation in *Death by Hanging* differs from Soni Kum's own narration and representations in her video works.

2. THE (IN)VISIBILIZED TEXT: *TSUMI TO SHI TO AI TO* (CRIME, DEATH, AND LOVE), EDITED BY BOK SUNAM

Death by Hanging itself is a film into which many different types of citations have been interwoven; the main texts that it cites are the trial transcripts from the Ri Chin'u Incident, the trial verdict, and *Tsumi to shi to ai to*, published by Bok Sunam in 1963. The correspondence *Tsumi to shi to ai to* between Ri Chin'u, the condemned man, and Bok Sunam, who campaigned for Ri's rescue and was a member of the North Korean community in Japan, is an especially important text—without it this film would probably not have come into existence. Despite the fact that the correspondence was not acknowledged in the film credits by Oshima, it was well known that the film was made based on that correspondence.[25] In other words, circumstances at

us. As if someone might rape her! (Laughter.) She was probably seeing [us] through that kind of eye" (*Oshima Nagisa 1968*, 173). He also said, "For me, emotionally, feminism is something that has existed around me since childhood. Because my father passed away when I was seven, the environment I grew up in was very close to what you might call a female culture. That kind of thing came out naturally in *A Street of Love and Hope* (1959) and *Cruel Story of Youth* (1960). The problem in *Night and Fog in Japan* (1960) was that the student movement in Japan was premised on a kind of male chauvinism. I think I just filmed it the way it was. If it is true that women have a low profile ... it was probably because of the way Sōzōsha was structured at the time. ... It is probably true that Sōzōsha's dramaturgy at the time was based on the exclusion of women" (ibid., 174).

25. In *Oshima Nagisa 1968*, Oshima writes disparagingly, "The way that woman speaks represents the highly ideological (Japanese Communist) Yoyogi way of thinking. There's something funny about a woman doing that. In that sense, Bok Sunam was that kind of character." He adds on page 167, "Bok Sunam is one of the Sōren (General Association of Korean Residents in Japan) people. Although I took my subject matter from her book, I didn't mention it. There was no reaction to that from Bok. That's odd, too (laughter). It suggests how closed the society of North Koreans in Japan is. At the same time, it can be said that our way of dealing with that society is also closed. I presented a reaction against that in the film, though." (Translator's note: Here Oshima alludes to the fact that Bok was a member of the General Association of Korean

the time were such that even people who had not read the correspondence knew that it was the basis for the film.

In their letters, Ri Chin'u calls Bok Sunam "Sister," an appellation borrowed by Oshima to use in his film. In the film, Sister is the one who explains to R the history behind the status of *zainichi* Koreans, as well as the discrimination directed toward them, urging R to assume his ethnic identity. Yet this Sister is not exactly the same person as the Bok Sunam in the correspondence. Rather, she transmutes into an existence that might even be called Sister Oshima. For example, let us read the following lines:

> Woman: "As a Korean in Japan, I am angry and sad that this person has become like this! R, you're not R anymore. You've lost R's spirit! Lost the Korean spirit! You're now only a culprit! A murderer! No, you wouldn't even be able to commit a deed like this! That's right! You never did commit a crime! How could you have? The real R, after committing his murders, called the police, as if he had been challenging all Japan! What do you think about that!"
>
> R: "... ..."
>
> Woman: "R's crime was a Korean crime. A dark and detestable one! But, that was the only way that the persecuted Koreans could make the Japanese pay with blood for the Koreans' blood shed because of them. In the name of the Japanese nation-state, the Japanese have murdered innumerable Koreans. However, for us, who do not have a nation, there is nothing else we can do except to make the Japanese bleed using our own, individual hands. That is what is called a crime! Yes, there is something distorted about this! But even in such a crime the pride and sorrows of the Korean people are concentrated. R! Your crime was that kind of crime, was it not? Answer me!"
>
> R: "Sister, what you are talking about is getting further and fur-

---

Residents in Japan, which was sympathetic to North Korea.) Oshima also says, "From start to finish I never had a single meeting with Bok. You would think that we had to meet, since I cited her work. But I decided never to meet her. At that point in time, I wouldn't have been able to demolish her positions no matter how much I wanted to. The very fact of meeting her would have been a loss for me and a plus for her. Nothing could possibly trump this woman's lines— "Please repent of your sin and become a splendid Korean." It's probably fair to say that I'm completely put off by that kind of thinking, instinctively. But there are people who can't help but fall in love with such logic after hearing it" (ibid., 172).

ther away from R. If what you described is really the way R is, then I feel that I'm not R at all."[26]

My intention is not to point out the fact that Bok Sunam did not write the above lines in her letters. To be very accurate about what Oshima did, I should say that—using a perfectly common representational strategy—he borrowed the character Sister from Bok's correspondence and used her to explicitly express a theory of rebellion that corresponded to his own theories of nation and revolution. That he did this is linked to the image of Sister in the film, who is Oshima's stereotypical nationalist, which is a problem.[27]

The first half of the speech of Sister Oshima reflects the antiestablishment thought and notion of revolt held by Oshima and his coproducers, and resonates with the radicalism of the 1960s New Left and underground counterculture. Her agitation in the form of her negations—"You're now only a culprit! A murderer! No, you wouldn't even be able to commit a deed like this!"—affirms the association of crime with an act of revolt. This, at the same time, is linked to the glorification and romanticization of the criminal as a hero whose rebellious actions have encroached upon the order of the state. We could call these lines the bombast of Sister Oshima, who is seeking an outlaw hero (who is simultaneously rebel and criminal).

Moreover, in the second half of her speech, Sister emphasizes a similar definition of the rebel and nationalist. "But, that was the only way that the persecuted Koreans could make the Japanese pay with blood for the Koreans' blood that was shed because of [the] Japanese"—this speech of Sister, alleging that R's crime is of this type, is distant not only from R, who expresses a feeling of discomfort with her statement in the film, but also from the Sister who was the historical Bok Sunam.

---

26. The citations of the scenario of *Death by Hanging* used in this essay are from *Sekai no eiga sakka 6*. The page numbers for the script are not indicated.

27. Yang Insil, "Sengo nihon eiga ni okeru 'zainichi' joseizō" [The image of the *zainichi* woman in Japanese postwar cinema], *Ritsumeikan sangyō shakai ronshū* 39, no. 2 (September 2003), 35–55. He writes, "'Sister' is not only the spokesperson for R's ethnic identity but also speaks lines that question the legitimacy of the nation-state named 'Japan,' which can be seen as a message from the director. Furthermore, when such lines come from the mouth of a woman in the *chima jeogori* dress, we can assume they take on more persuasive power for the audience" (41). In his article, Yang brings up the problem of the absence of attention to *zainichi* Korean women in critical writing on the film, although in the film they are made present through the *chima chogori* and the dialogue.

In any case, in the theory of Sister Oshima in the film, R's crime, although distorted in its form, is given the status of an act of revolt by a persecuted Korean who has been crushed by the state, and is justified in that context. Seen in these terms, R is an innocent existence countering a state that forever makes him a criminal. In this sense, the antistate logic in *Death by Hanging* is coherent.

R's last words in the film are also suffused with Oshima's vision of vanquishing the state. R's argument that "as long as there is something that wants to sentence me guilty, in other words, as long as there is the state, I remain innocent" embodies a philosophy of revolt that seeks to challenge the state's right to judge and punish. The Public Prosecutor's response to Ri— "We cannot allow thinking like this to exist"—demonstrates the absolute consistency of the logic of the state, which cannot tolerate revolt or subversive thinking. Martyrdom is necessary if the state's consistency in this logic is to be represented. At the conclusion of the film, R takes upon himself the role of martyr in order to counter the state and overcome its logic.[28] The intertitle "R ACCEPTS BEING R FOR THE SAKE OF ALL Rs" inserted in this scene conveys nothing less than a theory of martyrdom.

What has been made invisible in Oshima's film, however, is a different logic of how to counter the state, the logic maintained by Bok Sunam. Bok's logic accepts the contradictions of Ri's life in their entirety and, facing a Ri who was directly confronting his own crimes, struggles to bring him back to an awareness of that contradiction-filled reality. Inherent in this is a philosophical project that stands at the other extreme of the logic of martyrdom. Moreover, the projects of awakening and ethnic self-awareness Bok advocates exist on a different register from the logic of the "inner state" denounced in their own ways by Yajima and Oshima. The awakening that Bok Sunam, in her letters, seeks from Ri Chin'u is one in which he would recover his ethnic identity while at the same time coming to terms with the crimes of rape and murder that until then he had only been able to feel as "something seen through a veil," thus making the dignity of his female victims come alive once more within his own life. That something like this was experienced by R is acknowledged in *Death by Hanging* in the segment titled "R FINALLY BECOMES R," a segment based on Ri Chin'u's own words written to Bok

---

28. Nozaki Rokusuke's *Ri Chin'u nōto—shikei ni sareta zainichi chōsenjin* [Notes on Ri Chin'u: A *zainichi* Korean executed in Japan] (Tokyo: San'ichi shobō, 1994), 67–71, deals with the topic of "the political martyr in *Death by Hanging*." Nozaki notes critically that in this film, there is no need to ask whether R is guilty or not, for he is described as a political martyr.

Sunam. Ri's letter to Bok dated August 7, 1962, was a long one that he had been intermittently working on since August 3 of that year. In that letter, Ri stated that through the emotions he himself was experiencing, which he described as "falling in love with Sister [Bok Sunam]," the existence of "the murdered girls" was being brought back in his heart.[29]

> It was I who did it. The I who thinks this is the I who did it. However, why is it that I can only feel the idea that "they were killed by me" as if it were from the behind a veil?[30]

> I can't express well what I wanted to say. But when I felt something strong for you, Sister, through those feelings I was able to feel close to the victims, who up until now had been distant to me. By deepening my feelings for you, I wanted to bring that matter right into my heart.
> It was in this way that I tried to bring the victims back to life in my heart.[31]

Bok Sunam was both witness and supporter of a process in which a young man, who at the time of the killings was seen as a "fiendish murderer who was 'neither Japanese nor Korean,' and whose inner self was so divided that his own experience of the killings was 'as distant as a dream within a dream,'" delved into his own self.[32] In response to the way people like Bok Sunam reached out to him, that young man's body, "little by little, began to move," as Bok Sunam later wrote.[33] Moreover, Bok Sunam's gaze is also directed toward "the girls who were killed," of whom Ri wrote, "When the value of my own existence, of which I had been robbed, began to pulsate again, the value and dignity of the lives of the girls that 'I killed' became one with it and began to breathe."[34] This gaze is what is missing from Sister Oshima.

---

29. Bok, *Tsumi to shi to ai to*, 156.

30. Letter dated August 6, 1962, in ibid., 155–156.

31. Ibid., 159.

32. Bok Sunam, "Shinpan no tame no maegaki" (Preface for the new edition), in ibid., 3.

33. Bok Sunam, "Kaisetsu—Komatsugawa jiken, Ri Chin'u to mou hitori no R-tachi" [Commentary: The Komatsugawa Incident, Ri Chin'u, and another R], in *Ri Chin'u Zenshokanshū* [Ri Chin'u's collected letters], ed. Bok Sunam (Shinjinbutsu ōrai sha, 1979), 67.

34. Ibid., 69.

At that time in the 1960s, Bok Sunam was a nationalist active in the struggle to seek unification of the homeland on the split Korean Peninsula. However, it turned out that in the course of her efforts to save the life of Ri Chin'u, she was repudiated by the same "homeland" that repudiated Ri Chin'u as an "outrageous criminal" who should not be allowed to exist. This repudiation of Ri Chin'u, convicted as "a fiendish rapist and killer," meant that he could never be a "citizen" of North Korea, and Bok Sunam's action of reaching out to such a criminal as a compatriot was also repudiated.

In this way, Bok Sunam experienced what she described as a "sad exile similar to a deportation" from the North Korean community in Japan.[35] She wrote that she endured "being pelted by stones of denial" wherever she went, and a persecution that was "close to being a witch hunt." She described being "like a beast with serious wounds all over its body," from which she "licked off the blood while gnashing her teeth." Whereas Bok Sunam presented Ri Chin'u (who was being cast as someone who "deeply disgraced and hurt the prestige and dignity of our people") as "a lonely beast" or "a hungry beast," she also spoke of herself as "a beast with deep wounds all over its body" during this time when her very existence, as someone who was reaching out to Ri Chin'u, was denied by the logic of the "state" and when she was forbidden to "speak out."[36]

The struggle of the people Bok calls "unrecognized," of people like Bok herself, who experienced "doubled denial and exile" from both the Japanese state and the "homeland," offers a perspective that allows us to objectify our "states within." Bok Sunam wrote that, as someone "continuously living with contradictions and conflicts" that exist in the gap between one state and another, she longed "to create a new existence that has yet to be named."[37] This struggle of the lonely beast "with deep wounds all over its body," moreover, also slips into Soni Kum's work.

3. THE MONOLOGUE OF THE "BEAST": *KEMONO TO NARITEMO/ BEAST OF ME*

Although Kum's video work *Beast of Me* (2005) was made in California, she appears in it wearing a Korean ethnic school uniform—the *chima jeogori*

---

35. Bok Sunam, "Hosetsu—nijū no hi'nin to tsuihō o ikite, ninchisarenai mono-tachi" [Appendix: Surviving the dual denial and exile—people who are not recognized], in ibid., 452.

36. Ibid., 446–452.

37. Ibid., 455.

dress—and is herself its narrator. To borrow Lee Chonghwa's words, in the monologue of Kum's "beast of me," we hear the mumbling of "memories of the wounds engraved in the *chima jeogori* and of the body that has become the *chima jeogori*." Kum's way of expressing herself here is "to mumble," or "to complain—*neokduri*."[38]

The traditional Korean *chima chogori* dress is used as the uniform of Korean ethnic schools in Japan. It has become a symbol of ethnic resistance within a Japanese society that is full of discrimination against *zainichi* Koreans, and has thus become a target of violence by the Japanese. Female students who wear the *chima jeogori* uniform and go to or from school every day during rush hours are particularly vulnerable to this kind of violence, including abusive language, beating, slashing, and sexual harassment by Japanese men. *Beast of Me* makes this vulnerability of the *zainichi* Korean female students its focal point. At the same time, Kum's video exposes a body which is not in harmony with the compulsory policy of the Korean ethnic schools, which force only young women compatriots to wear the *chima jeogori* as an ethnic uniform, in an effort to maintain the schools as a space within Japanese society where Korean ethnic identity can be cultivated.

Beast of Me opens with a scene of singing and dancing performances by girls from a Korean ethnic school. In this group performance, the schoolgirls, from their position under a hostile "foreign" sky, sing and dance while they look at the heavens, thinking of the "homeland" that is far away, with patriotism burning in their hearts, vowing their faith, and wishing long life to their leader. In contrast to this vivid dancing scene is the scene which follows, in which we see the figure of Soni Kum, wearing a simple black-and-white *chima jeogori* dress, sitting alone amid clumps of grass with her arms around her knees.

Kum's narration is neither directed toward the camera nor toward the spectators. It is not addressed to anybody, but is rather a mumbling. What comes to our ears is multilingual—we hear Kum's voice in Japanese, English, and Korean at the same time. The least audible of these is Korean, and can

---

38. Lee Chonghwa, *Ritsumeikan Gengo Bunka Kenkyū*, 51–52, note 2: "I wanted to talk a little more just about the way she sits—how she pulls on her hair, sitting there. It is as if there is some 'trace of madness there'; in my words, she is 'mumbling' (*tsubuyaku*) or 'complaining,' or, in Korean, *neokduri*. *Neokduri* refers to the mumbling sounds that come out of people's mouths at the instant when their souls fly away or when they are gripped by a certain emotion. In Soni Kum's video, too, these sounds are a mixture of Korean, Japanese, and English. Although narrated in her normal voice, the sounds seem to go on and on."

hardly be heard. The most clearly heard is English. However, all of the languages vibrate through Kum's body that is strangely tensed up yet brooding.

Kum's hands clasped tightly together while they rest on her knees emanate raw emotion. When she starts to narrate, these clasped hands on her garment take on a reddish color, as does her tense-looking face. The gaze of the camera closing in on her body exudes the same tension and anxiety. The camera does not focus in on a certain point, but instead creates a blur, moving from the side of her body to the front, to her long black hair, her neck, throat, chest, the whole upper body under the white *chogori*, and the pleats of the black *chima*.

What Kum mumbles about to no one in particular is the senseless, unhappy experience of wearing her *chima jeogori* uniform and becoming the target of a molester on her way to school. She describes how every morning, in order to avoid hostile glances and behavior from the Japanese, she had "concentrated her mind, trying not to look anyone in the eye, and just moved her feet forward."[39] Having been forced to live under the constant tension of being exposed to violence, she encountered the day during rush hour when she was molested and, cowering with fear, found herself too frightened to scream. She describes her sense of shame and displeasure in being the object of unwanted sexual attention, and in looking behind herself in the bloodshot eyes of the drunken molester, "intensely desirous of my body." Moreover, she tells us that her mother had questioned why only the girl students in Korean ethnic schools were required to wear the national dress as their uniforms, and had demanded that the school withdraw the policy in order to protect students from violence, only to find her request ignored. Here was seen both a violence descending relentlessly from the outside and one invisibly hidden within. Her narration is a monologue that is almost impossible to hear, slipping out from a "beast with serious wounds all over its body," who has been enduring a "doubled denial."

In this video work, we find a representation of several other bodies in contrast to Kum's body. As mentioned earlier, we first see the dancing bodies of the girls singing aloud of Korean national identity in the opening scene. Although this is in strong contrast to the body of Kum, who sits alone outside, the girl dancers are not represented as something completely different and estranged. For Kum, who since childhood had been trained in Korean dance at her school, the bodily comportment, womanliness, faithfulness,

---

39. Quoted from Soni Kum's naration in *Beast of Me* (2005).

gracefulness, obedience, and orderliness seen in the dances were inscribed as such on her body. It is Kim's own awareness that her own body and those of the dancers have been gendered and nationalized in the same way that allows her to set them in contrast. Hers, then, is not a gaze that looks at the girls' bodies as Other.

This is linked to the question of what kind of gaze we ourselves direct toward the representation of these schoolgirls. When women artists make use of women's traditional ethnic costumes, dances, mannerisms, gestures, and makeup in their work, we are apt to criticize them for essentialism in their representations of gender, national identity, or ethnicity. In our eyes, these seem to be bodies separate from our own; they are particular, and characterized by their otherness. But can we simply relegate the qualities of having been gendered and nationalized to the "oppressed"? Put differently, can we really say that the processes of gendering and nationalizing are not pertinent to ourselves? The narration and representations of the body in Kum's videos require us to question what kind of positionality and gaze would allow us to confront the pain and scars our own experiences of being gendered and nationalized have left us with.

Another kind of body used as a point of contrast in Kum's video is the flock of goats, which gives the sense of being a representational strategy intended to decenter the boundaries we ascribe to bodies. Overlapping with the scene of the seemingly peaceful flock of goats grazing in a pasture is the voice of a woman victim of U.S. nuclear testing in the Marshall Islands.[40] The voice-over tells of her multiple experiences of pregnancy, miscarriage, and stillbirth. We hear of a deformed shape attached to her placenta, not even recognizable as human; of a son who did not survive a month after being born; of residents of the island who were transported to a large American army hospital and used as guinea pigs in medical experiments. The contrast here is between the bodies of humans who were treated like animals and the "bodies" of the carefree goats "placidly" eating grass. Yet here the body exposed to violence does not just refer to human beings but also includes animals, plants, and the land—that is, the body "damaged" by radiation.

The last contrasting body is introduced through the citation of images from the feature film *Wolmido* (Gyong-sun Cho, 1983) made in North

---

40. From the documentary film *Half Life* by Dennis O'Rourke (1985). It is a film about the testimony of the residents who were affected by nuclear fallout, because they were not relocated during the testing of nuclear weapons at the U.S. military base in the Marshall Islands.

Korea. *Wolmido* is a state-produced action film, depicting the heroic battle of North Korean soldiers, all of whom sacrificed their lives to defend the island of Wolmido from an American army during the Korean War. The film contains a scene in which a young female signal corps member is singing to comfort her fellow soldiers, while we see the image of a hometown for which the soldiers' longing is evoked by her song. In *Beast of Me*, as a female signal corps member sings—"Ah / My hometown / The hill covered by blooming wildflowers / My one and only homeland"—the image of a hill covered by blooming wildflowers appears, together with images of the signal corps member and her younger sister, wearing blouses and skirts, reading a book and talking to each other with bright smiles on their faces. Coming at the conclusion of *Beast of Me*, however, Kum has removed the soundtrack from this scene. Instead, the images are accompanied by her own voice-over reading Yu Chihwan's line—"even if it make a beast of me"—as the final line of the work.

These cited fragments of film and poetry, taken out of context, do not leave spectators like ourselves (who do not know the contexts) with the sense that the film concludes as a satisfying whole. Together, they throw into vivid relief a longing for an as yet unrealized, because partitioned, "hometown ... my one and only homeland." At the same time, however, when we juxtapose these fragmentary images and lines in Kum's concluding segment with the opening scenes of the schoolgirls' patriotic dance, with Kum's monologue (as the "beast with serious wounds all over its body," tensed up in the face of its "doubled denial"), with the image of the silent flock of goats, and with testimony of the female Marshall Islands victim, they resonate with each other while functioning on different registers rather than collapsing into some unitary meaning. These contrasting representations of bodies that continue to be exposed to different types of violence, including the silent flock of goats, serve to decenter the boundaries and outline of the embodied self that has endured "even though it makes a beast of me." Let me now turn to *Foreign Sky*, where Kum takes the same strategies to a different level.

4. FUNERAL: *FOREIGN SKY* (IKYŌ NO SORA)

The experimental documentary film *Foreign Sky* (2005) starts with Soni Kum's narration in Japanese. We are told that "this story is one that is not written in any formal documents in this society."[41] What will be narrated are the memories and history of Kum herself, who has "grown up listening to people's voices in a space where their history had been nullified, amidst forces that sought to erase their existence." The narrator explains that when she left this community and was exposed to the outside world, she was told her memories were "incorrect," and thus could not speak of them. The film was produced with the clear aim of "illuminating, one by one, the memory fragments that others have told me are mistaken."

A striking visual representation accompanies this brief narration in the opening scene. On the screen there is the sky, covered by dark clouds, and the surface of a wavy sea that reflects the sky. These images are intercut with images from the bicycle scene of R and Sister in *Death by Hanging*. Moreover, the fantasmic afterimage of the faces of R and Sister as the two roll down the slopes of the Arakawa River are superimposed on the image of a Jewish woman, lying down and clad in a slip or negligee.[42] This montage creates a very unique visual impression. The Japanese script (from the intertitles of *Death by Hanging*) is written over that body. In the close-ups of the face, breasts, and wrists of this woman, we see grimaces of pain so vivid one might say that they represent lost histories in contradistinction to official ones.

The montage that consists of the fantasy image from *Death by Hanging* scrolling over the body of the Jewish woman is repeated one more time in the second half of *Foreign Sky*. There it overlaps with a voice-over by Kum that tells about the same violence brought up in *Beast of Me*, the violence directed

---

41. Quoted from Kum's voice-over in *Foreign Sky*.

42. The woman is Kum's classmate, whose name is Loren Hartman. Hartman has made her career as an artist. I learned from Kum that Hartman is the descendant of concentration camp survivors. The two had discussed "how Hartman's work was linked to trauma which one inherited, a kind of contagious trauma, and how customs in a traditional Jewish family were related to Korean ones." Kum herself was striving to look at the Japan-Korea relation within the global historical context, and while becoming interested in postcolonial theory, was also thinking about the Holocaust in relation to the massacres of Koreans (interview with Kum, September 2, 2008). The close relationship between the two is evident from the fact that they appear as subjects in each other's video work. I should caution, however, that these detailed considerations are completely my own arbitrary reading. Moreover, in analyzing the woman's body as Jewish in spite of the fact that the image in the video is not really clear to the spectator, I am taking the risk of determining ethnic identity in an essentializing way. I have wanted to consider this image also in relation to the sexual abuse of Jewish women in Nazi concentration camps, a matter that has not yet been clearly discussed. But I should be fully aware of the violence that could be implicit in such arbitrary interpretations.

toward the bodies of Korean ethnic schoolgirls in the *chima jeogori* uniform. We hear the unidentified voice of a Japanese male, who has made a telephone call to a Korean school, threatening, "It is not a crime, no matter how many Korean pigs we kill!" and "Stop talking so big! You guys are just cockroaches," followed by the suggestive image of a torn-apart *chima*. Then we see, just as in the opening scene, the barely legible intertitles from R in *Death by Hanging*, R and Sister on their bicycles, and the faces of the two rolling down the riverbank, repeatedly superimposed on the body of the woman.

Such unexpected effects in Kum's work are probably not something accidental. We can certainly look at them in connection with different images that appear in *Death by Hanging*. In *Death by Hanging*, Oshima plays the voice-over of a speech by Hitler over images of the Korean community.[43] Oshima's striking idea of projecting Hitler's speech over the slum-like Korean community in postwar Japan can be read as producing an obvious analogy between it and the Jewish ghetto in Europe during World War II. Kum's insertion of the Jewish woman's body in *Foreign Sky* can be seen as creating the same kind of relationship and defamilizarizing effect. By introducing the body of a Jewish woman (not a Korean woman like Kum), she evokes other bodies colonized in the same way as a result of the violence of the Second World War. Here we are probably also reminded of Agamben's concept of *homo sacer*, or "the life that may be taken but which is impossible to sacrifice."

> The Jew living under Nazism is the privileged negative referent of the new biopolitical sovereignty and is, as such, a flagrant case of a homo sacer in the sense of *a life that may be killed but not sacrificed*. ... The Jews were exterminated not in a mad and giant holocaust but exactly as Hitler had announced, "as lice," which is to say, as bare life. The

---

43. Oshima wrote about these images of the Korean community in *Death by Hanging*, "They were filmed at Ri Chin'u's home. Although we were very open about what we were doing and there shouldn't have been any concerns about it, we used hidden cameras. ... We didn't do a trial run, but the shoot turned out to be okay without any rehearsal. When we left and walked toward the Arakawa River shore, we could feel on our backs the gaze full of questions and accusations from the people living in the Korean community. (Ri Chin'u's mother was said to be among them.)" See Matsuda Masao, "A Filmmaker's Diary—*Death by Hanging*, II," in *Eiga Hyōron*, June 1968, as cited in *Oshima Nagisa 1968*, 95. Oshima also mentions, in *Oshima Nagisa 1968*, that he inserted the soundtrack of a speech by Hitler, and sounds of the Vietnam War into the film.

dimension in which the extermination took place is neither religion nor law, but biopolitics.[44]

Sonia Ryang has introduced Agamben's *homo sacer* in discussing the massacre of Koreans at the time of the great Kanto earthquake, under the regime of the modern Japanese nation-state. While touching upon the constitution of the "sovereignty of the citizen (or subject)" under the emperor, she states the following:

> Each individual killer of Koreans *acted as sovereign* who killed homo sacer that did not belong to the political order and hence, killing them did not violate anything. As such, it would be erroneous to understand the mass killing of Koreans in 1923 as violence. It did not even constitute violence, in the sense of the term violence as a violation of the person of a free man.[45]

"Rather than being an unexpected hiccup in the process of Japanese modernity," the massacre of the Koreans who were excluded from the "sovereignty of the citizen (or subject)" of imperial Japan at the time of the great Kanto earthquake was "a logical and ordinary outcome of the way Japan emerged as a modern nation, in the form of an exclusively Japanese nation, where *sovereignty is indissolubly connected with nationality*."[46] The threat that we hear in *Foreign Sky* from the unidentified Japanese male who called the Korean ethnic school to say, "It is not a crime no matter how many *Korean pigs* we kill" and "Stop talking big! You guys are just *cockroaches*," reveals the consciousness of "sovereignty" that the Japanese "citizen" possesses, which has not changed although it has been eighty years since the Great Kanto earthquake. The striking strategies of representation that Oshima and Kum invoke call attention to the fact that even in the postwar, Japanese citizens continue to behave as "sovereign" in relation to the the "bare life" of Koreans who had been subjected to the colonial control of Hirohito's Japanese em-

---

44. Giorgio Agamben, *Homo Sakeru: Shuken kenryoku to mukidashi no sei* [Homo sacer: Sovereign power and bare life], trans. Takakuwa Kazumi (Ibunsha, 2003), 161, author's emphasis.

45. Sonia Ryang, *Korean diasupora: Zainichi chōsenjin to aidentiti* [Korean diaspora: Zainichi Koreans and identity], trans. Nakanishi Kyoko (Akashi Shoten, 2005), 41, author's emphasis.

46. Ibid., 45, author's emphasis.

pire. They seem to suggest that these behaviors are comparable to the barbarous actions whereby Jews were massacred "just as if they were lice" in Nazi Germany.

The documentary film *Foreign Sky* is a text that consists of the citations of various historical materials. It constitutes an archive drawing on media such as visual materials and photographs with historical significance, including Japanese and foreign films, TV programs, documentary films, feature films, and videos of hearings held by international tribunals. Kum's text calls attention to both continuities and discontinuities in a way that heightens defamiliarizing effects. Thus *Foreign Sky* itself is an archive that reconstitutes all kinds of memories, temporalities, and spaces. Buried in that archive, however, in addition to footage from the television news programs of the type we are accustomed to watching every day, are also quite a few historical materials that will be unfamiliar to most spectators. Kum uses these selectively for their visual and/or aural effect. Nevertheless, her reconstitution of those familiar and unfamiliar materials does not convey a complete, official history.

Rather, by interweaving messages from various media, the film once again reminds us that in our daily lives, we select images and information from what is circulating generally in the mass media, reconstituting them as history by ourselves. Having been raised in a North Korean ethnic community in Japan, Kum brings many sources into play, including those we are not ordinarily exposed to. But what she directs her gaze to are the disparities, the biases, and differences that exist between and among these images and information sources. Rather than designating which are the correct ones, she clarifies the historical contexts and the sources of her information, allowing us to see what kind of information or image is produced from what kind of position.

Among the representational strategies used in *Foreign Sky*, what especially stands out is the way Kum mixes together images from news and documentary films and images from feature films. News films and documentary films do not in and of themselves equal unmediated truth. Instead, they are processed and edited by the producer, and come into being based on the disposition of the camera's gaze, angles, and frames. It is as true of documentary as of fictional films that in all of them the producer's vision and representational strategies are involved in producing whatever reality they present. In Kum's experimental documentary, then, what is consistent is her drive to destabilize the represented images by opening them up and exposing them to their historical contexts, thus denaturalizing them and historicizing them. I also want to touch on the estranging effects produced by the use of multiple languages in this film. Kum's own narration is in Japanese throughout; but there are subtitles in English, and the English and Korean languages can also be heard in the segments extracted from documentary films and fictional films. These plural languages mix and resonate with each other not only in the formal historical documents Kum refers to, but also in the confidential, private relationships she depicts. The video in this way becomes a space open to heterogeneous spectators and listeners, while at the same time creating a kind of contested site where languages compete with and cancel each other out. It is a space where we may test our own politics of listening.

One of the topics about which Kum has most emphasized the existence of disparities, gaps, and differences between and among available images and information is the Korean War. Drawing on footage made during that period that had barely been known to us previously, she tries to answer questions about how the Cold War division of Korea along the thirty-eighth parallel impacted those who had been fighting in both the North and South at the time. For example, the video shows film produced during an investigation carried out in 1951, at the height of the Korean War, by the International Women's Inquiry Commission, an offshoot of the border-crossing peace movement of the time.[47] The documentary made by the commission provides accounts of the massacre of civilians by American soldiers in the South in the period preceding the start of the war.

Other footage, the sources of which are made very clear, also shows investigations into the status of Korean War victims. One is the video recording of the international gathering organized by some members of the South Korean

---

47. The International Women's Inquiry Commission, which included representatives from seventeen countries, is discussed in detail in the chapter, "Amerika-gun no zangyaku kōi: Kokusai fujin chōsadan" [Atrocities committed by the U.S. Army: The International Women's Inquiry Commission], in *Kokuren-gun no hanzai: Minshu/josei kara mita chōsen sensō* [Crimes by United Nations forces: The Korean War seen through the eyes of women and ordinary people], ed. Fujime Yuki (Fuji Shuppan, 2000). Fujime touches upon the fact that "crimes by soldiers of the United Nations forces" during the Korean War have been hidden from view, and that the truth has been hard to reveal. She writes, "Especially when discussions about 'North Korea's responsibility in starting the war' became popular in the 1990s, the simple facts that the Korean War would not have happened without Japan's and America's invasions, and that the peoples of South/North Korea suffered greatly because of the invasion of the United Nations forces, seem to have disappeared somewhere" (10). According to Kum, the video of the field investigation by the International Women's Inquiry Commission used by her is an excerpt from a documentary about the Korean War made in North Korea. In North Korea, the Korean War is called "the war to liberate the homeland."

government's Truth Commission, together with American and European activists, for the purpose of hearing testimony about these matters some fifty years after the end of the war. The video reveals that certain groups of witnesses from both North and South Korea were denied entry to the United States on the occasion of the Korean International War Crimes Tribunal convened in New York on June 23, 2001, and that to compensate for that footage was displayed at the gathering of a public hearing of such testimony held in Pyongyang.[48] In this video, we see a team of international investigators listening to the testimony of a North Korean woman who was shot by American soldiers when she was seven years old and lost both of her arms.

In addition to the testimony of victims, Kum cites other documentaries which present testimonials from perpetrators. There is a scene in which two American soldiers who fought in the Korean War testify that, following their superior's command to "kill everyone," they shot soldiers and civilians indiscriminately, including young girls. In these scenes, we hear how the soldiers have been haunted by nightmares of the young girls they killed. As a contrast to the former soldiers' facial expressions, which register pain as they speak about their memories of children whom they cannot forget even if they try to, a scene of contemporary girl students in North Korea singing the praises of their country is shown by Kum. In the alternation between these two scenes, the gaze of the audience is destabilized. As a result, we start to question our own positionality and viewpoint as spectators of *Foreign Sky*, while being constantly made aware of the mediating and editing functions carried out by the video's producer.

While the Korean War, in which so many Korean lives were lost, left the Korean Peninsula exhausted, it brought an economic recovery to Japan, because of special procurement contracts Japan received. Here, too, Kum includes documentary footage to illuminate the contrast. In the scenes presented we see fully operating factories manufacturing war supplies, and also

---

48. On June 23, 2001, the Korean International War Crimes Tribunal organized an international tribunal in New York to interrogate war crimes committed by the American military between the end of World War II and the Korean War. In the footage we see in *Foreign Sky*, the focus is on the Sinchon Massacre (1950), but the long-term focus of the tribunal itself has been on war crimes committed under the American military occupation which commenced as soon as the Pacific War ended. The tribunal also calls attention to war crimes committed by the Korean Army with the backing of the American military, including the Jeju April 3 Massacre and other incidents (http://www.iacenter.org/Koreafiles/ktc-contents.htm). A different set of facts concerning the Sinchon Massacre has been delved into by novelists and historians in the wake of the tribunal hearings.

zainichi Korean workers who survive by scavenging for iron scraps in garbage dumps. During the Cold War, Japan regained its status within international society by shouldering the burden of supporting the maneuvers of the U.S. military. These were the circumstances under which, according to the 1951 Treaty of San Francisco, Japan unilaterally deprived *zainichi* Koreans of Japanese nationality, forcing them to choose to identify with either the North Korean or South Korean regimes, while those who did not were subject to repressive administrative policies as "refugees." At this juncture, the Korean ethnic schools, built in various places in Japan so that *zainichi* Koreans could learn the language, history, and culture they had been deprived of under colonialism, were pressured to close by the Japanese government, but the move was resisted. Rare footage of this struggle has also been inserted into *Foreign Sky*.

Kum uses newsreels and documentaries to represent the Repatriation to North Korea Project which the North Korean government commenced in 1959. But she also includes a scene from Urayama Kirio's fictional film *Kyuupora no aru machi* (Foundry Town, 1962), in which we hear the voice of a Japanese girl who goes to see off a *zainichi* Korean girl and her younger brother who are leaving Japan.[49] Images showing the faces of *zainichi* Koreans boarding ships going to the North, as well as of the people seeing them off and farewell scenes at the harbor, are superimposed on the excerpts from Urayama's film. Kum here, however, does not actually show the characters in the film, but only lets us hear the words of farewell that are exchanged between the girls. Out of the darkness on the screen emerges Kum's voice, stating that "many *zainichi* Korean compatriots, fired up by the dream of rebuilding their communist homeland, returned to the North, after which they were never able to return to Japan." This moment opens up a space where we can entertain the illusion that those people who will never be represented in either documentary or fictional films somehow exist.

Kum experiments with a different way of linking voice and sound in the segments where she herself visits the "homeland" for the first time during an excursion from her Korean high school. Here, unlike in the segment just described, she features no sound or narration at all, and creates a purely visual exposition composed by shooting filmed images with her video camera.

---

49. *Kyuupora no aru machi* [Foundry town, 1962] was the debut film of Urayama Kirio (1930–1985). It deals with the parting between the protagonists—a Japanese girl (played by Yoshinaga Sayuri) and her younger brother, and a Korean girl and her younger brother who are moving to the North with their family.

The smiling faces of Korean high school students, the clear sky, the paddy fields with the stalks of rice waving, the dancing and singing of the North Korean children who welcomed them, and the scenery observed from the bus windows are all represented without sound. Consequently, we spectators feel something impedes us from going closer to the silent objects under the video camera. Kum's voice-over only cites her diary to describe her impressions at that time, and this itself increases our sense of estrangement from the objects being filmed.

Kum also focuses on the gap between what she herself saw and heard during her school trip and what has been reported about North Korea in Japan's media. Breaking news about North Korea in 2002 was conveyed in shots taken by a hidden camera, depicting starving children and black markets in North Korea. Another news program about purges of Japanese wives of *zainichi* returnees, and of political criminals, features the testimony of someone who claims to be a former spy in North Korea. But neither Kum nor we spectators have the ability to tell whether these reports are true or false. Instead, Kum gives attention to the anti–North Korean sentiment such media reports provoke in Japanese society. That is because every time North Korean issues are taken up in the Japanese media, such sentiment transforms into violence against *zainichi* Koreans, especially against female students wearing the *chima jeogori* uniforms.

Just as in *Beast of Me*, Kum in these segments expresses her discomfort with the gender hierarchy within the *zainichi* community that makes it the female students' obligation to wear the *chima jeogori* uniforms as "a link in the chain of resistance" against the layers of discrimination and brutality directed against them. At the same time, the fact that it was a Japanese friend close to Kum who exploded at her in anger toward North Korea urges us to pay attention to the violence that can be bred by the very lack of historical knowledge about Japanese colonialism among younger generations of Japanese. Moreover, by inserting into this narration the images of the Jewish woman's body overwritten by images from *Death by Hanging* (as I described earlier), Kum provides a doubled image of the female body that is exposed to different types of violence.

In another contrast to the media reports, we are told the story of a relative of Kum who was arrested and executed as a political prisoner. Kum discovered an old letter addressed to her mother from a female relative who returned to the North and never came back. In that letter "there is not a single word that tells of the harshness of life in North Korea or criticizes the current regime." As we see the relative's letter written in Hangul, we hear the voice of an absent female speaking Korean, accompanied by English subtitles, while Kum's voice-over calmly speaks of a relative who was executed in North Korea. This introduces new rifts among the different sources of information introduced in the video: the footage from TV and other media, as well as the historical videos, photographs, and images from the past. Here we encounter words exchanged within individual and private space, such as the letters and information found in the private space of Kum's family and relatives, which differ from the kinds of information circulated in the discursive space of public media.

As a way of wrapping up the succession of disparate and defamiliarizing citations from various media she has used, Kum switches for her last scene to a highway in Los Angeles, where she lived in early 2000. In the automobile-centered U.S. world, the road Kum walks on is not designed for pedestrians. The fear she experienced as she walked this highway to reach her university, with cars roaring by, was similar to the tension she felt wearing her *chima chogori* uniform to school in Tokyo, but also different, Kum says. Ironically enough, along the highway we are shown a sign designating it a Korean War Veterans Memorial Highway. Moreover, our eyes are assaulted by the images of small animals that have been hit by cars and left lying in the lanes. Kum's voice-over states, "I wonder if the people in those cars know that they have hit an animal, if they feel the pain of the animals they hit, or perhaps just don't realize they hit anything." In this final segment, we see Kum herself for the first time, picking up the dead body of one of the small animals heart-lessly hit and left to die beside the highway. She carries it to a small hill, digs a grave, and buries it. The teeth, limbs, and claws of the small body lying in the hole are striking. While mounding soil onto the grave, Kum prays that the animal can return to the earth, absorb sunlight and water, and live again as nourishment for plants.

In *Beast of Me*, a focus was put on such things as the flock of goats, and the situation of local residents who had been exposed to fallout from nuclear testing and treated as animals. In *Foreign Sky*, too, the bodies of silent animals that have been run over and thrown to the side of the road by cars are made a focal point. They are the "bare lives" exposed to the violence of a callous, speeded-up modernity. Ultimately, in *Foreign Sky*, Kum goes beyond expressing her grief over the "cannibalism" of human beings, who annihilate each other with the advanced killing techniques they have mastered in the modern civilization of the machine (for whose invention wars were the provocation), and attempts to mourn for its innumerable "victims" that include small animals and "beasts."[50]

Kum's documentary film opens with scenes of Seoul and the surrounding countryside under Japan's colonial rule in the early 1920s and, by incorporating a massive amount of historical materials and citing images and information from various media, challenges our assumptions as spectators. Kum's personal narration regarding historical events that have so far received little coverage introduces rifts into the official narratives, and opens up a space available for hallucinations and imaginings of the "bare lives" of countless people/"beasts" whose existences have been erased. It is both an individual and a collective archive of memories. However, the work stands and is supported by a certain methodology. While maintaining full awareness that memory itself is "always being reconstituted and narrated" on the basis of omissions, new emphases, and new scriptings, Kum says, "I sought to develop fictional materials in the manner of a documentary, and thus to allow for a sharing of my own 'vulnerability' with the spectator."[51] It seems to me that, in confronting Kum's video works, we as spectators are also able to attain the profound gaze into the "vulnerability" that is an inevitable product of our own historical existences.

Kum's *Foreign Sky* attempts to "tell, through a personal narrative, the typical story of a girl who was commuting to a Korean ethnic school in Japan." It is "a fiction based on facts" (as Kum put it), that draws on her and her family's individual and collective experiences and memories, as well as on her own imagination. Exposed to the violence of being torn mentally by

---

50. Grief over cannibalism is described in the chapter "Cannibal" in Soni Kum's *Funeral* (2006). Kum produced *Funeral* as an essay in a creative writing course she took, while reading Deleuze and Guattari's *A Thousand Plateaus: Capitalism and Schizophrenia*, trans. Brian Massumi (Minneapolis: University of Minnesota Press, 1987), and Theresa Hak Kyung Cha's *Dictée* (Berkeley: University of California Press, 1982). The essay is a "lament" over the "cannibalism" of human beings who annihilate each other with the superior killing techniques developed during a century of wars. Kum here also takes up and discusses the links between violence directed toward women within the *zainichi* community and the construction of masculinity in *zainichi* families as a by-product of colonialism in the era of Japanese empire. These same issues of nationalization and gendering carried out within the community are described in *Beast of Me* and *Foreign Sky*.

51. Interview with Kum, September 2, 2008.

encountering the reports and representations of North Korea in the Japanese media, Kum has protested by reconstituting this "fiction." Her work is a powerful "counterattack" (in her words) which hides within itself "the quiet violence of a minority woman" who must endure being "a beast with deep wounds all over its body" while struggling to overturn that very situation.

TRANSLATED BY JUNLIANG HUANG AND BRETT DE BARY.

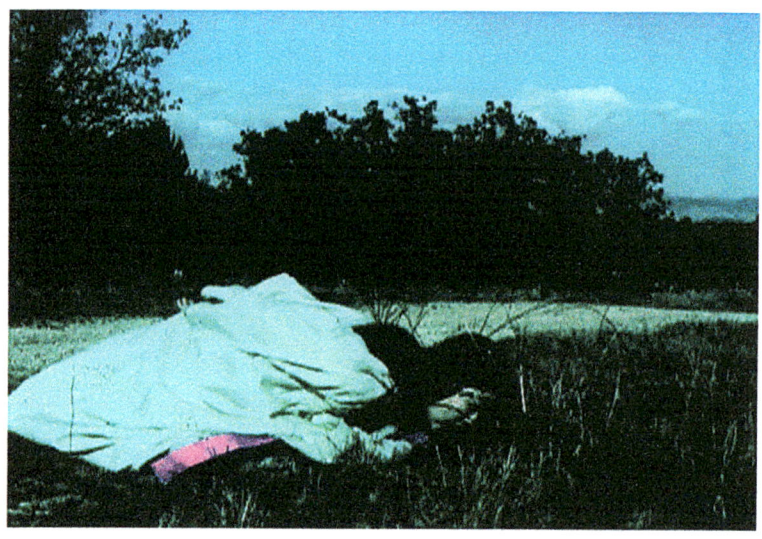

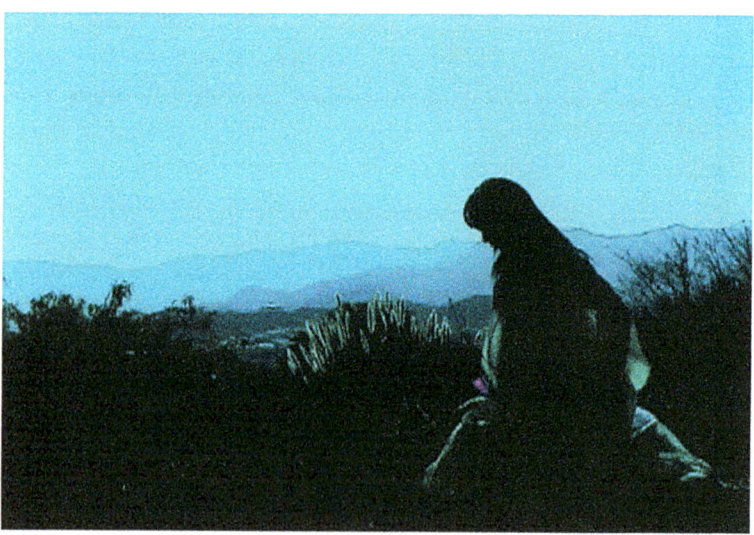

Soni Kum, *Sheep*, 2002, video, 6 min.

CHAPTER 7

"Postmemory" in the Work of Oh Haji and Soni Kum

Rebecca Jennison

INTRODUCTION

This chapter focuses on the work of two third-generation *zainichi* artists, Oh Haji and Soni Kum. In thinking about where to locate these artists, Homi Bhabha's description of "borderline artists" is useful. Bhabha paid tribute to the work of borderline artists when discussing cultural diversity in the arts within the European context in the early 1990s, arguing that their explorations of personal histories and experiences of migration and displacement speak to larger issues facing contemporary European societies. His essay was part of a project that aimed to reenvision the role of art and participation by artists in European cities. Bhabha writes,

> The borderline artist performs a poetics of the open-border between cultures. She displays the 'interstices,' the overlappings and interweavings, the hither and thither that is part of the history of those people whose identities are crafted from the experience of social displacement.[1]

This is a slightly abridged and edited version of the original essay. See Ikeuchi Yasuko's essay (chapter 6, this volume) and interviews with the artists on the DVD.

1. Homi Bhabha, "Beyond the Pale: Art in the Age of Multicultural Translation," in *Cultural Diversity in the Arts: Art, Art Policies and the Facelift of Europe* (Royal Tropical Institute, The Netherlands, 1993), 24.

Although emerging from a very different context, these artists draw on personal experiences of borders between cultures; moreover, in the "interstices" we come to glimpse through their works, we discover traces of complex and contested histories that still haunt the present. On the relationship of past and present in works by such artists, Bhabha goes on to write,

> [The borderline work of art] does not merely recall the past as social cause or aesthetic precedent, it renews the past, refiguring it as a contingent 'in-between space' that innovates and interrupts the performance of the present. The past-present is part of the necessity, not the nostalgia of living.[2]

Though Oh Haji and Soni Kum work in different media and are evolving unique artistic practices, both third-generation *zainichi* artists explore the specific "in-between" experiences of Koreans in Japan in ways that "refigure the past." They each draw on personal and family memories as well as historical narratives, making reference to experiences of migration and displacement, yet their works are hardly "nostalgic." Rather, I will try to show that their works both "innovate and interrupt the performance of the present." In doing so, they also interrupt the myth of Japan as a monoethnic society.[3]

Much scholarly work in English in recent years has contributed to a better understanding of questions surrounding the history, legal status, civil rights, and identity "dilemmas" of Koreans in Japan.[4] Scholars of literature who study Japan have also begun to turn their attention to the writings of *zainichi* writers.[5] In the field of contemporary visual arts, Yong Soon Min's curatorial project, *There*, a collaborative effort that resulted in a major exhibition of artists of the Korean diaspora from five different locations—including *zainichi* Koreans—at the 2002 Gwangju Biennial, opened up new ways to consider the dilemmas faced by Koreans in Japan through art. In recent years, other seminars and projects bringing together contemporary artists

---

2. Ibid., 28.

3. Naoki Sakai, "Introduction: Nationality and the Politics of the 'Mother Tongue,'" in *Deconstructing Nationality* (Ithaca, NY: Cornell East Asia Series, 2005), 1.

4. Sonia Ryang, *Koreans in Japan* (2000), *North Koreans in Japan* (1997), *Diaspora without Homeland* (2009); Lee, Befu, and Shigematsu, *Japan's Diversity Dilemmas* (2006); Tessa Morris-Suzuki, *Exodus to North Korea* (Rowman and Littlefield, 2007).

5. Carol Hayes, "Cultural Identity in the Work of Yi Yang-ji," in Ryang, *Koreans in Japan*.

and scholars to discuss contemporary art, gender, and diaspora in Japan have helped pave the way for the Asia, Politics, Art project.[6]

In one such seminar, Korean Canadian artist Jin-me Yoon spoke about her conviction that art can be fertile ground for the interrogation of history and memory in both the public and private spheres. The artist explained that through her photo and video installation works she aims to give expression to "the psychic and intergenerational effects that linger after war and dislocation." In a subsequent e-mail exchange with the artist, Yoon explained that she found the notion of "postmemory," developed by Marianne Hirsch through her work with photographic images and personal and family memories of Holocaust survivors, to be useful in her own work.

Along with the notion of "borderline artist," Hirsch's and Yoon's concept of postmemory may also be useful as a tool to approach a reading of selected works by Oh Haji and Soni Kum. In this essay, I will discuss the metaphors, materials, and media these artists have used to explore personal and family histories and to suggest that the creative artistic practices of these two young artists constitute imaginative interventions in the larger, public sphere of Japanese society where the myth of a "monoethnic" society persists.[7] The works of these artists help us to reimagine both past histories and present-day lived experience as well as links between them.

"FROM A SINGLE STRAND OF THREAD": IDENTITY AND MEMORY IN OH HAJI'S TEXTILE AND INSTALLATION WORKS

Trained primarily as a textile artist, Oh Haji uses a range of weaving, dyeing, and stitching techniques to create works that continue to evolve in scale and concept. With these materials and techniques that require exacting skill and substantial amounts of time, the artist has forged inventive ways to fuse the demands of the medium with her conceptual and artistic aims. In her graduation work for her master of fine arts degree, Oh drew on motifs from "hybrid" Japanese and Korean ethnic dress to create original garments, material manifestations of her identity. Like many Koreans in Japan, she had used a Japanese "passing" name, but from around that time, she began using the

---

6. Yong Soon Min, *There*, Project 2, exhibition catalog, Gwangju Biennale, 2002. Yong Soon Min, Jin-me Yoon, and Jane Jin Kaisen spoke at seminars held in Tokyo and Kyoto between 2004 and 2006.

7. Sakai, "Introduction."

name "Oh/Okamura," in itself a representation of the history she and her family have lived: "In Japan, I am often asked which name I use. My Japanese family name, Okamura, was forced on us by history, and my Korean family name, Oh, is in our family tree. But both names are mine, so I use them both."[8]

After her grandmother's death in 2001, Oh became more concerned with the themes of personal history and memory and began exploring techniques that would allow her to integrate them into her work. While continuing to develop textile techniques, she also began to introduce the use of photographs and other photographic techniques in her installation works,

In her study *Family Frames*, Marianne Hirsch looks closely at theories of photography and uses the notion of postmemory as she examines specific uses of family photographs by artists and Holocaust survivors who try to process traumatic personal and family histories. Hirsch defines the concept of postmemory as follows:

In my reading, postmemory is distinguished from memory by generational distance and from history by deep personal connection. Postmemory is a powerful and very particular form of memory precisely because its connection to its object or source is mediated not through recollection but through an imaginative investment and creation.[9]

Hirsch goes on to write,

Postmemory characterizes the experience of those who grow up dominated by narratives that preceded their birth, whose own belated stories are evacuated by the stories of the previous generation shaped by traumatic events that can be neither understood nor recreated.[10]

---

8. Oh/Okamura Haji, "Unbound," *Kyoto Journal*, Special Issue on Gender, no. 64 (2006), 22. As Oh/Okamura currently uses her Korean family name, I will refer to her as Oh Haji hereafter. Both Oh Haji and Soni Kum might be seen as a new generation of *zainichi* artists who have received higher degrees from (former) national art universities. Until the mid-1990s, non-Japanese nationals were not eligible to apply to such institutions.

9. Marianne Hirsch, *Family Frames: Photography, Narrative and Postmemory* (Cambridge, MA: Harvard University Press, 1997), 22.

10. Ibid.

For Oh, both her deep personal connection to her grandmother and her generational distance from her grandmother's actual experiences and memories prompted her to probe her own postmemory through creative means. The narratives preceding her birth and the sometimes painful and awkward silences she had experienced growing up in a *zainichi* family were somehow linked to her to innovations in art.[11]

In *Three Generations* (2004) the artist introduces photographs of herself in the work: three "self-portraits" taken in a landscape on Jeju Island, the ancestral home of her grandmother. Oh is seen wearing three different *hanbok*, or traditional Korean dresses—her grandmother's, made of the white, synthetic fabric popular at the time; her mother's on the right, and the third in the center, handmade by the artist herself with bright red fabric. The work gives powerful expression to the notion of three different generations of women, with overlapping but distinct relationships to the garment worn and the place depicted.

Though inaccessible to the artist in the present time, through attempting to re-create or perform them, Oh imaginatively attempts to come nearer to the lives of her mother and grandmother. But as viewers we are left with many questions to ponder: What does each *hanbok* mean for each generation? What relationship does each figure have to the road on which she is standing? Is the road itself a metaphor for forced migration, or for return? Why are the frames on either side of the three portraits empty? What lies behind, or ahead? The work both literally and metaphorically frames the images, drawing our attention to these provocative questions.

In another piece shown as part of an installation where these works were exhibited, *Three Times* (2004), the artist used a photo silkscreen technique to print photographic images on a long strip of linen cloth traditionally used to honor the dead.[12] Again we see images of the artist herself wearing three different *hanbok* as she walks along a road that is perhaps symbolic of the lives and times of her mother and grandmother; though their memories and experiences can never be fully known, her link to them is clearly conveyed. In her

---

11. Oh Haji, "Ippon no ito kara minzoku isho wo tsukuru—zainichi kannkokujinn to shite no watashi no seisaku" [From a single strand of thread—my creative work as a *zainichi kankoku-jin*], *Aida* 110 (February 2005), 18–24.

12. Oh's grandmother had prepared this cloth to be used in the traditional way at her funeral.

discussion of the particular effects of photographs as expressions of post-memory, Hirsch writes as follows:

> Photographs in their enduring 'umbilical' connection to life are precisely the medium connecting first and second-generation remembrance, memory and postmemory.[13]

In the absence of actual family photographs that might trigger recognition of places or experiences from which Oh is inevitably separated by time and geography, the artist has ingeniously created her own "umbilical" connection to the past, thus establishing imaginative links to the lived present.

In a large, mixed-media installation piece titled *Memory* (2006), Oh again addresses this theme, using textiles, objects, a photograph, and text. The artist began with the repetitive and painstaking task of imprinting the flower pattern on the synthetic white cloth of the dress that spread from one wall across the floor of the room. On a small table with a glass mirror top sits a spool of white cord, its twisted form suggestive of an umbilical cord, and the unraveling threads seem like tresses of white hair. On one wall hangs a small photograph of her grandmother's *jeogori* or jacket.

In an interview, Oh explained that the inspiration for this work came from her grandmother's *chima jeogori*, one that Oh had kept hanging in her room:

> In the past I have made works by unraveling my grandmother's *chima jeogori* and making new garments. But I was ready to try something else, and just kept it hanging in my room. ... I began to feel that she was actually there, "physically present." That was the inspiration for this work. ... Technically speaking, I took photographs, both with an ordinary reflex camera and with a camera that I could manually adjust so that it was slightly out of focus. I tried both and decided to use the latter because it conveyed the sense of the physical presence.[14]

In Hirsch's discussion of ways in which photographs can become vehicles for the expression of postmemory, she cites Roland Barthes's reflections on photography:

---

13. Hirsch, 22.
14 Interview with the artist, November, 2008.

The photograph is literally an emanation of the referent. From a real body, which was there, proceed radiations which ultimately touch me, who am here; the duration of the transmission as insignificant; the photograph of the missing being, as Sontag says, will touch me like the delayed rays of a star. A sort of umbilical cord links the body of the photographed thing to my gaze: light, though impalpable, is here, a carnal medium, a skin I share with anyone who has been photographed.[15]

For Oh, the use of photography, and the discovery of a particular technique, allowed her to convey a stronger sense of the "physical presence" of her grandmother, transmitted through an object that she had kept.

In this installation piece, the artist also experimented with the use of printed text in Korean and Japanese, again seeking material technique to give expression to memory, this time of her experience of living between two languages. In an interview, Oh explained as follows:

I wanted the texts to appear as if they were floating up to the surface, or as if they had been rubbed into the wall. I was recalling the feeling of frustration when I couldn't understand what my grandmother was saying to me. ... I was also imagining my grandmother's experience, coming to Japan, being forced to use Japanese every day, even though her native language was Korean.[16]

In the wall text itself, Oh describes the process of trying to grasp fragments of memory, or postmemory, a gesture that is, as Hirsch writes, "obsessive and relentless."[17]

Memory

The fragments spill
Etched on each one
A memory that
Floats, then falls

---

15. Hirsch, *Family Frames*, 4–5; Roland Barthes, *Camera Lucida: Reflections on Photography* (Vintage Classics, 1980), 80–81.

16. Interview with the artist, November 2008.

17. Hirsch, *Family Frames*, 23.

Again and again.
I scoop up the fragments
Hold them in cupped hands
Again they spill, again they rise[18]

In February 2007, Oh exhibited a new mixed-media textile work titled *Kahan* (Flower Spot) at the Kyoto City Art Museum. The combination of Chinese characters used in the title—花 (flower) and 班 (mark or bruise)—is the original invention of the artist. She again chose to use the polyester organdy with imprinted flower patterns of the *chima jeogori* seen in *Memory*, which forms the base of the abstract form of the work. Strands of white fiber appear to rise out of the sculpted form of the fabric; the strands or fibers are threaded through needles that pierce the rounded surface of a cushion that seems to hover in the air above the base of the work. In the material and metaphor, a moment of pain and tension is re-created, in which needles pierce the soft skin cloth, and threads, suspended precariously, topple down into the folds of white cloth below. The artist's statement again points to the underlying theme of memory:

Kahan

A sensation of warmth floats upward, fades along with time's passing. *Kahan*—a trace of memories that never fade, that marks memories unheard, unwritten.[19]

As we have seen, Oh has continued to explore themes of identity, diasporic experience, and memory. Integrating material, metaphor, and image, we might say that she is creating what Hirsch would call an "aesthetics of postmemory," or "a diasporic aesthetics of temporal and spatial exile that needs simultaneously to (re)build and to mourn."[20] The following section shows how Soni Kum, though using very different materials and media, is also engaged in the process of inventing such an aesthetics.

---

18. Oh Haji, *Memory*, mixed-media installation, Voice Gallery, Kyoto. My translation.
19. Oh Haji, *Kahan* (Flower Spot), artist's statement. My translation.
20. Hirsch, *Family Frames*, 245.

HER BODY ON THE BORDERLINE—
SELECTED WORKS BY SONI KUM

Soni Kum writes that her video and performance pieces were inspired in part by her desire to "tell a story about a missing piece from the official record."[21] Like Oh Haji, she had to begin by interrogating the gaps and silences transmitted "intergenerationally" to her as a third-generation *zainichi* Korean raised in the Chongryun North Korean community in Tokyo. Her experiences both in and outside of that community, and the conflicting versions of history and current events she continued to encounter after leaving it, are translated into the metaphors and materials of her artistic practice. To again borrow Hirsch's notion of postmemory, Kum seeks to excavate her personal story from the "stories of the previous generation shaped by traumatic events that can be neither (fully) understood nor recreated."

Kum began her schooling in Korean ethnic schools in Tokyo and, after graduating from high school, studied at a Japanese university there. She then decided to pursue the study of contemporary art, and entered the MFA program at the California Institute of the Arts. It was while studying there that she began to experiment with performance and video art, producing a number of works that proved pivotal in her career. In a comment about her work at that time, she writes:

> I started making short video works in 2002. At that time, I was trying to transform what I wanted to say, what I wanted to change, through using metaphors as much as possible. Growing up in Korean schools, I watched the adults around me engage in struggle with Japan to gain their civil rights. But often, the issues were not resolved as hoped, and it felt like tensions and knots of frustration were just accumulating. Rather than trying to overcome ethnic discrimination by confronting things head on, I was looking for new and different ways to address the issues. I held the hope that art would provide a way to do that.[22]

---

21. Soni Kum, English narration for *Foreign Sky* (2005), courtesy of the artist.
22. Interview with the artist, November 2007.

Kum also found that without much money or other resources, the most readily available medium she could use was her own body; she could perform and have a trusted woman friend film her.

In Kum's early video pieces—*Story of Light* (2001), *Sheep* (2002), and *Flour* (2004)—we see the artist's first attempts to develop the vocabulary of visual images, film techniques, and unique performative practices she has gone on to use in works that make reference to different "fragments" of history and personal experience. In *Sheep*, the figure of a woman (Kum herself) appears unexpectedly in an unidentified landscape. Short filmic shots show the figure from different angles; the angle of the camera shifts sharply, and in several of the shots (not necessarily in direct sequence) we see Kum, wearing a *chima jeogori*, first standing, and then down on her knees, or taking bits of grass into her mouth like an animal grazing—creating another uncertainty, an unexpected and disturbing association. The viewer ponders the image: Why is the woman there? What is the association with a grazing animal, with sheep? Is this female figure the object of a gaze that controls, fears, or desires her? Am I, the viewer, making her the object of my gaze, as "other"? In *Flour*, Kum again uses the image of a female figure in white, this time in an interior setting. Here, too, the image of the female figure, covered with white flour as she crawls and moves in the narrow frame of the film segment, is both powerful and disturbing.

In *Red Hunting* (2004), we see Kum herself in a white *hanbok*, enclosed in a narrow interior space, covered with a thick layer of white flour. Throughout this ninety-minute performance, Kum continues to crawl on all fours, enclosed in the narrow space that is covered by a knee-high sheet of clear plastic. One by one, Kum uses only her mouth to pick up bright red candies that have been scattered in the white flour, in her mouth; and one by one, she carries them to the center of the space and drops them in a circle at the center, forming a large image of the Japanese Rising Sun flag.

Only a short segment of a video documentary of this piece remains, but I imagine Kum's repetitive gesture might have been seen as the repetitive task of a laborer or "beast of burden." From above, her figure would have been less clearly visible, clouded by the rippled, not-quite-transparent plastic sheet. Placed on stands above the sheet of plastic were two television screens, one with a video loop showing the ABC newscaster Tom Brokaw, reporting on the "North Korean Threat," and the other showing short segments of a documentary produced in North Korea.

Kum has explained that she had been thinking about one of the many disturbing, unresolved fragments in the history of Koreans in Japan when she began to work on this performance piece. The particular incident she had in mind is known as the Ukishimamaru Incident, which occurred in late August 1945. More than 500 Koreans who had been conscripted as laborers in Aomori during the war were on a ship bound for Busan where they were to be repatriated. They died when the ship exploded and sank, but the cause of the disaster remains unexplained.[23]

While in *Red Hunting* Kum makes no direct reference to this incident, she uses powerful visual and performative metaphors to convey the palpable sensation of fear and uncertainty that was widespread among Koreans in Japan after the war. In the artist's imagination, such fragments of memory and history resurfaced alongside representations of North Korea in the U.S. mainstream media, and in North Korean film. Kum has gone on to use this technique of juxtaposing visual image, performative gesture, and narratives from a range of sources in her work.

In *Beast of Me* (2005) and *Foreign Sky* (2005), Kum began to introduce the element of narration in her own voice recorded over original film and performance video clips, fragments of documentary, and other films to create powerfully original filmic montages. Through the use of her body and voice, and the juxtaposition of these fragments and metaphors, Kum began to forge a unique "aesthetics of postmemory."

Elsewhere in this volume, Ikeuchi Yasuko has done an excellent, in-depth analysis of the filmic and narrative texts Kum used in these works, so I will limit my comments here to the question of how they might be understood in relation to Hirsch's notion of postmemory. In *Beast of Me*, Kum links five filmic segments in a kind of collage referring to personal and collective memory and trauma, as well as to issues that were current when she produced this work at CalArts.

In the first segment of *Beast of Me*, we see an unedited piece of a performance at a school recital in which *zainichi* Korean schoolgirls perform a song and dance dedicated to the North Korean leader. Pride and patriotism are embedded in the lyrics of the song, which stream in English translation across the bottom of the screen. The smiling young girls mouth their devotion to their Dear Leader, in whose name they wear their Korean school

---

23. E-mail exchange with the artist, November 2007. See Naitoh Hisako, "Korean Forced Labor in Japan's Wartime Empire," in *Asian Labor in the Wartime Japanese Empire*, ed. Paul H. Kratoska (New York: M.E. Sharpe and NUS Press, 2007), 97.

uniforms; the lyrics explain the importance of the girls' costumes as symbols of patriotism and resistance: "We are generously blessed by our Leader. By wearing Korean clothes as a school uniform ... we respect and follow the spirit of our father land. Our scouts' motto is always one: ... even though foreign enemies attack us, we are going to keep our Korean clothes until the end."[24]

In the second segment, we see Kum herself wearing a *chima jeogori*, seated on a grassy hillside. Gentle breezes blow her hair and garment, as the camera tentatively shifts angles, never showing her face or figure completely. Kum narrates the original text in three languages: English, Japanese, and Korean. Her voice is also tentative, as if frightened that she might be overheard, as she relates the traumatic experience of being physically and sexually harassed while commuting to school in her Korean-style school uniform on a crowded train in Tokyo. Kum begins by explaining the context of discrimination against Koreans in Japan:

> Japanese tend to consider Koreans as a lower race. ... Japanese have been trying any possible way to eradicate Korean ethnicity from Japan. Their method has been taking away our consciousness as a Korean, taking away our names, taking away our languages, and taking away our lives. Thus, Korean girls wearing Korean clothes is a kind of antithesis against Japanese government.[25]

Kum goes on to explain that her mother questioned the policy requiring only girl students to wear ethnic dress as the school uniform, but because "Korean ethnicity has a trait of dominance of the male over the female, as an idea ... my mother's struggle was disputed." It was while riding a crowded subway in Tokyo that a Japanese man sexually harassed her, leaving her feeling "disgusted and angry ... and scared. But I couldn't find my voice. My voice couldn't come out because I was ashamed and angry." For Kum, her life "in between" the majority Japanese society and the minority Korean community meant crossing borders on a daily basis; like other young women in her community, her own body became the target of ethnic and sexual violence.

In the third segment of the piece, the artist turns to the immediate situation she was facing in the "post-9/11" United States. Viewed by the U.S.

---

24. Soni Kum, English text for *Beast of Me*, courtesy of the artist.
25. Ibid.

administration as a part of the "Axis of Evil," some of Kum's friends were worried that the United States would now attack North Korea, as it had Iraq. Here Kum explained her view that in reality, an attack by the North, unable to even feed its people, would be suicidal. In the midst of intense mainstream media attention directed toward the possible development of a North Korean nuclear program and again caught between differing versions of events, Kum decided to "shift the gaze" and try to film a nuclear facility in Southern California. Unable to come closer than the outside wall of the facility, the artist turned her camera toward the "foreign" sky. In the third segment of the film, we see shots of the night sky above the plant, lights flickering softly as Kum narrates:

> I was looking at the light in the absent way. It was very beautiful. The way light goes straight up to the sky. I was thinking about my relatives, living in North Korea, who are hungry, and incarcerated [beyond] the borderline.[26]

In the fourth section of the work, we see a flock of goats grazing on a grassy hillside. The sudden shift in the visual image is made even more surprising by the voice of a woman who tells her story of how she suffered multiple miscarriages and stillbirths caused by exposure to high levels of radiation. We come to understand that the speaker is from the Marshall Islands, where the United States conducted extensive nuclear tests and where several generations of islanders have continued to suffer from the effects of radiation. The woman's story of her infant son, who was treated like "an animal in an experiment," is juxtaposed with images of animals grazing, as I follow the artist's thoughts and associations.

In the short, final section of the work, Kum inserts a short segment from the North Korean film *Wolmido* (1983) and reads lines from a poem by Yu Chi-Hwan that were written during the time of Japanese colonial rule. Kum saw the film in Los Angeles, and it was there that she first encountered the phrase "beast of me" in lines of Yu's poem translated into English in the subtitles: "Like Cain, long pursued, even though it makes a beast of me, I will endure this suffering."[27]

---

26. Ibid.

27. See Ikeuchi Yasuko's insightful analysis (chapter 6, this volume). Soni Kum, English narration for *Foreign Sky*, courtesy of the artist.

Kum's use of performative and filmic techniques to express this metaphor of the "beast" links the fragmented segments as they lead viewers to consider multiple, interweaving histories of colonization and militarization.

While both *Beast of Me* and *Foreign Sky* clearly demonstrate Kum's concern with reimagining histories, in *Foreign Sky*, the artist goes further to create a filmic collage of "missing pieces from an official record."[28] Again, read with Hirsch's notion of postmemory in mind, we might think of these fragments as "the leftovers, the fragmentary sources and building blocks, shot through with holes, of the work of postmemory. They affirm the past's existence and in their flat, two-dimensionality, they signal this unbridgeable distance."[29]

In the opening narrative to the film, Kum explains that when she left the community she had grown up in, she faced a conflict: "My version of history and their version of history do not correspond." She begins with narrative and filmic segments that explain her own grandmother's and great-grandmother's stories. Other segments of films excerpted from a range of sources discussed in detail by Ikeuchi (chapter 6, this volume), trace the history of liberation from Japan and reveal atrocities committed by the U.S. military documented in video recordings of field investigations by the International Women's Inquiry Commission.[30]

Kum uses short excerpts from different types of film, juxtaposing and interlinking narratives such as the testimony of a North Korean woman who was shot by U.S. soldiers at the age of seven and an interview with a retired U.S. serviceman describing his recurring nightmare about a young Korean girl he shot during the Korean War. Later, in a clip from Kum's video diary of a visit she made with high school classmates to Pyongyang, North Korea, we see a long segment without narration in which *zainichi* Korean girls perform in traditional dress for Kim Il Sung, singing "The First Song I Learned." In the next segment, Kum again narrates, explaining that upon her return to Japan she was struck by the starkly different representations in the Japanese media of North Korea. In an excerpt from prime-time Japanese news, well-known news commentator Chikushi Tetsu reports on tensions that were building between North Korea and the United States over the nuclear issue. In quick succession follow images of the slashed uniform of a *zainichi* Korean

---

28. Hirsch, *Family Frames*, 22.

29. Ibid.

30. In addition to the testimonies cited in chapter 6, see Charles J. Hanley and Jae-Soon Chang, "Summer of Terror: At Least 100,000 Said Executed by Korean Ally of US in 1950," *Japan Focus*, July 23, 2007, http://www.japanfocus.org/-J_S_-Chang/2827.

schoolgirl, with voice-overs of violently racist, anti-Korean comments made by anonymous callers. Here, as if to underscore the violence inherent in the gaze that is directed toward the bodies of the young Korean girls, Kum interrupts the stream of documentary images with a segment showing the body of a woman over which is projected scenes from Oshima Nagisa's *Death by Hanging*. Through this intervention, Kum seems to ask the viewer to reflect on her or his own gaze at these disturbing images and fragments of media and history. It is here that Kum elaborates on the attacks that she and other female students wearing Korean school uniforms experienced in Tokyo.

Kum also reflects on disturbing news from Pyongyang heard several years after her visit there that further complicates the narrative: two of her relatives were sent to a camp as political prisoners, where one later died. Kum explains,

> They were among a group who left Japan in the 1960s to return to North Korea. In Japan, they had faced discrimination as Koreans, but in North Korea they were ostracized for being 'half Japanese.'[31]

Then, Kum tells us (in Japanese, with English subtitles) about a letter from her relative that she found when looking for old photographs of her mother.

> *Dear Ryosu,*
> *What is the lesson I learned from my experiences ... living in capitalism for 17 years and in socialism for 40 years? The iron in my house is better than gold in other's houses. I found the truth. We prosper when we believe in our own ability ... and lose when we rely on another's ability. In any social system, the most important things are human relationships and the next important thing is money. I wonder what this money is, which made us suffer so much. What is this money, which separates us? When I was in Japan, money allowed us to see each other. Our lives seem long but are short. Don't die until we can see each other again.*[32]

In the narrative, Kum comments that she was unable to find any criticism of the government in the letter; then a series of alternating images show

---

31. Soni Kum, English narrative from *Foreign Sky*, courtesy of the artist. See Morris-Suzuki, *Exodus to North Korea*.

32. Soni Kum, English narrative from *Foreign Sky*.

an evening sky at sunset and shots of a handwritten letter in *hangul* characters on orange paper. Gradually, the sunlight fades and the sky grows darker
until finally it is completely dark.

The final section of the film is set along a freeway in southern California.
Kum describes what she sees walking along the freeway outside Los Angeles
on her way to school, and comments on tensions in U.S. and North Korean
relations:

> Although there is no war today, North Korea and the United States
> are officially in the middle of a war. I wanted to know more about the
> United States from the inside. President George Bush stated that
> North Korea and Iraq are the Axis of Evil. ... I didn't have a car for
> half a year when I first came to California. I found people must rely
> on cars to live in the United States. It is even hard to go to school and
> to the supermarket without a car. I sometimes needed to walk to
> school. It was as scary as going to school wearing Korean clothes.[33]

The narration moves quickly, linking the issues of ongoing tensions between North Korea and the United States to Kum's present, everyday life
walking to school along freeways not intended for pedestrians.

The final images in the film show the bodies of animals lying beside the
freeway; in one short segment, Kum carefully buries one of them. In another
still shot, we see the cars rushing past a dead animal, and on the side of the
road a sign reading, "Korean War Veterans"—an unexpected image, linking
the stories that have brought her to the present moment. Now under another
"foreign sky," Kum asks whether any of those who go rushing past even notice the suffering and death of these animals.

CONCLUSION

I began this essay by suggesting that Homi Bhabha's notion of the borderline
artist might prove useful in a discussion of the works of these two third-
generation *zainichi* artists, Oh Haji and Soni Kum. Though each artist is
unique in her use of materials, themes and techniques, both collect and cre-
atively reinterpret fragments of family narratives, personal memory, and conflicting versions of history as they try to make sense of their identities and

---

33. Ibid.

experiences. When viewed in the larger context of the Asia, Politics, Art project, these "borderline works of art" by Oh and Kum help make visible the terrain that lies between private and public memory, a terrain that cannot help but disrupt the myth of Japan as a monoethnic society. At the same time, Oh and Kum both seek ways to communicate cross-generationally through their art, interrupting "the performance of the present" as they revisit and renew the past. Similarly, they experiment in the formation of what Marianne Hirsch calls an aesthetics of postmemory that on the one hand signals "absence and loss" but also makes it possible to "rebuild, reconnect, bring back to life."[34]

When I consider once again the context of our seminar and the Asia, Politics, Art project, and the particular ways in which these works speak to the value and meaning of life, I am also reminded of questions posed by Judith Butler in *Precarious Life*, a collection of essays written in response to the war in Iraq. Judith Butler draws on Giorgio Agamben's notion of bare life, asking us to consider, "Who counts as human? Whose lives count as lives? And, finally, what makes for a grievable life?"[35] Although coming out of a different context, both Oh and Kum ask us to look at these questions in relation to the historical and political context of East Asia.

Butler also points to ways in which "official" media and historical narratives (in the post–9/11 U.S.) have been used to achieve hegemonic consensus and to control "the way in which people see, how they hear, what they see."[36] Here, too, Oh and Kum refigure "official" things that have not been "admissible," as well as to attempt to see beyond the boundaries of circumscribed, hegemonic "public spheres" that have hidden forgotten or ungrievable lives.

As the dialogues and responses generated by the Asia, Politics, Art project have already shown, art has the potential to activate new levels of understanding across generation, location, gender, and ethnicity. Encouraged by the responses received through this project, Oh and Kum continue to create new works and show them both in and outside of Japan. I hope that the English version of *Still Hear the Wound* will help their works reach a wider audience and spark further dialogue about an "Asia, politics and art to come."

---

34. Hirsch, *Family Frames*, 245–246.
35. Judith Butler, *Precarious Life: The Powers of Mourning and Violence* (New York: Verso, 2004), 20.
36. Ibid.

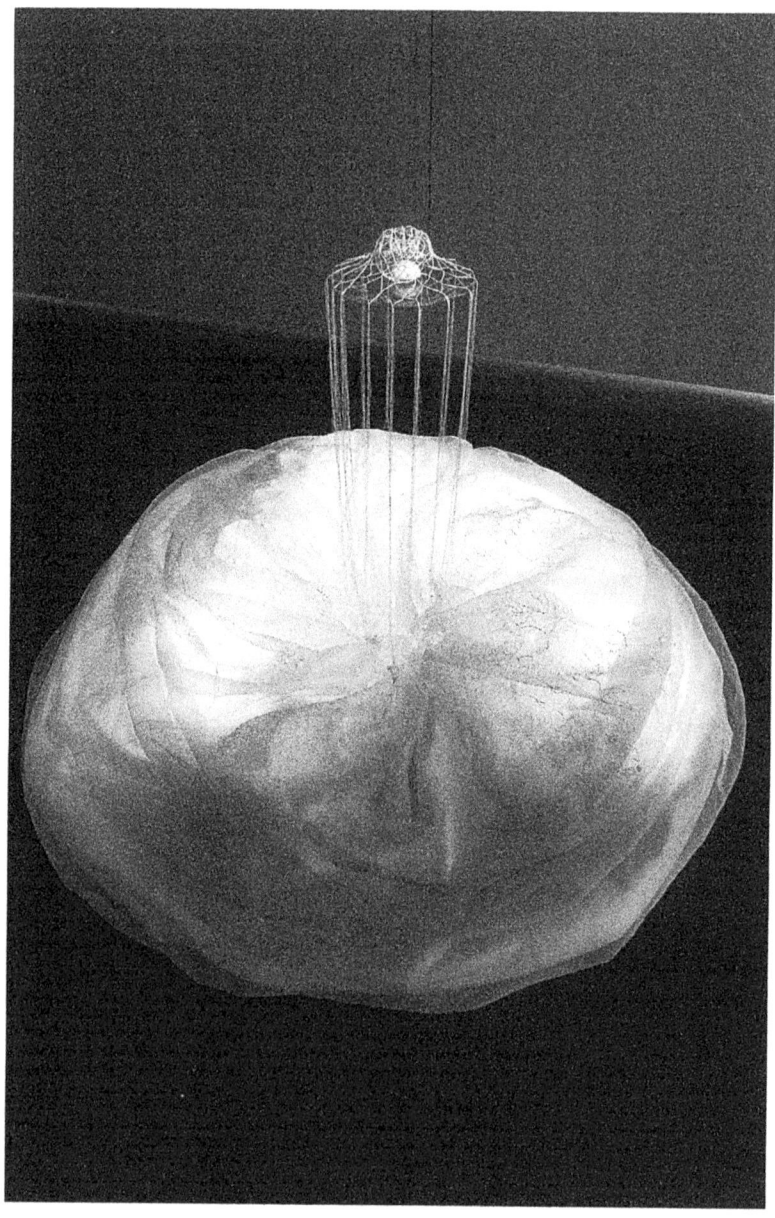

Oh Haji, *Kahan* (Flower Spot), detail, 2007.

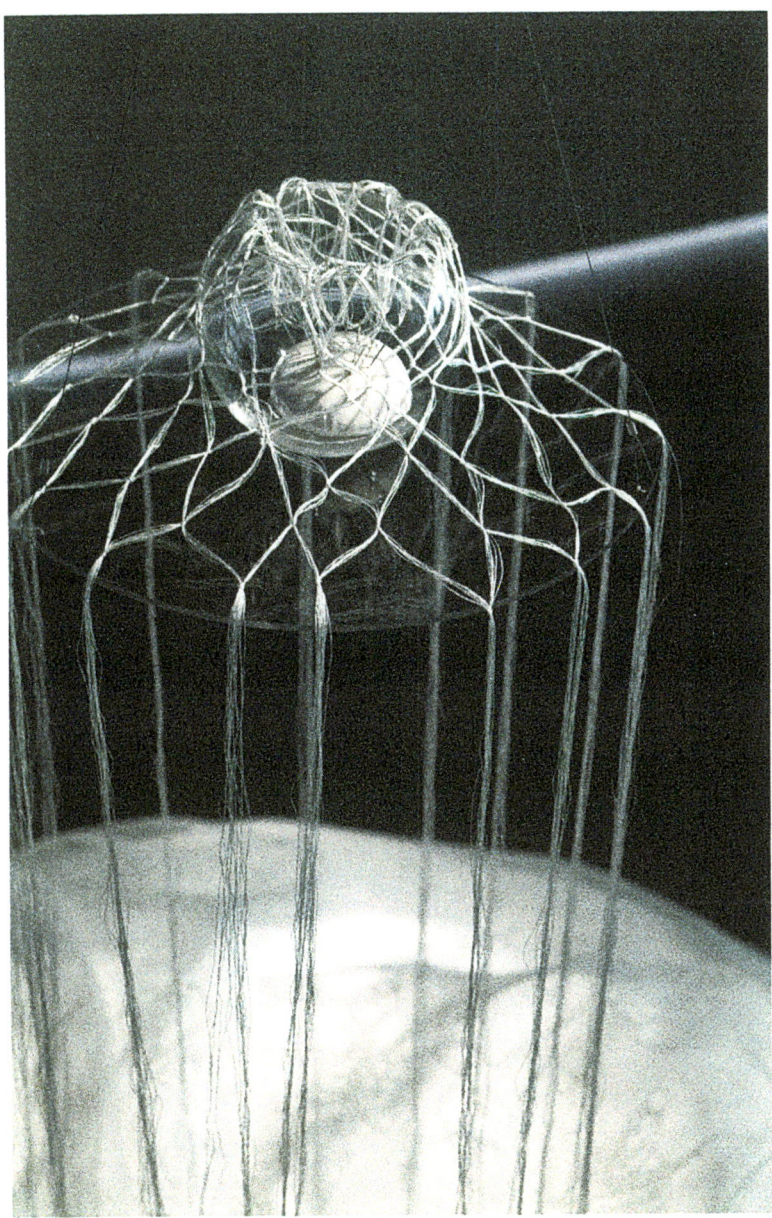

Oh Haji, *Kahan* (Flower Spot), 2007. Silk, pincushion, sewing needles, acrylic board, wire, bulb, embroidery, macrame (2007); 150 x 150 x 180 cm. Photo: Toyonaga Seiji.

PART II

Still Hear the Wound II DVD

Produced and edited by Soni Kum

As in the original Japanese version of *Still Hear the Wound*, readers will find a DVD of Soni Kum's film of the same title, and artists' works and interviews inserted inside the back cover of this volume. Because the contents of the two sections of this DVD are an integral part of the Asia, Politics, Art project that both inform and inspire the essays selected and translated here, we strongly recommend that readers take the time to view them. Our aim to publish the volume in a timely manner prevented us from including interviews with two of the artists, Kitajima Sumiko and Miyagi Akira, but we have included still images of their works in the volume.

The first section of the DVD, *Still Hear the Wound*, was filmed by Soni Kum at the Sakima Art Museum in 2008. Kum's camera takes us on a journey through a series of stunning details from the Maruki Iri's and Toshi's mural painting, *Picture of the Battle of Okinawa* (1984, 8.5 × 4 meters), while the soundtrack she composed creates a powerful audio environment for the images. In the latter part of the film, Takahashi Yūji's composition inspired by Nakaya Kōkichi's poem "Last Note" is performed by Suigyū Gakudan, a group of musicians founded and led by Takahashi.

The second section of the DVD consists of five segments with interviews and works by artists who participated in the Asia, Politics, Art project. The interviews were conducted and filmed by Soni Kum in Okinawa and Tokyo.

Ito Tari's performance of *I will not forget you* was filmed by Desirée Lim in Tokyo in 2006. The final segment by Soni Kum was produced by the artist early in 2015 for this volume. Each segment can be viewed independently or in sequence.

DVD CONTENTS

Section 1
Still Hear the Wound
Maruki Iri, Maruki Toshi, Takahashi Yūji and Soni Kum
(23 min.)

Section 2
Five Artists (113 min.)

Oh Haji (20 min.)
Yamashiro Chikako (19 min.)
Kinjō Mitsuru (16 min.)
Ito Tari (30 min.)
Soni Kum (28 min.)

Subtitles by Jooyeon Hahm and Andrew Harding

Contributing Authors

Brett de Bary Professor of Asian Studies and Comparative Literature at Cornell University. She is senior editor of *Traces: A Multilingual Series of Cultural Theory and Translation*. Recent publications include critical essays on the women writers Morisaki Kazue in the volume *Kikyō no monogatari/idō no katari: Sengo nihon ni okeru posuto-koroniaru no sōzō*, edited by Hirata Yumi and Iyotani Toshio (Heibonsha, 2014), and Tawada Yōko in *Translation/Transmediation: A Special Issue of Poetica*, edited by Atsuko Sakaki (Yushōdō, 2012). She is editor of *Universities in Translation: The Mental Labor of Globalization*, volume 5 of *Traces* (Hong Kong University Press, 2010), and coeditor with Naoki Sakai and Iyotani Toshio of *Deconstructing Nationality* (Cornell East Asia Series, 2005).

Lee Chonghwa Professor of Political Philosophy, Politics of Culture and Postcolonial Studies in the Department of Law, Seikei University, Tokyo. Born on Jeju Island, Lee came to Japan in 1988. Her publications include *Tsubuyaki no seiji shisō—motomerareru manazashi—kanashimi e no, soshite himerareta mono e no* (Murmurs as political thought—in search of ways to see the sorrow and things hidden, Seidosha, 1998); *Motome no Seijigaku—kotoba—haimau shima* (Toward a politics of supplication—in search of words—islands that crawl and dance, Iwanami Shoten, 2004). Lee's works have continued to draw attention because of the unique way that they integrate critical thought, poetry, and political philosophy. She is currently the director of the Center for Asian and Pacific Studies at Seikei University.

Shinjō Ikuo Professor of Okinawan and Japanese Literature at the University of the Ryukyus. His publications include *Okinawa bungaku to iu kuwadate: Kattō suru kotoba, shintai, kioku* (Undertaking Okinawan literature: Language, bodies and memories in struggle, Impaction, 2003); *Tōrai suru Okinawa—Okinawa hyōshō no hihan ron* (The advent of Okinawa—a cri-

tique of representations of Okinawa, Impaction, 2007); "The Ethics of Ecstasy: The Art of Yamashiro Chikako," in *Yamashiro Chikako, MAM Project
018* (Mori Art Museum, 2012); *Manazashi ni Fureru* (Touching on the gaze,
Suiseisha, 2014); *Okinawa no kizu to iu kairō* (Through the corridor of Okinawa's wounds, Iwanami, 2014).

Satō Izumi   Professor of Literature, Aoyama Gakuin University. Her publications include *Sōseki katazukanai (kindai)* (Soseki and unfinished [moder-
nity], NHK Books, 2002); *Sengo hihyō no meta hisutorii—kindai kioku o
kioku suru* (A metahistory of postwar criticism—remembering modern
memory, Iwanami Shoten, 2005); ed., *Kokugo kyōkasho no sengo shi* (Postwar
history of Japanese literature textbooks, Keisō Shobō, 2006); ed., *Ikyō no
nihongo* (Japanese language estranged, Shakai hyōronsha, 2009).

Yano Kumiko   Professor of Intellectual History and German Studies at
Ferris University. Her publications include *Hanna Aarento, aruiwa seijiteki
shikō no basho* (Hannah Arendt, or the site of political thinking, Misuzu
Shobō, 2002); "Monogataru—monogataru shintai to Aarento no manazashi" (Narration—narrating bodies and the gaze of Arendt), in *Seiji no hakken
(1): ikiru* (Discovering politics (1): Living), ed. Okano Yayo (Fūkōsha,
2010); "Naze Arento wa sengo doitsugo de 'kaku' koto ga dekitanoka" (Why
could Arendt 'write' in German after the war?), in *20 seiki no shisōkeikenin*
(The experience of thought in the twentieth century, Hōsei University Press,
2013); *Hanna Aarento: Sensō no seiki wo ikita seiji-tetugakusha* (Hannah Arendt: Political philosopher living in a century of war, Chuōkōronsha, 2014).

Choi Jinseok   Associate Professor, Graduate School of Integrated Arts and
Sciences, Hiroshima University. Born in Seoul and raised in Tokyo. Author
and actor who has performed with the theater group Yasen no Tsuki
Haibittsu. His publications include *Yi Sang sakuhin shū* (Collected works of
Yi Sang, ed., trans., Sakuhinsha, 2006); *Chōsenjin wa anata ni yobikaketeiru:
Heito supeechi o koete* (Chosenjin are calling out to you: Going beyond hate
speech, Sairyūsha, 2014). His recent performances include *Mo-nuke ten-
denko*, Tokyo, May 2013.

Higashi Takuma   Scholar and critic of music and cultural studies. Director
of the Hiroshima Peace Film Festival, he was born in Hiroshima. His publications include *Zen—sekai ongaku ron* (Music studies for the entire/world,

Seidosha, 2003); *Hiroshima dokuritsu ron* (Independence for Hiroshima, Seidosha, 2007); *Hiroshima de seibōryoku o kangaeru* (On sexual violence in Hiroshima, Women's Studies Center, Hiroshima, 2007); *Hiroshima nowaaru* (Hiroshima noir, Impaction, 2014).

Ikeuchi Yasuko   Professor Emeritus of Theater and Gender Studies at Ritsumeikan University. Publications include *Feminizumu to gendai engeki* (Feminism and contemporary theater, Tabata shoten, 1999); Theresa Hak Kyung Cha, *DICTEE* (Japanese translation, Seidosha, 2003); *Joyu no tanjo to shuen—pafoomansu to jendaa* (The birth and demise of the actress—performance and gender, Heibonsha, 2008); *Ikkyo o shintai: Theresa Hak Kyung Cha o megutte* (Foreign bodies: On Theresa Hak Kyung Cha, coedited with Masahiko Nishi, Jinbun shoin, 2006).

Rebecca Jennison   Professor of Literature and Gender Studies at Kyoto Seika University. Publications include *Imagination without Borders: Feminist Artist Tomiyama Taeko and Social Responsibility* (coedited with Laura Hein, Center for Japan Studies, University of Michigan, 2009). Translations include *MOVE—Ito Tari's Performance Art*, by Ito Tari (Impaction, 2012); *Voices of the Stones*, by Kinjō Mitsuru (Sakima Art Museum, 2010). Coorganizer of the Art of Intervention: Critical Enquiries into Private and Public Memory research project, and cocurator of *Art, Performance and Activism in Contemporary Japan* (Pump House Gallery, London, 2012).

Contributing Artists

Oh Haji   Textile and installation artist; Born in Osaka. She received a PhD from Kyoto City University of the Arts in 2012. A third-generation *zainichi* Korean, Oh uses textile techniques such as spinning, weaving, dyeing, and embroidery in innovative ways to create large installation works. Her solo and group exhibitions include *Orientity* (Kyoto Arts Center, 2004); *Zone-Poetic Moment* (Tokyo Wonder Site, 2005); *Kioku* (Memory, Voice Gallery, Kyoto, 2006); *Winter Energy* (Lennox Contemporary, Toronto, 2009); *HOME* (Aomori Contemporary Art Centre, 2009); *Inner Voices* (Kanazawa 21st Century Art Museum, 2011); *Shinshin to, tantan to* (Gesture in clothing, Aomori Contemporary Art Centre, 2013); *Tansu* (Breaker Project, Nishinari-ku, Osaka, 2012–2014); *Inhabiting the World* (Busan Biennale, 2014) (http://hajioh.com/).

Yamashiro Chikako   Video and performance artist. Born in Okinawa. Currently living and working in Okinawa. Solo and group exhibitions include *Okinawa TOURIST* (Maejima Art Center, 2004); the First Kurashiki Contemporary Art Biennale in Western Japan in 2005, of which she won an award; *Okinawa Prismed—1872–2008* (National Museum of Modern Art, Tokyo, 2008); *Into the Atomic Sunshine in Sakima: Post-War Art under the Japanese Peace Constitution, Article 9* (Sakima Art Museum, Ginowan City, Okinawa, 2009); *Art, Performance and Activism in Contemporary Japan* (Pump House Gallery, London, 2012); *Women in Between: Asian Women Artists, 1984–2012* (Fukuoka Asian Art Museum, 2012); *A Woman of the Butcher Shop*, MAM Project 018 (Mori Art Museum, Tokyo, 2012).

Kinjō Mitsuru   Artist working in a mixture of media including sculpture, painting, photography, and printmaking. Born in Okinawa, he received an MFA from University of the Ryukyus in 1993. He has exhibited work in Tokyo, Okinawa, and Seoul and has led workshops and collaborative projects at the Sakima Art Museum, including *Voices of the Stones*, *Mayoi no koi* (Carp losing their way) and *Tetsu no kioku* (Iron memory). Solo and group exhibitions include *Shiriizu domorie "kotoba no katachi"* (Stuttering paintings series: "The shape of words," Gallery Okinawa, 2006); *Sweet 400 Series* (2009). He was invited to participate in the Special Project for the Twentieth Anniversary of the Gwangju Biennale, 2014.

Ito Tari Performance artist. Born in Tokyo, Ito studied performance art in Europe and has continued to perform works in Japan, North America, Korea, Europe, and Southeast Asia. Her works include *Distant Skinship* (1995); *Self-portrait* (1995); *Where Is the Fear* (2003); *I will not forget you* (2006); *One Response—for Beh Boungi and Countless Other Women* (2008); and *I Guess It's Better That Radiation Doesn't Have Color* (2011). Her performances were featured in *Women in Between: Asian Women Artists, 1984–2012* (Fukuoka Asian Art Museum, 2012). Ito also established the Women's Art Network (WAN) and PA/F Space and has coordinated a series of events and exhibitions in Koganei City where Oh Haji, Yamashiro Chikako, and Soni Kum have shown their works.

Soni Kum Interdisciplinary artist. Born and raised in the North Korean community in Tokyo as a third-generation Korean. Kum obtained South Korean citizenship in 2006. She received an MFA from California Institute of the Arts and a doctorate in Fine Arts from Tokyo University of Arts in 2011. Her works have been exhibited in the United States, the United Kingdom, Japan, Korea, Cuba, Brazil, Denmark, Germany, the Philippines, China, and Myanmar. Recent exhibitions include *Art, Performance and Activism in Contemporary Japan* (Pump House Gallery, London, 2012); *Women in Between: Asian Women Artists, 1984–2012* (Fukuoka Asian Art Museum, 2012); "Going, Going Until I Meet the Tide," Special Exhibition (Busan Biennale, 2014). Her works include *Sheep* (2002), *Red Hunting* (2004), *Beast of Me* (2005), *Foreign Sky* (2005), *Slumber* (2008), *Vegetation* (2010), *Blood Sea* (2012), and *Heaven's Gate* (2014) (http://www.sonikum.com/).

Takahashi Yūji Composer and pianist. Studied composition with Shibata Minao, Ogura Roh, and Iannis Xenakis. He edited the quarterly *transonic* from 1974 to 1976, and established the Suigyū Band (Water Buffalo Band), which performed and recorded Asian protest songs from 1978 to 1985. He has produced over fifty albums and CDs of works by J. S. Bach, John Cage, Arnold Schoenberg, Erik Satie, and others. His publications include *Oto no seijaku, seijaku no oto* (The stillness of sound, the sound of stillness, Heibonsha, 2004); *Takahashi Yūji Korekushon 1970 nendai* (Takahashi Yuji collection: 1970s, Heibonsha Library, 2004); *Kikkake no ongaku* (Music that inspires, Misuzu shobō, 2008) (http://www.suigyu.com/yuji/).

CORNELL EAST ASIA SERIES

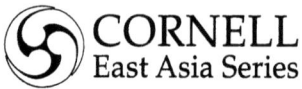

CORNELL
East Asia Series

eap.einaudi.cornell.edu/publications